CONTENTS

ACKNOWLEDGEMENTS

I am very grateful to all the following for their help.

The Nuffield Foundation and the Leverhulme Trust, for their financial support of the Primary Mathematics Project during a total period of eight years.

Ms Janet Ainley and Mr David Pimm, Research Associates during phases one and two, and my wife Valerie, Project Assistant during phase three, for their contributions to so many aspects of this project. (Janet Ainley is now Lecturer in Primary Mathematics at Warwick University, and David Pimm is Lecturer in Mathematical Education at the Open University.)

In the Solihull Local Education Authority: Mr Colin Humphrey, Director of Education, the late Mr Paul Turner and his successor Mrs Marion Idle, Mathematics Advisers, Mr Alan Stocks, Assistant Director of Education, Mrs Barbara Furniss, Head Teacher, and the staff and children of Bentley Heath Primary School; Mrs Rita Chapman, Head Teacher, and the staff and children of Lady Katherine Leveson's Primary School. In the Dyfed Local Education Authority, Dr David Finney, former Mathematics Adviser, Mrs A. Cole, Head Teacher, and the staff and children of Loveston County Primary School. In the Shropshire Local Education Authority: Dr David Finney, Science Adviser; Mrs Susan Boughey, Head Teacher, and the staff and children of Leegomery County Infant School; Mrs Ishbel Gamble, Head Teacher, and the staff and children of Holmer Lake County First School; Mr David Tyrrell, Head Teacher, and the staff and children of Leegomery County Junior School; Mrs Pamela Haile, Head Teacher, and the staff and children of St Lawrence Primary School. I am grateful to all who allowed me to work in their schools during the pilot testing of the project materials, and also for their advice, suggestions, and helpful discussions; and to the children for the many hours of enjoyment which I have had while working with them.

My colleague Professor John Eggleston, Professor of Education at Warwick University, and Advisory Editor for Routledge Education Books, for his encouragement and editorial advice.

And finally, but by no means least, yourselves, for allowing our efforts to find their hoped-for destination in your own classrooms.

STRUCTURED ACTIVITIES FOR PRIMARY MATHEMATICS

How to enjoy real mathematics

Richard R. Skemp

Emeritus Professor
University of Warwick

Volume 2

R

Routledge
London

First published in 1989 by
Routledge
11 New Fetter Lane, London EC4P 4EE

Typeset by Columns of Reading
Printed in Great Britain by T.J. Press (Padstow) Ltd.,
Padstow, Cornwall

British Library Cataloguing in Publication Data

Skemp, Richard R. (Richard Rowland), 1919–
    Structured activities for primary
    mathematics : how to enjoy real maths.—
    (Routledge education books).
    Vol. II
    1. Primary schools. Curriculum subjects :
    Mathematics
    I. Title
    372.7'3

0-415-02819-1

STRUCTURED ACTIVITIES FOR PRIMARY MATHEMATICS

opening hours

The author Richard Skemp is internationally recognised as a pioneer in the psychology of learning mathematics based on understanding rather than memorising rules. A former mathematics teacher, he has lectured in seventeen countries, is a former Professor of Educational Theory and Director of the Mathematics Education Research Centre at Warwick University, and a Past President of the International Group for the Psychology of Mathematics Education.

Routledge Education Books

Advisory Editor: John Eggleston
*Professor of Education
University of Warwick*

NOTES

Volume 1 is intended for use in infant and first schools, and Volume 2 for junior schools and the lower forms in middle schools. Because of the wide range of children's abilities, this division can only be very approximate. In particular, some of the later activities in Volume 1 will be found useful for children in their first year at a junior school, especially if they come from infant schools where this approach has not been used.

Since the English language lacks a pronoun which means either he or she, I have used these alternately by topics.

INTRODUCTION

1 Why this book was needed and what it provides

There is now a wide consensus, which was well expressed in the Cockroft report,[1] that practical work is essential throughout the primary years, and not just for younger children. There are now a number of these activities available, and individually many of them are attractive and worthwhile. But collectively, they lack two essential requirements for long-term learning: structure, and clear stages of progression. The present volume provides a fully structured collection of more than 300 activities, covering a core curriculum for children aged from five to eleven years old, which uses practical work extensively at all stages.

This collection is not, however, confined to practical work. Mathematics is an abstract subject, and children will need in the future to be competent at written mathematics. Putting one's thoughts on paper can be a help in organising them, as well as recording them for oneself and communicating them to others. What is important is that this should not come prematurely. It is their having had to memorise a collection of rules without understanding which has put so many generations of learners off mathematics for life, and destroyed their confidence in their ability to learn it. Practical, oral, and mental work can provide the foundation of understanding without which written work makes no sense. Starting with these, the present collection provides a careful transition from practical work to abstract thinking, and from oral to written work.

Activities for introducing new concepts often take the form of a teacher-led discussion. Many of the other activities take the form of games which children can play together without direct supervision, once they know how to play. These games give rise to discussion; and since the rules and strategies of the games are largely mathematical, this is a mathematical discussion. Children question each other's moves, and justify their own, thereby articulating and consolidating their own understanding. Often they explain things to each other, and when teaching I emphasise that 'When we are learning it is good to help each other.' Most of us have found that trying to explain something to someone else is one of the best ways to improve one's own understanding, and this works equally well for children.

This volume also provides the following:

(a)   A set of diagrams (concept maps) showing the overall mathematical structure, and how each topic and activity fits into this.
(b)   Clear statements of what is to be learnt from each group of activities.
(c)   For each activity, a list of materials and step by step instructions. (A volume of photomasters is also provided to simplify the preparation of materials.)

(d) For each topic, discussion of the mathematical concept(s) involved, and of the learning processes used.

The last of these will, it is hoped, be useful not only for classroom teachers, but also for advisory teachers, support teams, mathematics advisers, those involved in the pre-service and in-service education of teachers, and possibly also those whose main interests are at the research level.

2   The invisible components and how to perceive them

The activities in this collection contain a number of important components which are invisible, and can only be perceived by those who know what to look for. These include (i) real mathematics (ii) structure (iii) a powerful theory.

(i) *Real mathematics.*   Here I can begin to answer questions which may have arisen in your mind when you read the sub-title of this book. 'What do you mean by this? Is it just a puff?' I say 'begin', because a fuller answer depends on personal experience. If someone asks 'What is a kumquat?' I can tell them that it is a small citrus fruit, but two of the most important things for them to know are what it tastes like, and whether they like it or not. This knowledge they can only acquire by personally tasting a kumquat.

Real mathematics is a kind of knowledge. I can describe it, and I hope you will find this a useful start. But some of the most important things about mathematics people cannot know until they have some of this kind of knowledge in their own minds; and those who acquired real mathematics when they were at school are, regrettably, in a minority. A simple preliminary test is whether you enjoy mathematics, and feel that you understand it. If the answers are 'No', then I have good news for you: what you learnt was probably not real mathematics. More good news: you can acquire real mathematics yourself while using these activities with your children. You will then begin to perceive it in the activities themselves: more accurately, in your own thinking, and that of your children, while doing these activities. And you will begin to discover whether or not what you yourself learnt as a child was real mathematics.

Mathematics (hereafter I will use 'mathematics' by itself to mean real mathematics) is a kind of knowledge which is highly adaptable. In the adult world, this adaptability can be seen in the great variety of uses to which it is put. Mathematics is used to make predictions about physical events, and greatly increases our ability to achieve our goals. Our daily comfort and convenience, sometimes our lives, depend on the predictive use of mathematics by engineers, scientists, technicians, doctors and nurses. At an everyday level, we use mathematics for purposes such as predicting approximately how long we should allow for a journey. Highly sophisticated mathematics is required to project communication satellites into orbits whereby they hang stationary relative to the earth; and also in the design of the satellites themselves, whose electronic equipment allows us to watch on our television screens events many thousands of miles away.

Mathematics has also an important social function, since many of the complex ways in which we co-operate in modern society would not be possible without mathematics. Nuts could not be made to fit bolts, clothes to fit persons, without the measurement function of mathematics. Businesses could not function without the mathematics of accountancy. If the person in charge of this gets his calculations wrong, his firm may go out of business: that is to say, others will no longer co-operate by trading with them.

Another feature of mathematics is creativity – the use of one's existing knowledge to create new knowledge. Can you say what are ninety-nine sevens? Probably not, but if you think 'A hundred sevens make seven hundred, so ninety-nine sevens will be one seven less: six hundred and ninety three', then you are using your own mental creativity. Creating new mathematics which nobody ever knew before is creativity at the level of the professional mathematician; but anyone who has some real mathematics is capable of creating knowledge which is new to them, and this way of using one's mind can give a kind of pleasure which those who have not experienced it may find hard to understand.

These are some of the adult uses of mathematics, which make it so important in today's world of advanced science, technology, and international commerce. At school, most children still learn a look-alike which is called by the same name, but whose uses have little in common with the uses of real mathematics. School mathematics as it is experienced by children is mostly for getting ticks, pleasing teachers, avoiding reproofs and sometimes also the humiliation of being made to feel stupid. It is also used for passing exams, and thereafter quickly forgotten. Yet real mathematics can be taught and learnt at school. For an example of mathematics used predictively, try 'Missing stairs' (Org 1.5/1). Success in most of the games also depends largely on making good predictions. Mathematics is used socially in all children's work together in groups; and in some, e.g. 'Renovating a house' (Num 3.8/3), a social use is embodied in the activity itself. Examples of creativity I hope you will find in the thinking of your own children, when they are learning real mathematics.

(ii) *Structure.* This is an essential feature of real mathematics. It is this which makes possible all the features described in (i), so for emphasis I am giving it a section to itself.

By structure we mean the way in which parts fit together to make a whole. Often this whole has qualities which go far beyond the sum of the separate properties of the parts. Connect together a collection of transistors, condensers, resistances, and the like, most of which will do very little on their own, and you have a radio by which you can hear sounds broadcast from hundreds of miles away. That is, if the connections are right: and this is what we mean by structure in the present example.

In the case of mathematics, the components are mathematical concepts, and the structure is a mental structure. This makes it much harder to know whether it is there or not in a learner's mind. But the difference between a mathematical structure and a collection of isolated facts is as great as the difference between a radio and a box of bits. There is the same difference between a radio set and a wrongly connected assortment of components, but this is harder to tell by looking. The important test of the presence or absence of structure, i.e. of the right set of connections, may best be inferred from performance. This is also true for mathematics, and for its look-alike which goes by the same name. Of these two, only real mathematics performs powerfully, enjoyably, and in a wide variety of ways.

Each individual learner has to put together these structures in his own mind. No one can do it for him. But this mental activity can be greatly helped by good teaching, an important part of which is providing good learning situations.

The requirements of a good learning situation include full use of all the three modes of building conceptual structures. Mode 1 is learning by the use of practical materials; mode 2 is learning from exposition, and by discussion; and mode 3 is expanding one's knowledge by creative thinking. These categories are expanded and discussed more fully in *Mathematics in the Primary School*.[2]

The activities in this book are intended to help teachers provide learning situations of the kind described. They are also fully structured, meaning that the concepts embodied in each fit together in ways which help learners to build good mathematical structures in their own minds. This also includes consolidation, and developing mathematical skills.

(iii) *A powerful theory*.   In 1929, Dewey wrote 'Theory is in the end . . . the most powerful of all things';[3] and I have been saying the same for many years, even before I knew that Dewey had said it first. The activities in this book embody a new theory of intelligent learning. This had its origins in the present author's researches into the psychology of learning of mathematics,[4] and was subsequently expanded and generalised into a theory of intelligent learning which can be applied to the learning of all subjects.[5] It is not essential to know the theory in order to use the activities. But readers who are professional teachers will want to know not only what to do, but why. Mathematics advisers, or lecturers in mathematical education, will wish to satisfy themselves of the soundness of the underlying theory before recommending the activities.

This theoretical understanding is best acquired by a combination of first-hand experience, reading, and discussion. Each of the activities embodies some aspects of the general theory, so by doing the activities with children we can observe the theory in action. For school teachers, this is a very good way to begin, since the theoretical knowledge acquired in this way begins with classroom experience, and as it develops further will continue to relate to it. This also has the advantage that we get 'two for the price of one', time-wise: what might be called a 'happy hour' in the classroom! These observations can then form the first part of the trio

OBSERVE AND LISTEN   REFLECT   DISCUSS

whose value for school-based in-service education will be mentioned again in Section 5.

Reading helps to organise our personal experience, and to extend our knowledge beyond what can be gathered first-hand. A companion book to the present volume is *Mathematics in the Primary School*,[6] and this also offers suggestions for further reading.

3   How this book is organised and how to use it

These two volumes contain teaching materials for seven school years, together with explanations and discussions. This is a lot of information. Careful thought has therefore been given to its organisation, to make it easy to find as much as is required at a given stage, and to avoid feeling overloaded with information. Mathematics is a highly concentrated kind of information, so it is wise to take one's time, and to go at a pace which allows comfortable time for assimilation. The amount eventually to be acquired in detail by a class teacher would be no more than one-seventh of the total, if all children in the class were of the same ability. In practice it will, of course, be more because of children's spread of ability: but let us take this figure as a starting point. There are 326 activities in all, so if we spread these over a 30-week school year, allowing for times when the school is concentrating on other matters such as concerts, plays, seasonal festivities, sports, etc, this averages to about three new activities every two weeks. This should allow a fairly comfortable pace for the parts which need to be acquired in detail. It is also useful to have an overview of what went before, what comes after, and how it all fits together.

The aim has been to provide first an overview; then a little more detail; and then a lot of detail, of which many readers will not need all, nor all at the same time. This has been done by organising the subject matter at four levels, into THEMES, NETWORKS, TOPICS, and ACTIVITIES. The themes and networks are tabulated below.

THEMES	NETWORKS	CODES
Organising	Set-based organisation	Org 1
Number	Numbers and their properties	Num 1
	The naming and recording of numbers	Num 2
	Addition	Num 3
	Subtraction	Num 4
	Multiplication	Num 5
	Division	Num 6
	Fractions	Num 7
Space	Shape	Space 1
Synthesis of Number and Space	The number track and the number line	NuSp 1

The four main themes run in parallel, not sequentially, though some will be started later than others. Within the theme of Number, there are seven networks. For the other themes, there is at present just one network each; but I have kept to the same arrangement for consistency, and to allow for possible future expansion. By 'network', I mean a structure of inter-related mathematical ideas. It can well be argued that all mathematical ideas are inter-related in some way or other, but the networks help to prevent information overload by letting us concentrate on one area at a time.

Greater detail for each network is provided by a concept map and a list of activities. These begin at page 18, and it will be useful to look at a pair of these as illustrations for what follows. Each concept map shows how the ideas of that network relate to each other, and in particular, which ones need to be understood before later ones can be acquired with understanding. These interdependencies are shown by arrows. A suggested sequence through the network is shown by the numbers against each topic. Use of the concept map will help you to decide whether other sequences may successfully be followed, e.g. to take advantage of children's current interests. The concept map is also useful diagnostically. Often a difficulty at a particular stage may be traced to a child's not having properly understood one or more earlier concepts, in which case the concept map will help you to find out which these are. Another function of the concept maps is to help individual teachers to see where their own teaching fits into a long-term plan for children's learning, throughout the primary years: what they are building on, and where it is leading.

Below each concept map is shown a list of the activities for each topic. (I call them 'topics' rather than 'concepts' because some topics do not introduce new concepts, but extend existing ones to larger areas of application.) Usually these activities should be used in the order shown. An alphabetical list of the activities is also given, at the end of the book.

To find activities for a particular topic, the best way is via the concept maps and the lists of activities opposite them. Suppose, for example, that you want activities for adding past ten. For this you naturally look at the concept map for addition, and find adding past ten here as topic 6. On the adjacent page, for this topic, you will find seven activities. Not all topics have so many activities, but this indicates the importance of this stage in children's learning of addition. If on the other hand you want to find a particular activity by name, then the alphabetical index at the end of the book will enable you to do so.

The codes for each topic and activity are for convenience of reference. They show where each fits into the whole. Thus Num 3.8/2 refers to network Num 3, topic 8, activity 2. If the packet for each activity has its code written on it, this will help to keep them all in the right order, and to replace each in the right place after use.

4   Getting started as a school

Since schools vary greatly, what follows in this section and the rest of this introduction is offered as no more than suggestions, based on the experience of a number of the schools where the materials have already been introduced.

It has been found useful to proceed in two main stages: getting acquainted, and full implementation. Since the latter will be spread over one or two years at least, the first stage is important for getting the feel of the new approach, and to help in deciding that it will be worth the effort.

For getting acquainted, a good way is for each teacher to choose an activity, make it up, and learn it by doing it with one or more other teachers. (Different activities are for different numbers of persons.) Teachers then use these activities with their own children, and afterwards they discuss together what they have learnt from observation of their own children doing the activities. It is well worth while trying to see some of the activities in use, if this can be arranged. Initially, this will convey the new approach more easily than the printed page.

When you are ready to move towards a full implementation, it will be necessary to decide the overall approach. One way is to introduce the activities fully into the first and second years, while other teachers gradually introduce them into later years as support for the work they are already doing. This has the advantage that the full implementation gradually moves up the school, children being used to this way of learning from the beginning. Alternatively, activities may be introduced gradually throughout the school, individual teachers choosing which activities they use alongside existing text-based materials while they gain confidence in the new approach.

Arrangements for preparation of the materials need to be planned well in advance. This is discussed in greater detail in Section 5. A detail which needs to be checked in good time, because of the slowness of most educational suppliers, is whether the commercial materials needed, such as Multilink or Unifix and base ten materials, are already in the school in the quantities needed.

In considering the approach to be used, it is important to realise that while benefit is likely to be gained from even a limited use of the activities, a major part of their value is in the underlying structure. The full benefit, which is considerable, will therefore only be gained from a full implementation, with text-based materials moving into a subsidiary function.

5   Organisation within the school

Overall, the organisation of the new approach is very much a matter for the head teacher and staff of each individual school to work out for themselves; so as has already been emphasised, what follows is offered as no more than suggestions, based on what has been found successful in schools where this approach has been introduced.

Whatever organisation is adopted, it is desirable to designate an organiser who will co-ordinate individual efforts, and keep things going. It is a great help if this teacher can have some free time for planning, organising, advising, and supporting teachers as need arises.

One approach which has been found successful is as follows. The maths organiser holds regular meetings with the staff in each one- or two-year group, according to their number. Each teacher chooses an activity, makes it up if necessary, and teaches it to the other teachers in the group. They discuss the mathematics involved, and any difficulties. Subsequently they discuss their observations of their own children doing these activities, and what they have learnt by reflecting on these. This combination may be summarised as

OBSERVE AND LISTEN   REFLECT   DISCUSS

and is an important contribution to school-based in-service education. (So much so, that several leading maths educators have said that it should be printed on every page. As a compromise, I have printed it at the end of every topic.)

It is good if the maths organiser is also in a position to help individual teachers, since it is only to be expected if they sometimes feel insecure when teaching in a style which may be very different from that to which they are accustomed. Two useful ways to help are by looking after the rest of a teacher's class for a while, so that this teacher is free to concentrate entirely on working with a small group; and by demonstrating an activity with a small group while the class teacher observes, the rest of the class being otherwise occupied.

6   Getting started as an individual teacher

The most important thing is actually to do one or more activities with one's own children, as early on as possible. This is the best way to get the feel of what the new approach is about. After that, one has a much better idea of where one is going. If there are particular topics where the children need help, suitable activities may be found via the concept maps and their corresponding lists of activities. Alternatively, here is a list of activities which have been found useful as 'starters'.

The stages correspond roughly to years at school.

			vol	page
Stage 1	Lucky dip	Org 1.3/1	1	46
	'Can I fool you?'	Org 1.3/2	1	46
	Missing stairs	Org 1.5/1	1	49
Stage 2	Stepping stones	Num 3.2/3	1	105
	Crossing	Num 3.2/4	1	106
	Sequences on the number track	NuSp 1.2/1	1	214
Stage 3	The handkerchief game	Num 4.6/1	1	148
	'Please may I have. . .?' (complements)	Num 4.6/2	1	148
	Number targets	Num 2.8/1	1	97
Stage 4	Slippery slope	Num 3.6/3	1	120
	Slow bicycle race	NuSp 1.5/1	1	223
	Doubles and halves rummy	Num 1.9/3	1	50
Stage 5	Place-value bingo	Num 2.10/3	2	57
	Renovating a house	Num 3.8/3	2	76
	Constructing rectangular numbers	Num 6.4/1	2	151
	The rectangular numbers game	Num 6.4/2	2	152
Stage 6	Cycle camping	Num 3.9/2	2	79
	One tonne van drivers	Num 3.9/3	2	80
	Multiples rummy	Num 5.6/6	2	127
Stage 7	Cargo boats	Num 5.7/3	2	132
	Classifying polygons	Space 1.8/1	2	232
	Match and mix: polygons	Space 1.8/3	2	233

When the children are doing an activity, I recommend that you think about the amount of maths which they are doing, including the mental and oral activity as well as the written work, and compare it with the amount of maths they would do in the same time if they were doing written work out of a textbook.

Consideration also needs to be given to classroom management. I am assuming that your children are already sitting in small groups, and not in rows of desks facing the front. Even so, they may be more used to working individually than co-operatively, and if this is the case then their social learning will also need to be considered. Such things as listening to each other, taking turns, discussing sensibly and giving reasons rather than just arguing, which we may take for granted, may need to be learnt. The ways of learning mathematics which are embodied in this scheme both depend on, and also contribute to, social learning and clear speech. If some of the foregoing are already well established, then you are off to a flying start.

You will find that the activities fall into two main groups: those which introduce new concepts, and those which consolidate these and provide variety of applications. Activities in the first group always need to be introduced by a teacher, to ensure that the right concepts are learnt. Once they have understood the concepts, children can go on to do the second kind together with relatively little supervision. These activities could be introduced by another adult helper; and in some cases, children themselves can teach it to others with the help of the printed rules in each packet. The policy in one school I know, where these activities are being used with great success, is for a teacher to give (in the headteacher's words) 'high quality input' to each group once a week. For the rest of the time, the children learn mainly on their own. It is in fact one of the advantages of this way of organising your classroom that a teacher can only be with one group at a time. While with a group, it is very difficult, if one is a teacher, not to keep on actively teaching when it might be better to wait for children to do their own thinking. The kind of teaching involved here includes ways of managing children's learning experiences which are less direct, and more sophisticated, than more traditional approaches. They are also more powerful.

Management of the materials also need thought and organisation. Ways of storing these are discussed in Section 7. The children's contribution will include checking that all the materials for an activity are there at the beginning of an activity, and that they all go back in their right places at the end. I have been pleased to find how well most children respond when I point out the importance of putting everything back carefully, so that it is all there for the next people who do this activity.

So far, I have interpreted the heading of this section as meaning that the reader is an individual teacher within a school where most, or at least some, colleagues are also introducing the new approach. But what if this is not the case? When talking with teachers at conferences, I have met some who are the only ones in their school who are using this kind of approach to the teaching of mathematics.

This is a much more difficult situation to be in. We all need support and encouragement, especially when we are leaving behind methods with which we are familiar – even though they have not worked well for many children. We need to discuss difficulties, and to share ways we have found for overcoming them. So my suggestion here is that you try to find some colleague with whom you can do this. At the very least, you need someone with whom to do the activities before introducing them to the children; and further discussions may arise from this.

7   Making and storing the materials

Practical work and activity methods necessarily involve the preparation of physical materials. For the school as a whole, there will be quite a lot of these. Ideally, we would have liked to provide a complete set in ready-to-use form. Unfortunately, to do this for over 300 activities would have made the cost prohibitive. On the other hand, to prepare all the materials starting from nothing would be excessive in its demands on your time. So to give as much help as we can at reasonable cost, we provide with each volume a set of photomasters which will save you many hours of drawing. The other materials needed are of two kinds. The first is commercial materials such as Multilink, Unifix, number tracks to go with these, base ten materials. You are likely to have some of these already. The second is everyday materials such as thin cord for set loops, and little objects for sorting, such as acorn cups, shells, pebbles – we do not want children to think that mathematics only involves plastic cubes and other objects not found outside schools, useful as these materials are. You will also need plenty of plastic self-seal bags, usually one for each activity. The size is not critical, but they must take an A4 card with room to spare. To keep the photocopied material under control until it is all safely in its right bags, I suggest that you work on one network at a time. Initially, most schools make a complete set as a central resource; after which teachers have a model for making up additional sets according to their individual needs.

How the preparation of materials is organised is a matter for you to agree among yourselves. Some schools have had very useful help from parents: see Section 8. Here are some suggestions on matters of detail.

Our own materials are on cards of a number of different colours. This greatly helps to organise them, e.g. by having different packs of cards used for the same activity in different colours. You can do this by copying the photo-masters onto different coloured cards, if your copier will take card. If it will not, you can copy on white paper and stick this on coloured card. Though one side will be white, the back will be coloured and this will suffice for the organising function. We have not specified the colours to be used, since what you can obtain may be different from what was available to us. Instead, we have simply labelled the masters 'colour 1', 'colour 2', etc. You can then make your own list: 'colour 1 = blue, colour 2 = light yellow. . .'. Game boards will need to be protected by covering them with plastic film. Before doing this, it gives an attractive appearance to trim the white sheet a little, so that when stuck on card there is a coloured border.

For card games we find it best to cover the whole sheet, on one side only, with transparent plastic film before cutting out. As well as protecting the surface, it makes for easier handling, giving just the right amount of slipperiness. Covering both sides with plastic film is not as good. Anyone who is not familiar with plastic film is advised to experiment first.

To get different colours within the same activity, it has been necessary to spread some of the activities over more than one card. This also means that one card may have materials for more than one activity on it. It is therefore important to make sure that when cutting out, each set of cards stays with its own reference code. One good way is to put them straight into a small self-seal plastic bag with the code cut out and included, or attached to the bag with a small piece of the sticky film. Some teachers use cardboard box tops as trays to keep materials sorted. Rubber bands for the cards are also a help.

We have found that the best way to keep together all the materials for each activity is to have them in a labelled plastic bag. Usually a separate bag is used for each activity, but sometimes it is convenient to put two together. These can then be stored upright in a suitably sized open cardboard box. Alternatively, they can be suspended from a rail by a string attached to a clothes peg or bulldog clip.

In each bag, we find it useful to have the concept, ability, materials, and details of the activity (these may be rules for a game) written on coloured A4 cards which stay in the appropriate bags. This information can be read through the bags. The discussions of concepts and activities may be written on the back if desired. The card can be used for quick reference, and also serves as a reminder what has to go back in the bag afterwards. Underlining in red the materials (such as base 10 materials) which are not kept in these individual bags will indicate what else has to be collected at the start of an activity. These cards also give rigidity to the bags, which makes them easier to store upright. The colour of the instructions card may also be used as a colour code as to which network it belongs to.

It is worth remembering that the work of preparing the materials will not have to be repeated, except for occasional replacements. The time spent is a capital investment, which will pay dividends in years to come.

8 Parents

Parents are naturally interested in their children's progress at school. Written work is something they can see – what they cannot see is the lack of understanding which so often underlies children's performance of these 'rules without reasons'. Sometimes also they try to help children at home with their mathematics. Unfortunately, this often takes the form of drill-and-practice at multiplication tables, and pages of mechanical arithmetic. This is the way they were taught themselves, and some parents have been known to respond unfavourably when their children come home and say that they have spent their maths lessons playing games. As one teacher reported: 'Games are for wet Friday afternoons. Maths is hard work. They aren't meant to enjoy it.'

How you deal with problems of this kind will, of course, depend partly on the nature of existing parent-teacher relationships in your own school. When explaining to parents who may be critical of what you are doing, it also helps if you are confident in your own professional understanding, and if there is a good consensus within the school. These are areas in which Sections 2 and 5 offer suggestions. Some approaches which have been used with success are described here. They may be used separately or together.

A parents' evening may be arranged, in which parents play some of the games together. Teachers help to bring out the amount of mathematics which children are using in order to decide what move they will make, or what card to play. To do this well, teachers need to be confident in their own knowledge of the underlying mathematics, and this can be built up by doing the activities together, and discussing with each other the mathematics involved.

A small group of parents may be invited to come regularly and help to make up activities. This needs careful organising initially, but over a period it can be a great saving in teacher's time. When they have made up some activities, parents naturally want to do them in order to find out what they are for; so this combines well with the first approach described.

Some parents may also be invited to come into classrooms and supervise consolidation activities. (It has already been mentioned in Section 6 that activities which introduce new concepts should be supervised by a teacher.)

For parents who wish to help children at home with their mathematics, the games provide an ideal way to do this. Many of these can be played at varying levels of sophistication, which makes them suitable as family games; and there is usually also an element of chance, which means that it is not always the cleverest player who wins. None of the games depends entirely on chance, however. Good play consists in making the best of one's opportunities. Parents who help their children in this way will also have the benefit of knowing that what they are doing fits in with the ways in which their children are learning at school.

9   Some questions and answers

Q.   How long will it take to introduce these materials?
A.   The materials embody many ideas which are likely to be new to many teachers, in two areas: mathematics, and children's conceptual learning. So it is important to go at a pace with which one feels comfortable, and which gives time to assimilate these ideas to one's personal thinking and teaching. It took me twenty-five years to develop the underlying theory, three to find out how to embody it in ways of teaching primary mathematics, and another five to devise and test the integrated set of curriculum materials in this volume. If a school can have the scheme fully implemented and running well in about two years, I would regard this as good going. But of course, you don't have to wait that long to enjoy some of the rewards.

Q.   Isn't it a lot of work?
A.   Changing over to this new approach does require quite a lot of work, especially in the preparation of the materials. The initial and on-going planning and organisation are important, so that this work can go forward smoothly. As I see it, nearly all worthwhile enterprises, including teaching well, involve a lot of work. If you are making progress, this work is experienced as satisfying and worth the effort. As one teacher said, 'Once you get started, it creates its own momentum.' And once it is established, the fact that children are learning more efficiently makes teaching easier.

Q.   How were the concept maps constructed?
A.   First, by a careful analysis of the concepts themselves, and how they relate to each other in the accepted body of mathematical knowledge.[7] This was then tested by using it as a basis for teaching. If an activity was unsuccessful in helping children to develop their understanding, this was discussed in detail at the next meeting with teachers. Sometimes we decided that the activity needed modification; but sometimes we decided that the children did not have certain other concepts which they needed for

understanding the one we had been introducing – that is, the concept map itself needed revision. So the process of construction was a combination of mathematics, applied learning theory, and teaching experiment.

Q. Is it all right to use the activities in a different order?
A. Within a topic, the first activity is usually for introducing a new concept, and clearly this should stay first. Those which follow are sometimes for consolidation, in which case the order may not matter too much. Sometimes, however, they are for developing thinking at a more abstract level, in which case the order does matter. However, once the activities have been used in the order suggested, it is often good to return to earlier ones, for further consolidation and to develop connections in both directions: from concrete to abstract, and from abstract to concrete.

Whether it is wise to teach topics in a different order you can decide by looking at the concepts map itself. These, and the teaching experiments described, show that the order of topics is very important. They also show that for building up a given knowledge structure, there are several orders which are likely to be successful – and many which are likely to be unsuccessful.

Q. Is it all right to modify the activities?
A. Yes, when you are confident that you understand the purpose of the activity and where it fits into the long-term learning plan. The details of every activity have been tested and often re-written several times, both from the point of view of the mathematics and to help them to go smoothly in the classroom; so I recommend that you begin by using them as written. When you have a good understanding of the mathematics underlying an activity, you will be in a position to use your own creativity to develop it further.

Sometimes children suggest their own variation of a game. My usual answer is that they should discuss this among themselves, and if they agree, try it together next time: but that rules should not be changed in the middle of a game. They may then discuss the advantages and disadvantages of the variation.

Q. Can I use the materials alongside an existing scheme? And what about written work, in general?
A. Especially with the older children, I would expect you to begin by introducing these activities alongside the scheme you are already using and familiar with. With younger children, the activities introduce as much written work as I think is necessary, and for the first three years I envisage them as replacing written work from textbooks. Thereafter, existing textbook schemes can be put to good use for gradually introducing more written work of the conventional kind. But these should come after the activities, rather than before. Children will then get much more benefit from the written work because they come to it with greater understanding. (See again the second italicised passage quoted from the Cockcroft report, in note 1.)

Q. When children are working through a text book, it is easy to keep track of their progress. Have you any suggestions for progress records when using these activities?

A.   With the volume of photomasters there is one which I hope you will find helpful for this. With regard to textbooks, the page children have reached is not always a reliable indicator of their progress in understanding. Many teachers have found that observation of children while doing activities of this kind, with judicious questioning, is much more diagnostic of their thinking. Piaget was the pioneer of this approach.

Q.   What about measurement?

A.   My present thinking is that measurement is best used in the context of project work. It is one of the less abstract parts of mathematics, so I have concentrated initially on those areas where there are the greatest problems, and where primary school maths is particularly important as a foundation for understanding of later work.

Q.   Doesn't all this sound too good to be true?

A.   Frankly, yes. Only personal experience will enable you to decide whether it can become true for you yourself, and in your school. Each school has its own microclimate, within which some kinds of learning can thrive and others not. Where the microclimate is favourable to this kind of learning, what I have been describing can become true, and I think you will find it professionally very rewarding. Where this is not at present the case, the problems lie beyond what can be discussed here. I have discussed them at length elsewhere.[8]

Q.   What do you see as the most important points when implementing this approach?

A.   Good organisation; personal experience of using the activities; observation, reflection and discussion.

Notes

1. In the following extract from the Cockcroft report, the bold type is in the original; the italics are my own.

> 289   **Practical work is essential throughout the primary years if the mathematics curriculum is to be developed in the way which we have advocated in paragraph 287.** It is, though, necessary to realise at the outset that such work requires a considerable amount of time. However, *provided that the practical work is properly structured with a wide variety of experience and clear stages of progression*, and is followed up by the teacher by means of questions and discussion, this time is well spent. *For most children practical work provides the most effective means by which understanding of mathematics can develop.*

> 290 . . . It is therefore a mistake to suppose that there is any particular age at which children no longer need to use practical materials or that such materials are needed only by those whose attainment is low. It is not 'babyish' to work with practical materials while the need exists and *we believe that many children would derive benefit from a much greater use of these materials in the later primary years that occurs in many classrooms.*

3.5 . . . *a premature start on formal written arithmetic is likely to delay progress rather than hasten it.*
W.H. Cockcroft (Chairman of Committee of Inquiry), *Mathematics Counts*, London, HMSO, 1982, pp. 84, 85, 89.

2. R.R. Skemp, *Mathematics in the Primary School*, London, Routledge, 1989.
3. J. Dewey, *Sources of a Science of Education*, New York, Liveright, 1929.
4. R.R. Skemp, *The Psychology of Learning Mathematics*, Harmondsworth, Penguin, 1971, 2nd edn 1986.
5. R.R. Skemp, *Intelligence, Learning, and Action*, Chichester, Wiley, 1978.
6. Skemp, 1988, op. cit.
7. Skemp, 1971 and 1978, op cit. See chapter 2 of the first edition, or chapter 1 of the second edition.
8. Skemp, 1978, op cit., chapter 15.

Weight Act 5 P. 78 pack objects in smallest No of Containers are

CONCEPT MAPS AND LISTS OF ACTIVITIES

Activities in **bold** are in this volume.

Org 1 Set-based organisation

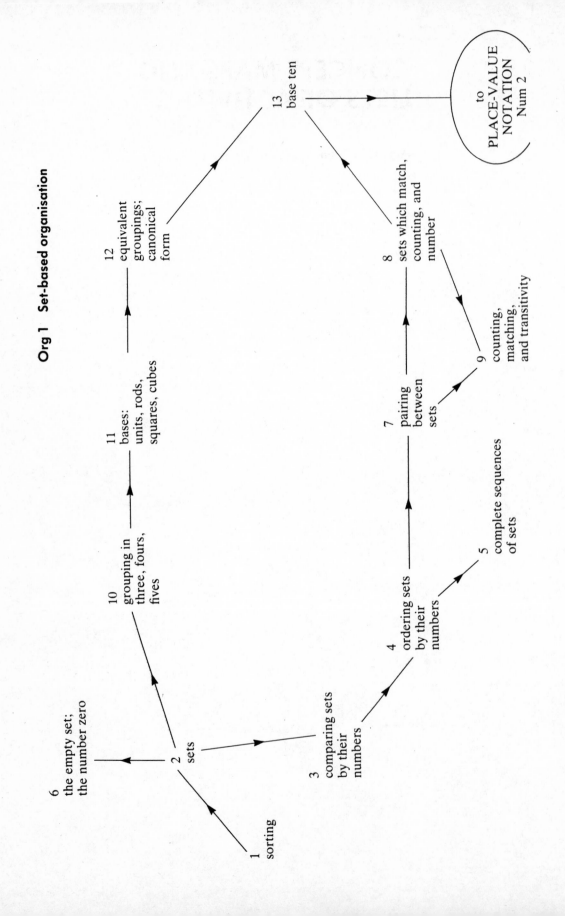

6
the empty set;
the number zero

2
sets

1
sorting

3
comparing sets
by their numbers

4
ordering sets
by their numbers

5
complete sequences
of sets

7
pairing
between
sets

8
sets which match,
counting, and
number

9
counting,
matching,
and transitivity

10
grouping in
three, fours,
fives

11
bases:
units, rods,
squares, cubes

12
equivalent
groupings;
canonical
form

13
base ten

to
PLACE-VALUE
NOTATION
Num 2

Num 1 Numbers and their properties

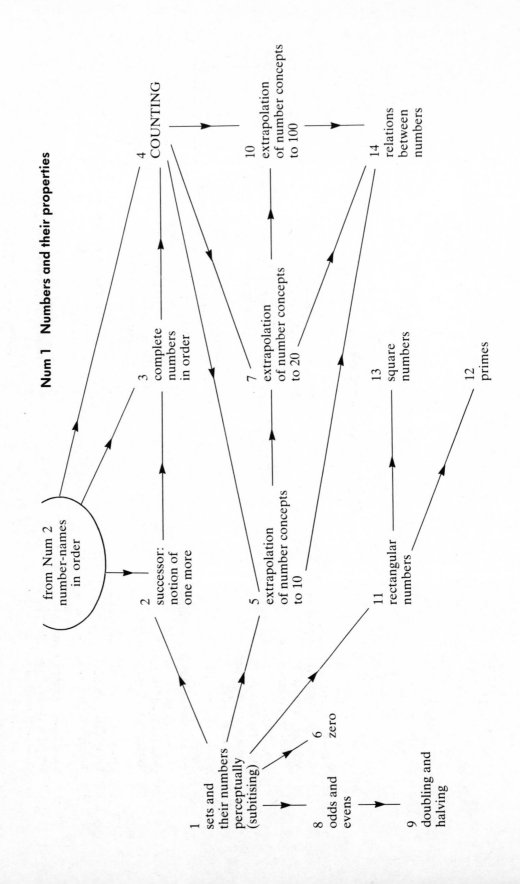

These activities will also be found in Num 6 (Division) in topics 6.4 and 6.5

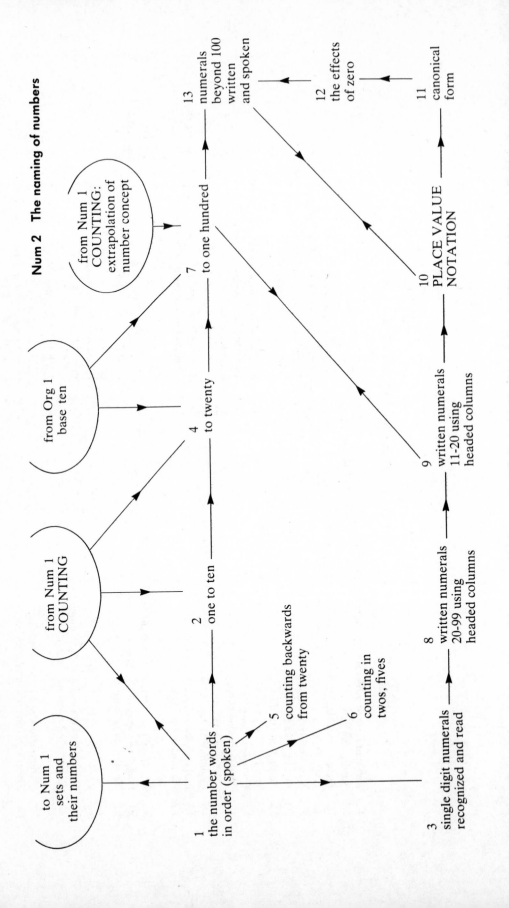

Num 2   The naming of numbers

from Num 1 COUNTING: extrapolation of number concept

from Org 1 base ten

from Num 1 COUNTING

to Num 1 sets and their numbers

1 the number words in order (spoken)

2 one to ten

4 to twenty

7 to one hundred

13 numerals beyond 100 written and spoken

12 the effects of zero

11 canonical form

10 PLACE VALUE NOTATION

5 counting backwards from twenty

6 counting in twos, fives

3 single digit numerals recognized and read

8 written numerals 20-99 using headed columns

9 written numerals 11-20 using headed columns

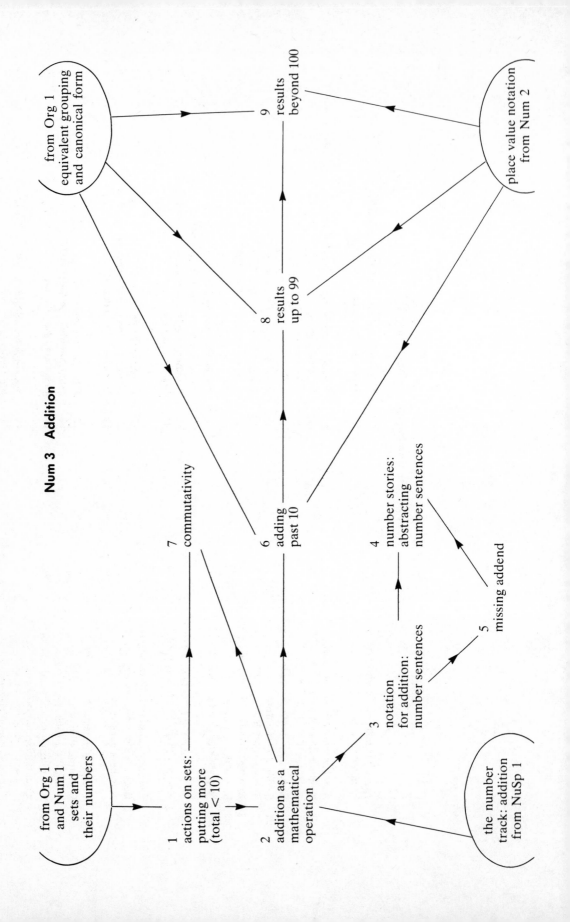

Num 3 Addition

1 actions on sets: putting more (total < 10)

2 addition as a mathematical operation

3 notation for addition: number sentences

4 number stories: abstracting number sentences

5 missing addend

6 adding past 10

7 commutativity

8 results up to 99

9 results beyond 100

from Org 1 equivalent grouping and canonical form

place value notation from Num 2

from Org 1 and Num 1 sets and their numbers

the number track: addition from NuSp 1

Num 3   Addition

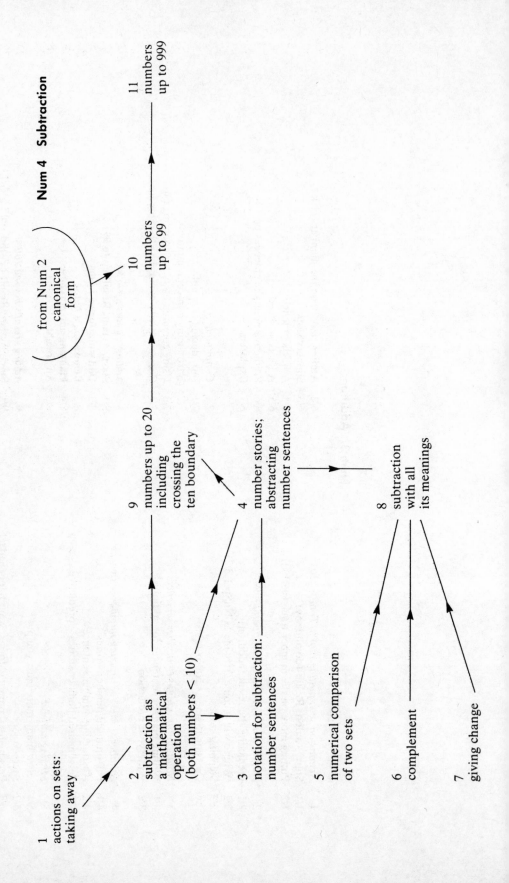

Num 4   Subtraction

1 actions on sets: taking away

2 subtraction as a mathematical operation (both numbers < 10)

3 notation for subtraction: number sentences

4 number stories; abstracting number sentences

5 numerical comparison of two sets

6 complement

7 giving change

8 subtraction with all its meanings

9 numbers up to 20 including crossing the ten boundary

from Num 2 canonical form

10 numbers up to 99

11 numbers up to 999

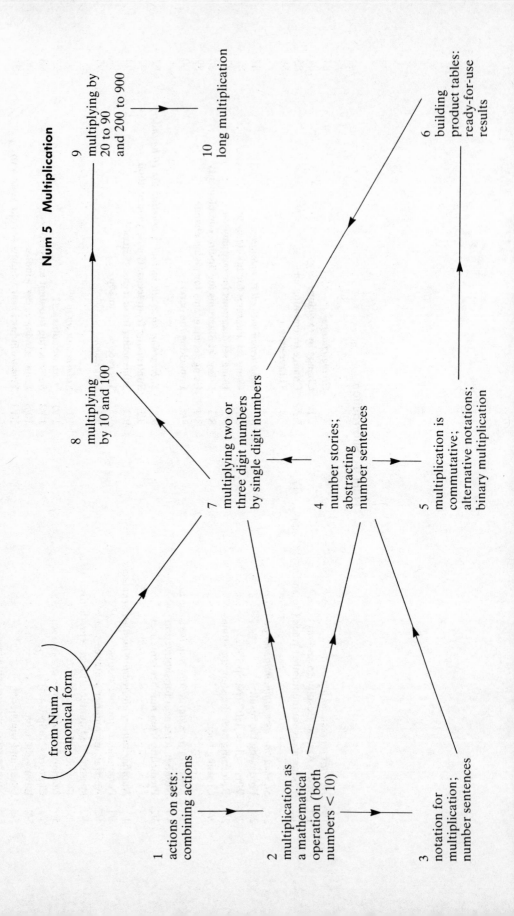

Num 5 Multiplication

9 multiplying by 20 to 90 and 200 to 900

10 long multiplication

8 multiplying by 10 and 100

7 multiplying two or three digit numbers by single digit numbers

6 building product tables: ready-for-use results

4 number stories; abstracting number sentences

5 multiplication is commutative; alternative notations; binary multiplication

from Num 2 canonical form

1 actions on sets: combining actions

2 multiplication as a mathematical operation (both numbers < 10)

3 notation for multiplication; number sentences

28

Num 5 Multiplication

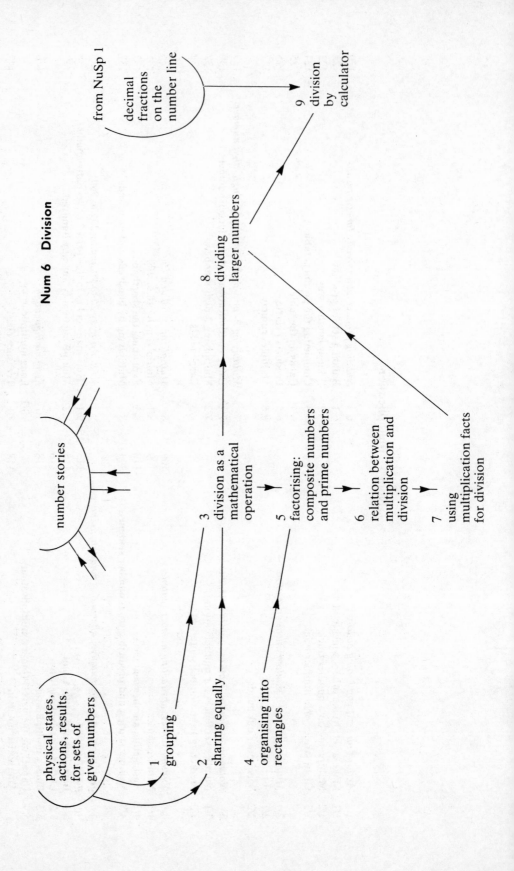

Num 6 Division

from NuSp 1

decimal
fractions
on the
number line

9 division
by
calculator

8 dividing
larger numbers

number stories

3 division as a
mathematical
operation

5 factorising:
composite numbers
and prime numbers

6 relation between
multiplication and
division

7 using
multiplication facts
for division

physical states,
actions, results,
for sets of
given numbers

1 grouping

2 sharing equally

4 organising into
rectangles

Num 6 Division

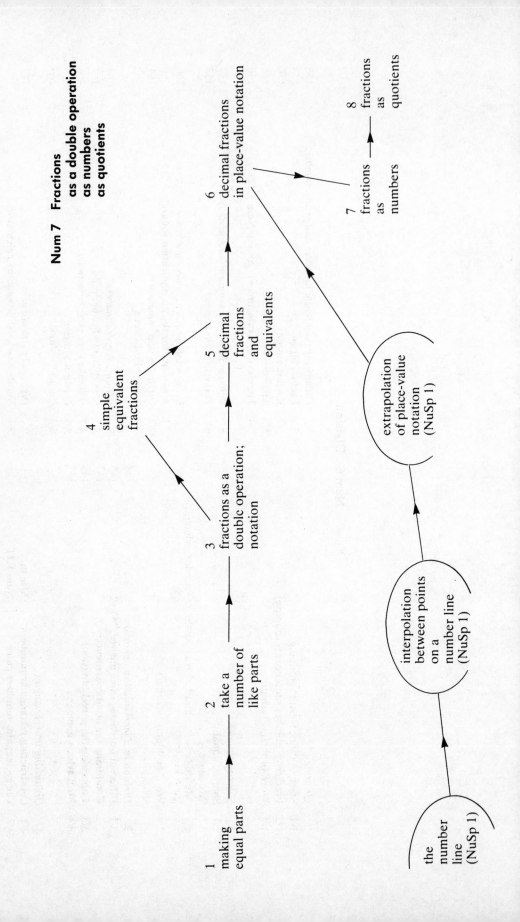

Num 7 Fractions
as a double operation
as numbers
as quotients

1 making equal parts

2 take a number of like parts

3 fractions as a double operation; notation

4 simple equivalent fractions

5 decimal fractions and equivalents

6 decimal fractions in place-value notation

7 fractions as numbers

8 fractions as quotients

extrapolation of place-value notation (NuSp 1)

interpolation between points on a number line (NuSp 1)

the number line (NuSp 1)

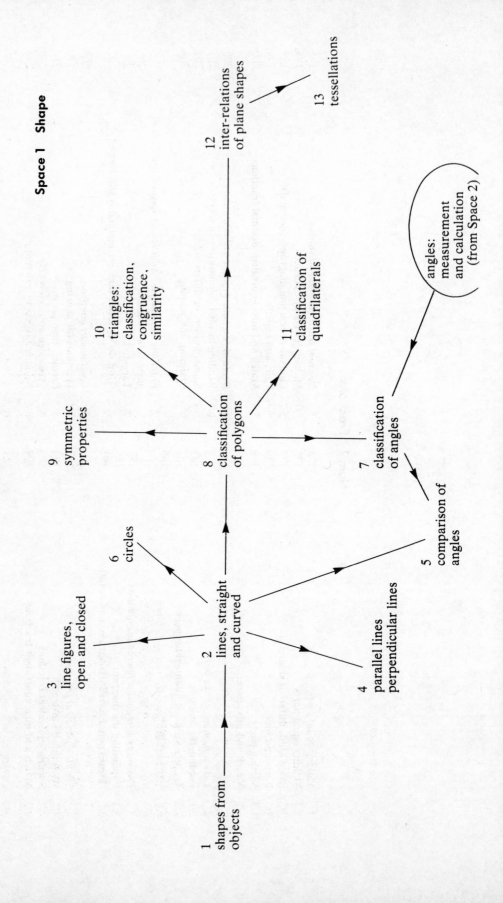

Space 1 Shape

1 shapes from objects

2 lines, straight and curved

3 line figures, open and closed

4 parallel lines perpendicular lines

5 comparison of angles

6 circles

7 classification of angles

8 classification of polygons

9 symmetric properties

10 triangles: classification, congruence, similarity

11 classification of quadrilaterals

12 inter-relations of plane shapes

13 tessellations

angles: measurement and calculation (from Space 2)

Space 1   **Shape**

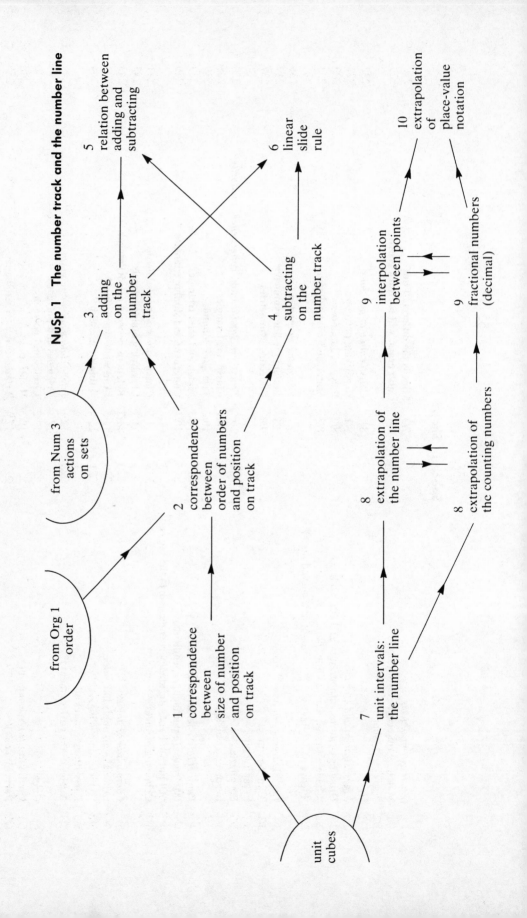

NuSp 1   The number track and the number line

THE NETWORKS AND ACTIVITIES

[Org 1] SET BASED ORGANISATION

Organising in ways which lay foundations for concepts relating to number

Org 1.13   BASE TEN

Concept   Tens, hundreds, thousands.

Abilities   (i)   To form and recognise sets of these numbers.
   (ii)   To recognise and match different physical representations of them, embodying different levels of abstraction.

Discussion of concept

Base 10 involves the same concepts as those used in bases 2, 4, 5. Practically, however, there are 3 major differences: (i) Our monetary system, and the measures used in commerce, technology and sciences, all use base 10; (ii) This base enables us to represent larger numbers with fewer figures; (iii) But 10 is too big to subitise. So manipulations which can be done perceptually for bases up to 5 depend on counting when working with base 10. Whether, using hindsight, it might have been better to choose some other base, may be for some an interesting subject for discussion. Many of us can remember the mixture of bases 4, 12, and 20 used by our former monetary system. Our measurement of time still uses bases of 60, 12, 24, 7, 30, 31, and 365! Computers work in base 2. This is not a good one for humans, who convert to base 16 (hexadecimal). But for most practical and theoretical purposes, base 10 is the established one, and it is an important part of our job as teachers to help children acquire understanding, confidence and fluency (in that order of importance) in working with base 10 in decimal notation. It is with this aim that the foundations have been so carefully prepared in topics 1 to 12 of this network.

Activity 1

Tens and hundreds of cubes

A teacher-led activity for a small group. Its purpose is to help children to transfer to base 10 the same thinking as they have developed for bases 2, 3, 4, in earlier topics.

Materials   • A large box of cubes. (Minilinks if available)

What they do   1.   Introduce this activity by asking if they know what base is most used in everyday life. Relate this to the fact that we have 10 fingers.
   2.   Ask them to make some ten-rods.
   3.   Ask them to join these up to make ten-squares.
   4.   Very likely they will run out of cubes: certainly they will not be able to make many ten-squares. This may surprise them! Tell them that the

number of single cubes in a ten-square is called a hundred, which (as they have discovered) is quite a large number. Tell them that we're now on our way to big numbers.

Activity 2   Tens and hundreds of milk straws

An activity for a small group. Its purpose is to repeat grouping into tens and hundreds with a different embodiment.

Materials
- A large number of milk straws cut into halves.
- Rubber bands.

What they do
1. Ask the children to find out how many hundreds, tens, and units there are.
2. Working together they group the straws first into tens with a rubber band round each ten.
3. They then group the tens into bundles of ten tens, with a rubber band around each big bundle.

Activity 3   Thousands

A teacher-led activity for a small group. Its purpose is to combine their concept of a base cubed with that of base 10 to give them the concept of a thousand.

What they do
1. Repeat activity 1, but ask them now to go on to see if they can make a ten-cube.
2. They will not have enough cubes to do this. Explain that the number of single cubes in a ten-cube is called a thousand: it is a very large number.
3. If we haven't enough single cubes to make a ten-cube, what can we do instead?
4. One possibility is to make a hollow cube using a ten-square for base and ten-rods for the other eight edges. We then have to imagine a solid cube, made from 10 ten-squares on top of each other.
5. Another possibility is to use the base 10 cubes from a multibase set. We then have to imagine all the cubes inside, indicated by the markings on the faces.

Discussion of activities

In the preceding topics, children developed the concepts of a base, and of rods, squares, and cubes, using bases small enough for all the grouping to be done physically. With base ten, this becomes laborious; and when it comes to the cube of base ten, impractical.

However, provided that the earlier concepts have been well established, they can be combined with children's concept of the number ten in such a way that the concepts which were learnt by using bases three, four, five expand to include base ten. This is what we have been doing in this topic. We have thus gradually been reducing children's dependence on physical objects for representing numbers and moving them towards representing them in other ways. We have also been extending children's concepts of numbers into the thousands. They have now come a long way, and should be allowed to return to the support of physical materials at any time when they feel the need. This will help to keep their concepts of numbers strong and active, and reduce the danger that when symbols become the main method for handling numbers, the concepts fade away.

OBSERVE AND LISTEN   **REFLECT**   **DISCUSS**

NUMBERS AND THEIR PROPERTIES

Numbers as mental objects which, like physical objects, have particular properties

Num 1.10   EXTRAPOLATION OF NUMBER CONCEPTS TO 100

Concept   The complete counting numbers in order to 100, grouped in tens.

Abilities   (i)   To state the number of a given set from 1 to 100.
(ii)   To make a set of a given number from 1 to 100.

Discussion of concept

Here we are concerned, not with a totally new concept (such as being odd or even) but with increasing the examples which a child has of his existing concept of number. Order and completeness provide a framework to ensure that these new examples fit the established pattern.

The key feature of the extrapolation is the idea that we can apply the process of counting, not only to single objects but to groups of objects, treating each group as an entity. So this topic links with all the topics in Org 1 (Set-based organisation) which are shown in the upper part of the network as leading to topic 16 (grouping in tens).

Activity 1   Throwing for a target

An activity for one player, two working together, or it may be played as a race between two players throwing alternately. Its purpose is to help children to extrapolate their number concepts up to 100, and to consolidate their use of grouping in tens.

Note   Before this activity, children should have completed Org 1.

Materials
- A game board, see figure 1.
- For stage 1, base 10 material.
- For stage 2, a variety of other materials as described below.
- 2 dice.
- Slips of paper on which are written target numbers, e.g. 137, 285. (It is best not to go above 300 at most, or the game takes too long.)

What they do   Stage (a)
1. The player throws the dice and adds the two numbers.
2. He puts down that number of units.
3. Each time he reaches 10 units he exchanges them for one 10, and likewise for tens.
4. He must finish with a throw of the exact number to reach the target number.

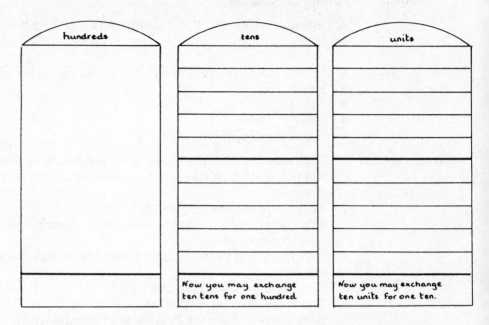

Figure 1 Throwing for a target

5.   If the number required is 6 or less he uses one die only.

Stage (b)
To prevent children becoming too attached to a particular embodiment, this game should also be played with other suitable materials, such as lolly sticks in units, tens with a rubber band around, and ten bundles of ten. Milk straws cut in half are good. Also coins: pennies, 10p pieces, and £1 pieces.

Notes
(i)   At stage 1, children will often put more than 10 units, and these should be available. E.g. starting with state on the left, and throwing 5, they put down 5 and get the state on the right. Then they remove the line of 10 cubes, exchanging these for a ten-rod which they put in the 10 column. This is a good way to begin.

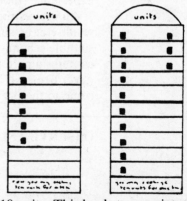

(ii)   However, at stage 2 provide only 10 units. This leads to a variety of strategies, which children should be given time to discover for themselves. It is important to restrain one's urge to tell them, or they may acquire the method but not its interiority. I recommend that you say something like this: 'When you find short cuts, as soon as you are sure they are correct you may use them.'

Activity 2 Putting and taking

A game for two players. It is a simple variant of activity 1, with the same purpose.

Materials
- 50 milk straws (halved) in bundles of ten, for each player.
- 5 more tens.
- 10 units.
- 2 dice.
- A box to put spares in.

What they do
1. Each player starts with 50 straws, in bundles of 10. They agree which will put, and which take, each working separately with his own set of straws.
2. They throw the dice alternately.
3. The 'putter' begins and puts down the number of units shown by the total shown on the dice.
4. The 'taker' plays next and takes away the total shown when he throws the dice.
5. The 'putter' wins by reaching 100.
6. The 'taker' wins by reaching 0.
7. Exchanging of 1 ten for 10 units will be necessary whenever they cross a ten boundary upwards or downwards.
8. If the game is played with the same requirement as in activity 1, that the exact number must be thrown to win, this could prolong the game unduly. It is therefore probably best to agree that a throw which would take the number past 100 or 0 is also acceptable.

Discussion of activities

Activities 1 and 2 both use the now-familiar concepts of grouping in tens, and canonical form (see Org 1) to lead children on to 100. Although they are extrapolating their number concepts, which is schema building by mode 3, this extrapolation is also strongly based on physical experience (mode 1 building). This is an excellent combination.

    An interesting feature here is that the physical experience by itself would not be sufficient to lead to the formation of these new concepts. A suitable schema is also needed which can organise this experience, and contains a pattern ready to be extrapolated by this experience. This has never been put better than by Louis Pasteur, when he said: 'Discoveries come to the prepared mind.'

OBSERVE AND LISTEN   **REFLECT**   **DISCUSS**

Num 1.11 RECTANGULAR NUMBERS

Concept   Rectangular numbers, as the number of unit dots in a rectangular array. (See example opposite.)

Ability   To recognise and construct rectangular numbers.

Discussion of concept

Here is another property which a number can have, or not have. The term 'rectangular' describes a geometrical shape, so when it is applied to a number it is being used metaphorically. Provided we know this, it is a useful metaphor, since the correspondences between geometry and arithmetic (also algebra) are of great importance in mathematics.

Rectangular numbers are closely connected with multiplication and with calculating areas. They provide a useful contribution to both of these concepts, and a connection between them.

Activity 1   **Constructing rectangular numbers**

An activity for a small group, working in pairs. Its purpose is to build the concept of rectangular numbers.

Materials   For each pair:
- 25 small counters with dots at their centres.
- Pencil and paper.

What they do   1. The activity is introduced along the following lines. Explain, 'We think of these counters as dots which we can move around.'
2. Put out a rectangular array such as this one.

3. Ask, 'What shape have we made?' (A rectangle.)
4. 'How many counters?' (In this case, 12.)
5. 'So we call 12 a rectangular number.'
6. Repeat, with other examples, until the children have grasped the concept. Note that the rectangles must be solid arrays like the one illustrated.
7. Next, let the children work in pairs. Give 25 counters to each pair, and ask them to find all the rectangular numbers up to 25.
8. If any of them think that a pattern like this might be a rectangle, remind them that the counters represent dots, draw these on paper, and ask: 'Would you say this is a rectangle?'
9. The question always arises whether or not squares are to be included. The answer is 'yes'. Both squares and oblongs are rectangles, in the same way as both girls and boys are children. This is discussed fully in the network on Shape, topic Space 1.11.
10. Finally, let the children compare and check their lists with each other's.

Activity 2   The rectangular numbers game

A game for two. It consolidates the concept of a rectangular number in a predictive situation. Children also discover prime numbers, though usually they do not yet know this name for them.

Materials
- 25 counters.
- Pencil and paper for scoring.

Rules of the game
1. Each player in turn gives the other a number of counters.
2. If the receiving player can make a rectangle with these, she scores a point. If not, the other scores a point.
3. If when the receiving player has made a rectangle (and scored a point), the giving player can make a different rectangle with the same counters, she too scores a point. (E.g. 12, 16, 18.)
4. The same number may not be used twice. To keep track of this, the numbers 1 to 25 are written at the bottom of the score sheet and crossed out as used.
5. The winner is the player who scores most points.

Discussion of activities

Activity 1 uses physical experience for building the concept of a rectangular number. Communication is also used to introduce the concept and to attach the accepted name. Schema building thus takes place by modes 1 and 2 in combination.

Activity 2 uses rectangular numbers as a shared schema which forms the basis of a game. Success at this game depends on predicting whether or not a given number is rectangular. Each prediction is tested (mode 1) as part of the game.

OBSERVE AND LISTEN   **REFLECT**   **DISCUSS**

Num 1.12   PRIMES

Concepts
(i) A prime number as one which is not a rectangular number.
(ii) A prime number as one which is not the multiple of any other number except 1 and itself.
(iii) A prime number as one which is not divisible by any other number except 1 and itself.

Abilities
(i) To use these criteria to recognise prime numbers.
(ii) To give examples of prime numbers.
(iii) To be able to construct the set of primes less than 100.

Discussion of concepts

This is a negative property, that of not having a given property. Children will already have formed this concept while playing the rectangular numbers game. In this topic we give the concept further meaning by relating it to other mathematical ideas.

Activity 1   Alias Prime

A game for up to 6 players. Its purpose is to introduce children to the difference between composite and prime numbers, and give them practice in distinguishing between these 2 kinds of number.

Materials   ● 3 counters for each player.

Rules of the game   1. Begin by explaining the meanings of 'composite number' and 'prime'. These concepts have been well prepared in earlier activities, and children have usually invented their own names for them.
2. Explain that 'alias' means 'another name for', often used to hide someone's identity. In this game, all prime numbers use the alias 'Prime' instead of their usual name.
3. Start by having the players say in turn 'Eight', 'Nine', 'Ten' . . . round the table.
4. The game now begins. They say the numbers round the table as before, but when it is a player's turn to say any prime number, they must not say its usual name, but say 'Prime' instead.
5. The next player must remember the number which wasn't spoken, and say the next one. Thus the game would begin (assuming no mistake) 'Eight', 'Nine', 'Ten', 'Prime, 'Twelve', 'Prime', 'Fourteen', 'Fifteen', 'Sixteen', 'Prime', 'Eighteen' and so on.
6. Any player who makes a mistake loses a life – i.e. one of his counters. Failing to say 'Prime', or saying the wrong composite number, are both mistakes.
7. When a player has lost all his lives he is out of the game, and acts as an umpire.
8. The winner is the last player to be left in the game.

Note   When the players are experienced, they may begin counting at 'One'. This gives rather a lot of primes for beginners.

Activity 2   The sieve of Eratosthenes

An activity for children working individually. As they get better at 'Alias Prime', they will come to numbers about which they are doubtful whether these are prime or not. This is a method for constructing a set of primes by systematically eliminating multiples.

Materials   ● For each child a 10 by 10 number square on which are written the numbers in order from 1 to 100. They can make these themselves.

What they do   1. They begin by crossing off all the multiples of 2 except 2 itself.
2. Then they cross out all the multiples of 3 except 3 itself, and so on.
3. After 7, they will find that there are no new ones to cross out. Let them discover this. Why is it so? (This is quite a hard question.)
4. When finished, children check their results against each other's.
5. They then make a separate list of the primes below 100.

Activity 3   Sum of two primes

A game for two. Its purpose is to give a further opportunity for thinking about prime numbers.

Materials   • Number cards 2 to 20.

What they do   *Stage (a)*
1. The cards are shuffled and put on the table face down.
2. Player A turns over the top card and puts it down face up. (Say, 14.)
3. He now tries to express this as the sum of two primes, and if successful he scores a point. In this case he can: 13 + 1.
4. If B can do so in a different way, he also scores a point. In this case he can: 3 + 11.
5. B then turns over the next face-down card, and the game is continued as above.

Stage (b)
This is played as above, but using two dice to give larger numbers. These are of different colours, and one determines the tens, the other the units.

Discussion of activities

The concept of a prime number was implicit in the rectangular numbers game (Num 11.1/2) when children encountered numbers which are not rectangular numbers. Here this negative property is made explicit and given a name. Activity 1 ('Alias Prime') centres attention on prime numbers in a game based on this concept, and the concept is tested by mode 2 (comparison with the schemas of others, leading sometimes to discussion).

Primes were initially conceptualised in relation to rectangular numbers, which is a physical and spatial metaphor. In activity 2 they are thought of in a different way, that of not being multiples. They are therefore not divisible except by 1 and themselves. Multiplication and division are abstract mathematical operations, so the concept of a prime has now become independent of its physical/spatial beginnings. Independent does not however mean permanently detached from physical embodiments. While learning to climb a mountain higher and higher, we must always retain the ability to come down again. We also need to be able to put our mathematics to work, and this means relating it once again to physical embodiments.

Activity 3 is an abstract game with numbers, of a kind which only mathematicians enjoy. So if the children we are teaching do enjoy this game, we may congratulate both them and ourselves.

OBSERVE AND LISTEN   REFLECT   DISCUSS

Num 1.13   SQUARE NUMBERS

Concept   A square number as a particular kind of rectangular number, in which the corresponding rectangle has sides equal in length (i.e. is a square).

Ability   To construct and recognise square numbers.

Discussion of concept	Since a square is a particular kind of rectangle, we are now distinguishing a particular kind of rectangular number, using the term 'square' metaphorically as was the case for 'rectangle'. Note that 'a three-square' is a kind of square, whereas 'three squared' is a number: the number of dots in a three-square. The latter is the result of an operation on the number 3 (multiplied by itself); compare 3 doubled and 3 halved.

Activity 1 Square numbers

An activity for a small group. Its purpose is to introduce the concept of a square number.

Materials
• 50 counters.
• Pencil and paper for each child.

What they do
1. Ask the children to make the rectangles for the numbers 4, 9, 16.
2. Put these in the centre of the table, and ask the children what they notice.
3. Explain that since these rectangles are squares, their numbers also are called squares.
4. Ask the children each to make a list of all the square numbers up to 100. They may use counters if they wish, and if there are enough.
5. When they have finished, they compare lists. If there is any discrepancy, it is discussed.

Activity 2 An odd property of square numbers

This is an interesting investigation which can be done singly or in pairs. It relates the sequence of square numbers (present topic) and of odd numbers (topic 8, volume 1).

Materials
• Cubes: about 30 in each of several colours.
• Paper and pencil.

What they do
1. Ask the children to continue the following, each time adding the next odd number, until they have seen a pattern.

$$
\begin{aligned}
1 + 3 &= 4 \\
1 + 3 + 5 &= 9 \\
1 + 3 + 5 + 7 &= 16
\end{aligned}
$$

2. When they have seen the pattern, ask them to try and find out why it is that adding the next odd number gives the next square number. This is difficult without the following hint: make a staircase of the odd numbers, using different colours for adjacent rods. The step from this to an explanation is shown in the diagram below; but if children can discover this for themselves, it is a pity to deprive them of this pleasure.

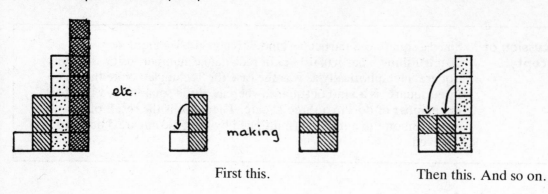

etc.

First this.   making   Then this. And so on.

HINT   EXPLANATION

3. A further step is to see that the sum of the first N odd numbers is equal to the square of N. This is difficult to express tidily in words without the use of N to stand for 'any number'.

Discussion of activities

Activity 1 shows a familiar pattern. A new concept is introduced by examples of several physical embodiments. Children then use the concept to find more examples for themselves, first with and then without the help of physical embodiments. All 3 modes of schema building are thus brought into use.

Activity 2 introduces not just a property of certain numbers, but a relation between two patterns. One pattern is formed by the successive left-hand sides, the other by the successive right-hand sides of the equations.

This result can also be obtained starting from the other end, i.e. beginning with the explanation shown after step 2, and deriving the sequences of numbers on the left and right-hand sides. But I think that the way I have presented it makes it more intriguing, and increases the pleasure of discovering why.

For your own interest

Here is a question which has come up a number of times in discussion with teachers.

As explained in the discussion of the concept, 3 multiplied by itself is called 3 squared.

So 2 squared = 4
3 squared = 9
4 squared = 16 and so on.

The inverse relationship is called a square root.

So the square root of 4 = 2
the square root of 9 = 3
the square root of 16 = 4 and so on.

As long as we are talking about the counting numbers, only certain numbers have a square root. These are called perfect squares. So 4, 9, 16 . . . are perfect squares. They are also non-prime.

Are all perfect squares non-prime? In particular what about 1? You might like to think about this, and perhaps discuss it with others, before reading on. The discussion is probably more important than the result. Here are my own thoughts on the matter. 1 is not a square number, since a single dot can hardly be described as a square. However, 1 multiplied by itself is equal to 1, i.e. 1^2 is 1. So we now have the paradox that 1 is a perfect square arithmetically, but geometrically it is not a square number. By any definition, 1 is prime.

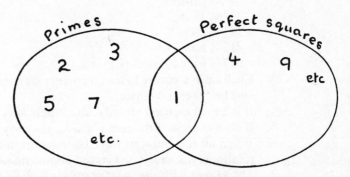

In this context, 1 is unique.

OBSERVE AND LISTEN **REFLECT** **DISCUSS**

Num 1.14 RELATIONS BETWEEN NUMBERS

Concept That all numbers are related, in many ways.

Abilities (i) To find several relationships between a given number and other numbers.

(ii) To find several relationships between two given numbers.

Discussion of concept	From the second topic of this network onwards, there has been emphasis not only on individual numbers but on relationships between them. This is an example of one of the major emphases of this approach: that learning mathematics involves learning, not isolated facts, but a connected knowledge structure.
	The relationships dealt with specifically in this topic are straightforward ones such as successor and predecessor, half and double. In other networks we meet (e.g.) sum and difference, multiple and factor. In this topic we go further, to bring forward a very general property of numbers: that every number is related to every other number, not just in one way but many. Indeed, the only limits to how many relationships we can find are those of time and patience.

Activity 1   'Tell us something new'

A game for a small group. Its purpose is to give practice in thinking about properties of numbers, and their relationships with other numbers.

Materials
- A bowl of counters, say 3 per player.
- A pack of number cards (or any other way of generating assorted number). How high they should go depends on the ability of the players.

Rules of the game
1. The first card is turned over, e.g. 17.
2. Each player in turn has to say something new about this number, e.g.
    '17 is prime.'
    '17 is 10 + 7.'
    '17 is 20 − 3.'
    '17 is half 34.'
    '17 is four fours plus 1.' etc.
3. Each time a player makes a correct statement, the others say 'Agree' and he takes a counter.
4. If it has been used already, the others say, 'Tell us something new'.
5. If an incorrect statement is made, they say, 'Tell us something *true*'.
6. When all the counters have been taken, many different properties and relationships have been stated about the same number.
7. The player with the most counters is the winner.
8. Another game may then be played with a different number.

Activity 2   'How are these related?'

A game for a small group. It is a variation of activity 1, but harder.

Materials   As for activity 1.

Rules of the game   As for activity 1, except that two numbers are used at a time. Players now have to say how these are related.

E.g. 25 and 7
    '25 is more than 7'
    '25 is 18 more than 7'
    '3 sevens plus 4 makes 25'
    'Both 25 and 7 are odd numbers'
    'The sum of 25 and 7 is an even number.' etc.

Discussion of activities   These activities develop fluency and inventiveness in the handling of numbers. In activity 1, children can choose to keep well within their domain (the mental region where they feel confident), or to stretch their abilities by devising more difficult answers and thereby to expand their domains. This is under each child's control, so confidence is maintained and developed further. Activity 2 allows less choice, so it is more demanding.

They also increase the interconnections within children's schemas. This makes much use of mode 3 activity – the creative use of existing knowledge to find new relationships. Testing is by mode 2, agreement and if necessary discussion, which in turn is based on mode 3 – testing by consistency with what is already known.

OBSERVE AND LISTEN   **REFLECT**   **DISCUSS**

THE NAMING OF NUMBERS

in ways which help us to organise them and use them effectively

Num 2.10   PLACE-VALUE NOTATION

Concept   That a particular digit can represent a number of units, tens, hundreds, according to whether it comes first, second, third in order reading from right to left.

Abilities   (i)   To identify separately which digits represent units, tens, hundreds, by their positions relative to each other.
(ii)   To read aloud two and three digit numerals.
(iii)   To match these with physical representations.
Note   Hundreds are not included until the second time round, after Num 2.13.

Discussion of concept

Provided that we have only one digit in each column (which may be a zero), we can leave out the headings and ruled columns and still know what each digit stands for. The result is a brilliantly simple notation, whose brilliance is easily overlooked just because it is so simple. The Greek mathematicians, excellent though they were in many ways, did not think of it; nor did the Romans, nor the earlier Egyptians nor the Babylonians. As a result, they made relatively slow progress in arithmetic and algebra.

It is also a condensed and abstract notation, and this is why it has been approached with such careful preparation in volume 1.

Activity 1   **'We don't need headings any more'**

A teacher-led discussion for a small group. Its purpose is to introduce children to place-value notation, as described above.

Materials   ● Pencil and paper.

Suggested sequence for the discussion   1.   Write some number between 21 and 99, with headed columns, as below.

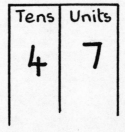

2. Ask, 'Can you say this number?' Accept either 'forty-seven' or 'four tens, seven units'.
3. Then say 'Can you say it another way?' to get the alternative reading. (At this stage we want both, every time.)
4. Repeat with other numbers, including ones between 11 and 19. Numbers such as 30 should be read as 'Three tens, zero units; thirty'.
5. Fold the top of the paper under so that the headings for tens and units do not show, and write another number. Ask the children if they can still say the numbers as before. Practise this until they are confident, and then do the same without the dividing line.
6. If the children are fully proficient in the new notation, say 'So we don't always need the headings now, though they are still useful sometimes' and continue to Activity 3. Children who have progressed through the earlier topics in this network should have no difficulty at this stage. For those who do, it would be best to go back to topics 8 and 9, which will be found in volume 1, to ensure that they are fully prepared. They should then do activity 2 of this topic.

Activity 2   Number targets using place-value notation

The children should now play again the number targets game, exactly as in Num 2.8/1 and Num 2.9/2, but with plain number cards and plain paper.

Activity 3   Place-value bingo

A game for 5 or 6 players. Its purpose is to consolidate children's understanding of the relationships between written numerals in place-value notation, the same read aloud, and physical embodiments of the numbers.

Materials
- Number cards 0 to 59.
- Base 10 material, tens and units.
- Die 0 to 9.*
- Die 0 to 5.*
- Shaker.
- For each player, pencil and A4 paper.
* Spinners may be used instead.

Rules of the game

Stage (a)

Preparation
1. The players fold their papers once each way to make 4 rectangular spaces. These are used as bingo cards.
2. The first player throws the two dice. The 0 to 5 die gives the tens, the 0 to 9 die gives the units.
3. Suppose that he gets 2 tens and 4 units. He takes the corresponding ten-rods and units from the box and puts these into the first space on his bingo card.

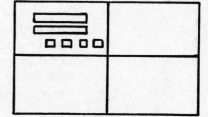

4.   The other players do likewise in turn.
5.   Steps 2, 3, 4 are repeated until each has filled all his spaces.

The game

1.   The pack of number cards is shuffled and put face downward on the table.
2.   The players in turn turn the top card over, calling each two ways. E.g. 'Three tens, five units, thirty-five.' 'Seven tens, zero units, seventy.' 'Zero tens,* four units, four.'
3.   It is important to speak each number in these two ways. After calling, the cards are put face down in another pile.
4.   When a number is called corresponding to the ten-rods and units, in one of a player's spaces, he takes these off and writes the numeral for them.

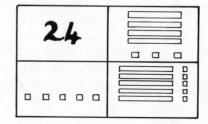

5.   The first player to replace all his ten-rods and units by numerals is the winner. He calls 'Bingo.'
6.   The game continues until all the players have done likewise.

Notes

* The question of whether zero may be omitted is considered later, in Num 2.12.

(i) The game can be played with cards from 0 to 99, but this uses a lot of ten-rods and no new ideas are involved.

(ii) The paper may be folded to make 6 spaces if desired.

Stage (b)

This is played in the same way as stage (a), except that instead of ten-rods and units, 10p and 1p coins (actual or plastic) are used.

Discussion of activities	Activity 1 introduces the final step into place-value notation, in which an important part of the meaning of each digit (namely whether it means that number of units, tens, hundreds . . .) *is not written down at all*, but is implied by relative position. It is therefore very important that this meaning has been accurately and firmly established, which is the purpose of all the preparatory activities in earlier topics. Also, that the connection of the new notation with this meaning is established and maintained. Since the tens and units no longer appear visibly, children now have to use their memory-images instead. These images are exercised and consolidated by having the children speak aloud (e.g.) 'four tens, seven singles' every time. Activity 2 relates the new notation to the individual meanings of each digit both as expressed in words (five tens, three units) and as embodied in physical materials (ten-rods and single cubes).

Activity 3 uses all these connections:

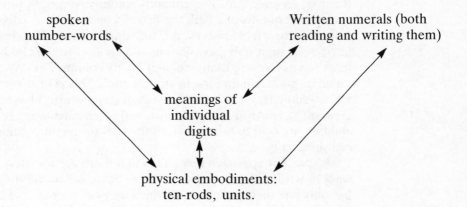

spoken
number-words

Written numerals (both
reading and writing them)

meanings of
individual
digits

physical embodiments:
ten-rods, units.

All three modes of schema building, and all three modes of testing, are brought into use for this final step into place-value notation.

Mode 1 building	The new notation is related to physical embodiments.
Mode 2 building	In activity 1, the new notation is communicated, both verbally and in writing by a teacher. Activities 2 and 3 consolidate the shared meaning of this notation, by using it in a social context as basis for two games.
Mode 3 building	The new notation is an extrapolation of the headed columns notation which they already know.
Mode 1 testing	In activity 1, children see column headings which confirm the accuracy of their readings in the 'tens, units' form.
Mode 2 testing	Activities 2 and 3 are games in which the players check the accuracy of each others' actions.
Mode 3 testing	This is implicit in the transition from headed columns to place-value, since if the new notation were not consistent with the one they already know, children would not accept it so readily as they do.

OBSERVE AND LISTEN   **REFLECT**   **DISCUSS**

Num 2.11   CANONICAL FORM

Concept   Canonical form as being one of a variety of ways in which a number may be written.

Abilities   (i)   To recognise whether a number is or is not written in canonical form.
(ii)   To re-write a number into or out of canonical form.

Discussion of concept

The interchangeability of headed column notation and place-value notation depends on there being one digit only in each column, so that the first, second, third . . . columns reading from right to left always correspond one-to-one with the first, second, third . . . digits reading from right to left. However, it is one thing to note the advantages of having one digit only per column, and another to tell children that 'We must not have more than one digit in any column', or 'We must not have numbers greater than nine in any column'. This is incorrect, because when adding (e.g.) 57 and 85, we shall (temporarily) have numbers greater than nine in both columns; and when calculating (e.g.) 53 - 16, children are told to take ten from the tens to the units column so that we can subtract 6.

The present approach recognises that there are a variety of correct ways of writing numbers, one of these being called canonical form. This has only one digit per column (which may be a zero), and has the advantage that in this case, and not otherwise, headed column notation can be replaced by place-value notation. For this reason, canonical form is used unless there is a reason for using one of the alternatives – which we often need to do as a temporary measure.

Here are some examples of the same numbers written in non-canonical and canonical forms. For a given number there is only one canonical form, but many non-canonical.

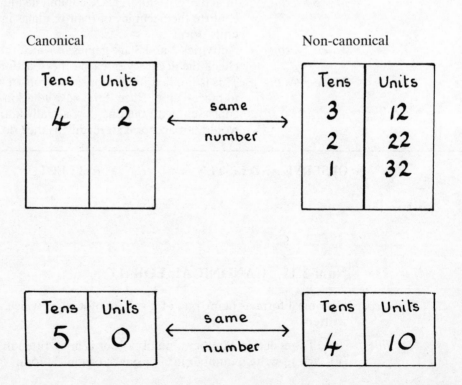

Canonical

Tens	Units
4	2

same number

Non-canonical

Tens	Units
3	12
2	22
1	32

Tens	Units
5	0

same number

Tens	Units
4	10

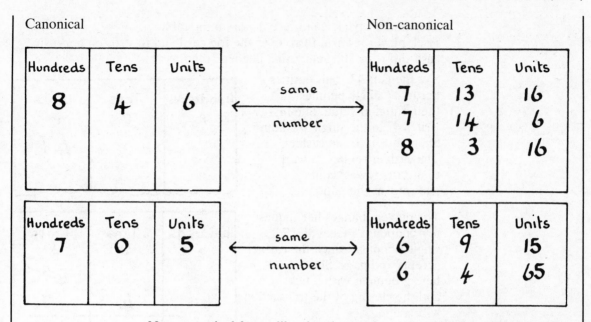

Canonical — Non-canonical

Hundreds	Tens	Units
8	4	6

same number

Hundreds	Tens	Units
7	13	16
7	14	6
8	3	16

Hundreds	Tens	Units
7	0	5

same number

Hundreds	Tens	Units
6	9	15
6	4	65

Non-canonical forms like the above often arise during calculations. To give the final answers in place-value notation, facility in converting to canonical form is required. But place-value notation depends on there being only one digit per column, so I think that headed column notation should be used whenever changes to and from canonical form are involved, until the children are absolutely clear what they are doing. The conventional notation, involving little figures written diagonally above, is a further condensation which may be quicker to write but is not consistent with this requirement. And now that calculators are readily available, it is understanding that is most important in written calculations. For speed, calculators are better.

A further complication, usually 'swept under the carpet', is that in non-canonical form place-value notation makes an appearance within the headed columns. There is no mathematical inconsistency, but we are now using two notations in combination. I see no objection to this provided that we show both of them clearly. This is what I have tried to do in the activities which follow.

Activity 1   Cashier giving fewest coins

A game for up to five players. Its purpose is to present canonical form in a familiar embodiment. Children should first have done Org 1.12 and 13.

Materials
- Play coins, 1p, 10p and later 100p (£1).
- Number cards 1-49, or 1-99 if preferred.
- Pieces of paper for cash slips.

What they do   Stage (a)
1. One child acts as cashier, and has a supply of 1p and 10p coins. (She should organise these to suit herself.)

2. The number pack is put face down on the table.
3. Each player in turn, turns over the top card and records on her own cash slip what she gets, using headed columns.

Say she gets 47. This entitles her to 47 single pennies, or their equal in value. She first writes 47 in the single p column. She hands it to the cashier. The cashier replies, 'I want to use the fewest coins', and returns the paper.

Hundreds p	Tens p	Units p
		47

5. The player changes her request to 4 tenpenny pieces and 7 single pennies, which the cashier accepts and pays. She records her agreement with a tick, and the closing of the transaction with a line.

Hundreds p	Tens p	Units p
		4̶7̶
	4	7✓

6. If a player turns a card showing less than 10, conversion is of course not required.
7. After three rounds, each player counts her money, and if she has more than nine coins of a kind, exchanges as appropriate with the cashier.
8. The winner is the one who has most, and she acts as cashier for the next round.

Extension

A bonus of 100p (£1) may be earned by first adding the three underlined amounts, converting, and predicting the result before checking physically.

When the game is established, players may forestall the cashier's refusal by making the conversion before passing her their cash slip. Both forms should however always be recorded: first the figure on the number card, then the equivalent value in canonical form. The whole object of this game is to establish that these are two ways of writing the same number.

Stage (b)

(Return to this after topic 13, numbers beyond 100.)

It is played exactly as for stage (a) except that two number packs of different colours are used, one signifying tens of pence and the other single pence.

The conversion to canonical form may now require several steps. Suppose a player turns

15 tens, 12 singles.

First we make separate conversions.

Then we combine their results.

Hundreds p	Tens p	Units p
	1̶5̶	1̶2̶
	1̶	2̶
1̶	5̶	
1	6	2

To begin with every step should be written, as above. In this case it makes no difference whether the 12 singles or the 15 tens are converted first. With proficiency, however, the process of combining can be done mentally, and it is then easier to work from right to left.

A player who turns (say) 46 tens, 71 singles will have further steps to take before conversion to canonical form is complete.

Hundreds P	Tens P	Units P
	4̶6̶	7̶1̶
	7	1
4̶	6̶	
4̶	13	1̶
5	3	1

(One step has been done mentally here.)

Activity 2   'How would you like it?'

This is similar to activity 1, except that the cashier behaves differently. Instead of paying out the amount in the smallest number of coins, she acts like a bank cashier who asks, 'How would you like it?' when we cash a cheque.

Suppose as before a player turns over 47, she records this, as before. But she might then ask for it to be paid like this

or this

or even like this.

Hundreds P	Tens P	Units P
		4̶7̶
	3	17
	2	27
	0	47

So the cashier needs to keep plenty of piles of ten single pennies. If the cashier runs out of change before all have had three turns, she will have to ask the customers to help by giving her back some change in return for larger coins.

This game can be played at stages 1 and 2, as in activity 1. In both cases the final counting, and conversion to canonical form, will now be complicated, so activity 2 should not be tackled until activity 1 is well mastered. At any time when a player has made a mistake, the conversions should be done with coins to check the pencil-and-paper conversions.

Discussion of activities

Children have already formed the concept of canonical form as it applies to the repeated grouping of physical materials, in Org 1.12 and the topics leading up to it; and for base 10, in Org 1.13. The present topic is concerned with the corresponding re-groupings done mentally, and recorded using the mathematical notation shown in activities 1 and 2.

This notation conveys, but more clearly, the same meaning as the makeshift devices which most of us learnt at school, such as this:

$$\overset{3}{\cancel{4}}\overset{1}{7}$$

Canonical form is concerned with different notations for representing the same numbers. The symbolic manipulations practised here all represent re-grouping exchanges such as those done in Org 1 with physical materials. Children now need to acquire facility at a purely symbolic level, so the base 10 physical material is replaced by coins. These provide an excellent intermediate material for the present stage, since they represent number values in a way which is partly physical, partly symbolic.

This topic forms cross-links with the various calculations which cause non-canonical forms to arise, and practice with these will be found in the appropriate networks. But canonical form is a major concept in its own right, and other examples of it occur in later mathematics. It needs to be presented in a way which allows children to concentrate on learning this important concept by itself, without having at the same time to cope with other mathematical operations.

OBSERVE AND LISTEN   **REFLECT**   **DISCUSS**

Num 2.12   THE EFFECTS OF ZERO

Concept   Zero as a place-holder.

Ability   In place-value notation, to recognise when zero is necessary for giving their correct values to other digits, and when it is not.

Discussion of concept

In place-value notation, it is the position first, or second, or third . . . in order from left to right which determines the value of a digit. So the numerals 04 and 4 both mean the same: 4 is in the units place in each, and there are zero tens – explicitly in the first, implicitly in the second. However, the numerals 40 and 4 do not mean the same, since 4 is in the tens place in the first and in the units place in the second. In the numeral 40, zero acts as a place-holder. By occupying the units position, zero determines the meaning of 4.

Though the zero in 04 is not necessary, it is not incorrect. Its use is becoming increasingly common, e.g. in digital watches, and in figures on cheques and elsewhere for computer processing.

Activity 1 **'Same number, or different?'**

A game for two or more players. They all need to see the cards the same way up. Its purpose is for children to learn when the presence or absence of a zero changes the meaning of a numeral, and when it does not.

Materials
- A double pack of single headed number cards from 0 to 9.
- A mixed pack of cards on which are the words 'same number' or 'different number', about 5 of each.
- An extra zero, of a different colour.

Rules of the game

Stage (a)

1. Both packs of cards are shuffled and put face down on the table.
2. The player whose turn it is has the extra zero.
3. He turns over one card from each pile. Suppose he gets these. He now has to put down a zero so that what is on the table still means the same number as before. (It does NOT tell him to 'add a zero'. This would mean something quite different.)

7 | same number

4. If he does this correctly, the others award him a point.

O 7 | same number

5. The circulating zero now goes to the next player, who might turn over these cards.

3 | different number

65

6. This would be his correct response.

3	0

different number

7. A player who turns over 0 from the pile, together with 'different number', still gets a point for saying, 'It can't be done,' and explaining why.
8. It is good for the players to speak aloud the numbers before and after putting down the zero. This makes it sound different if the numbers are different. E.g. in steps 3 and 4: 'Seven units.' 'Zero tens, seven units.' And in steps 5 and 6: 'Three units.' 'Three tens, zero units.'

Stage (b)
(Return to this after topic 13, numbers beyond 100.) This is played as in stage (a), except that they turn over *two* number cards from the pile and put them side by side.

Suppose a player gets this.

4	2

different number

In this case (though not always) there are two correct responses.

4	2	0

different number

If he gives both, and speaks both correctly, he is awarded 2 points.

4	0	2

different number

Activity 2   Less than, greater than

Stage (a)
A game for two players. Its purpose is to provide further examples of the effects of zero.

Materials   For each player:
• A pack of single headed number cards 1-9.
Shared between two:
• A single zero card.
• An 'is less than' card.
• An 'is greater than' card, both as illustrated below.

What they do   1. The 'is less than' card is placed between the two players. Also on the table is the zero card.
2. Both players keep their own pack face down. Each takes the top card from their pack and lays it on their side of the 'is less than' card.
3. The first player to have a turn then picks up the zero and must place it next to their own card to make a true statement.

Suppose that here it is the left-hand player's turn.

| 5 | $<$ is less than | 7 |

His correct response is:
For this he gets one point.

| 0 | 5 | $<$ is less than | 7 |

Had it been the right-hand player's turn, one correct response would have been:
(What is the other?)

| 5 | $<$ is less than | 7 | 0 |

In this case, only the right hand player can give a correct response.

| 5 | $<$ is less than | 3 |

If it was the left-hand player's turn, he could if he wished take a chance with an incorrect response. In that case, the other may say 'Challenge', and if the challenge is upheld the challenger gets two points.

When all cards have been used, the game is repeated using the 'is greater than' sign.

Stage (b)
(Return to this after topic 13, numbers beyond 100.)
As with activity 1, this can be played with larger numbers. Each player now begins by putting down two cards. Several correct responses may then be possible, and players get a point for each which is both tabled and verbalised.

For example,
in this situation

| 5 | 3 | $<$ is less than | 7 | 2 |

the right-hand player has three correct responses: 072, 702, and 720.

Discussion of activities

In this topic, children are now working at a purely symbolic level, without any support from physical materials. The activities involved are quite sophisticated, since they involve changing meanings for the same symbols. Agreement about these changing meanings depends on a shared schema for assigning values to symbols: this schema being (as we have noted) that of a condensed and sophisticated notation, in which much of the meaning is not explicitly written down at all, but is implied by relative positions.

Any difficulties will usually be best dealt with by relating these activities to the more explicit headed columns notation; and if necessary, by providing further back-up in the form of base ten physical materials. These can be used to make very clear what a great difference in meaning can result from quite small changes in the positions of symbols.

OBSERVE AND LISTEN   **REFLECT**   **DISCUSS**

Num 2.13 NUMERALS BEYOND 100, WRITTEN AND SPOKEN

Concepts

(i) That a particular digit can also represent a number of hundreds, thousands, ten-thousands, hundred-thousands, millions, according to whether it comes third, fourth, fifth, sixth, seventh in order, reading from right to left.

(ii) That each new position in this order (together with the associated word) represents groups of ten of the group just before.

Abilities

(i) To identify separately which digits represent hundreds, thousands, ten thousands, hundred-thousands, millions.

(ii) To read aloud numerals having up to seven digits.

(iii) To match these with physical representations.

Discussion of concepts

Here we are extrapolating the place-value concept from its limited application to tens and units successively to hundreds, thousands, ... The essence of this is a repetition, each time we move one place further from right to left, of the grouping process, each new larger group containing ten of the group just before.

This extrapolation can and should be begun physically. Since it is not likely that a million units are available, we are led naturally to an intermediate representation which is partly physical, partly symbolic.

Activity 1 Big numbers

This is a teacher-led activity for as many as can see the chart properly. Its purpose is to extrapolate children's use of place-value notation up to the seventh place, representing millions.

Materials

- A chart prepared as in the illustration below.
- Base 10 material.
- A skeleton metre cube (representing a million) would be very helpful if possible. This would have to be filled with units to represent a million physically.

millions	hundred-thousands	ten-thousands	thousands	hundreds	tens	units

hinged here

Stage (a)

1. Place the chart where the children can see it with the hinged section folded under so that only the right-hand section is visible (hundreds, tens, units).
2. Point to the units section, and (with the base-ten material on view) ask, 'Which do we put here?'
3. The answer is 'units', and you put a specimen unit in the space, saying 'Like these'.
4. Similarly for the tens and hundreds sections, the specimens in these cases being a ten-rod and a ten-square respectively. They will already know that the number of units in a ten-square is called a hundred.
   Now go straight on to stage (a) of activity 2, 'Naming big numbers'.

Stage (b)

5. Now open the chart out to show all the sections. Put a specimen from the base-ten material in the units, tens, hundreds.

millions	hundred thousands	ten-thousands	thousands	hundreds	tens	units
				□	▭	▫

6. Continue, pointing to the thousands space, 'What do we put here?' The answer is 'A ten-*cube*' and you put a specimen in the thousands space. The number of units in a ten-cube is called a thousand.
7. For the next space ten-thousands, a problem arises. Even if there are ten ten-cubes available, they would make a tall and unstable column. Ask the children whether, instead, they can *imagine* a ten-rod made up of thousands in this space.
8. Next we come to the hundred-thousand space. Ask 'Now, what should we imagine in *this* space?' (pointing). The answer is a ten *square* of thousands; and for the next (millions) space, a ten-*cube* of thousands.
9. It would be helpful to support their imaginations with a skeleton metre cube (representing a million).

Activity 2   Naming big numbers

For as many players as can see the material the same way up. (Otherwise the order gets reversed.)

Materials
- A chart as used in activity 1.
- A box of base 10 material.
- A pack of single headed number cards 0 to 9.

What they do   *Stage (a)*

1. The pack is shuffled and put face down on the table.

2. The first player picks
up the top card and
puts it face upward
beside the chart,
and says (in this example)
'Three units: three',
and puts the three units
into the correct space.

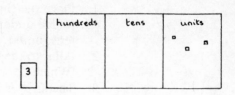

3. The next player picks
up the next card, and
puts it *on the right*
of the one already there.
She now says (in this example)
'Three tens, seven units:
thirty-seven', and puts down
material accordingly.

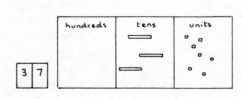

4. The next player picks
up the next card, and
again puts it *on the right*
of the one already there.
She now says (in this example)
'Three hundreds, seven tens,
zero units: three hundred and
seventy', and puts down
material accordingly.

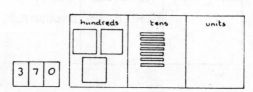

5. The chart is now cleared of material, and the cards returned randomly
   to the pack.
6. Steps 2 to 4 are repeated until the children have mastered this stage.
7. Now please read the directions at the end of stage (b).

Stage (b)

Materials
- As in stage (a) to begin with.
- Pencil and paper for scoring.

What they do
This is played a little differently. The base 10 material is no longer used.
For the first few rounds the chart from units to millions is left on display as
a reminder, after which it is put away and the game continued mentally.

1. The 0-9 pack is put face down on the table.
2. The players in turn pick up the top card and put it down *on the right* of
   those already there, as in stage (a).

3. The first player says
   'Five units: five.'

5

4. The next player says
   'Five tens, seven units:
   fifty-seven.'

5 7

5. The next player says
'Five hundreds, seven tens,
one unit: five hundred
and seventy-one.'

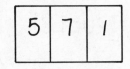

and so on.

6. This player should say 'Five
ten-thousands, seven thousands,
one hundred, six tens, two units:
fifty-seven thousand, one hundred
and sixty-two'.

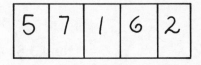

7. Scoring for a correct answer is 1 point for each correct digit.
8. If no one makes a mistake, the round continues to the millions, and the player to whom this falls will score seven points.
9. In this case the following round starts with the *next* player. This ensures that (provided that the number of players is not seven) the millions turn will come to a different player each time.

As soon as children are confident with activity 1 (Big numbers) stage (a), they should continue straight on to stage (a) of activity 2 (Naming big numbers).
After that, there are two paths open to them.
(i) They may return to Num 2.12 stage (b) doing these activities at the more difficult stages involving hundreds, tens, units.
(ii) They may continue to stages (b) of activities 1 and 2 (Big numbers, and Naming big numbers), and then follow path (i).
These two paths may also be followed alternately.

Discussion of activities

This topic makes considerable use of mode 3 schema building: extrapolation of an existing pattern, and combining ideas which they already have.

The pattern is that of repeatedly putting together the same number of groups to make the next group larger. This pattern was built up using physical materials (mode 1) in Org 1, topics 10 to 13. To start with it was based on numbers small enough to be subitised (perceived without counting). Then it was extended to base 10, using pre-fabricated physical materials so that the process of putting together physical materials to form larger groups was replaced by its mental equivalent.

In activity 1, stage (a), this pattern is picked up again, using physical materials by way of revision. In stage (b), it is continued much further. For this, we let go of the physical materials and we use our imagination. The children will in these activities be combining this extended pattern with words they have probably already heard: 'hundred', 'thousand', possibly even 'million'.

Note how in activity 2, every digit changes its place value at every turn, thereby emphasising how the meaning depends both on the digit itself and on its location.

OBSERVE AND LISTEN   **REFLECT**   **DISCUSS**

ADDITION

A mathematical operation which corresponds
with a variety of physical actions and events

Num 3.8   ADDING, RESULTS UP TO 99

Concept   Adding when the results are between 20 and 99.

Ability   To add 2-digit numbers, the results still being 2-digit numbers.

**Discussion of
concept**

What is new here is not the concept of addition, but extension of the
ability to do this with larger numbers.

Activity 1   **Start, Action, Result, up to 99**

This is a continuation of Num 3.6/1 (Start, Action, Results over 10) with
larger numbers.

Materials   • SAR board as illustrated below in step 1.
  • Start and Action cards with assorted numbers from 1 to 49.*
  • Base 10 material, tens and units.
  • Paper and pencil for each child.
  * I suggest that we may now replace arrow notation by a plus sign alone.

What they do   *Stage (a)   Headed columns and materials*
(The steps for this are same as in Num 3.6/1, and are repeated here for
convenience.)

What they do   1.   The Start and Action cards are shuffled and put in position as usual,
and the top two cards turned over.

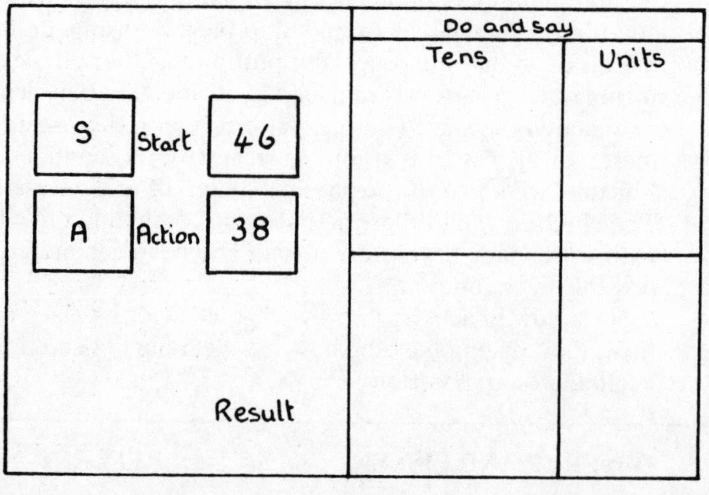

			Do and Say	
			Tens	Units
S	Start	46		
A	Action	38		
		Result		

2. Tens and units cubes are put down as shown on these cards by one of the children, who describes what she is doing and what it corresponds to on the SAR board. E.g. 'The Start card means put down four tens and six units.' The Action card means 'Put three tens and eight units more.' Each child records this on her own paper, which she first rules into headed columns. The board, and records, will now appear as below.

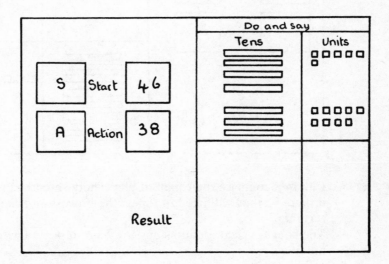

3. The next stage is shown below.

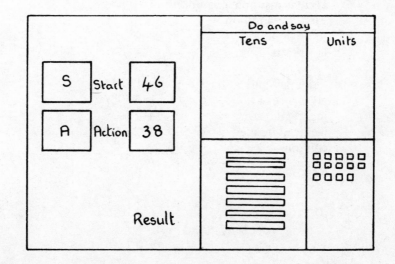

4. Finally, if there are (as in this case) more than ten units, ten of them are exchanged for a ten-rod. This is transferred to the tens column. The children again record this individually.

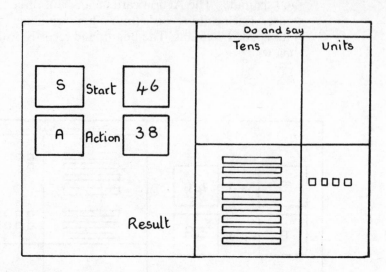

5. Children compare their final results. There should be no difference, but if there is, they will need to repeat the process and check each step together.
6. The board is cleared, and steps 1 to 5 are repeated with different numbers.

Stage (b)   Headed columns, no materials
1. The SAR board and base ten materials are no longer used.
2. Start and Action cards are turned over as before, and all the stages of addition are written in headed column notation as in stage 1.

Stage (c)   Place-value notation
1. Start and Action cards are turned as before. If the addition would result in 10 or more in the units position, a streamlined form of headed column notation is used.
2. Here is a simple example.
   First the addition
   to be done
   is written.

   $$\begin{array}{r} 3\;7 \\ +\,2\;5 \\ \hline \end{array}$$

3. Adding 7 and 5
   gives a result
   in 2 digits, so
   we need headed
   columns.

T	U
3	7
+ 2	5
5	12

4. Regroup

T	U
3	7
+ 2	5
5̶	1̶2
6	2

5. Finally write the
   result in place value
   notation

$$
\begin{array}{r}
3\ 7 \\
+\ 2\ 5 \\
\hline
6\ 2
\end{array}
$$

6. The whole may be set out like this.

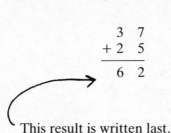

This result is written last.

Activity 2 Odd sums for odd jobs

A game for about four children. Its purpose is to use the skills learnt in activity 1.

Materials
- 1 die bearing only 1s and 2s. (For tens)
- 1 normal 1-6 die. (Or 0-9, if you have one.)
- 1 set of 'odd job' cards.*
- 1 set of 'target' cards.**
- Plastic money, 10p, 5p, 1p coins.
- Money boxes with a slit in the lid for all but one of the players.

* Written on these are jobs they might do such as 'Wash car,' 'Clean all downstairs windows'.

** Written on these are the kind of things they might be working for, such as 'Visit to baths, 60p', 'Present for sister, 78p'.

What they do
1. One child acts as 'Mum' or 'Dad'.
2. Each child picks a target from the target cards which are held in a fan or spread out face downwards on the table.
3. Then, starting with the child on the left of 'Mum' or 'Dad', the first 'does a job' by turning over a card, and since there is no fixed rate, throws the dice to see what she is paid.
4. The player acting as 'Mum' gives her the money in coins.
5. She puts these in her money box, which she may not open without permission.
6. Each takes her turn, putting the money in her box each time.
7. To know when she has enough money, each child keeps a record, adding on her earnings each time.
8. The first who thinks she has enough asks permission to open her money box, and her recorded total is checked by her 'parent' against the money in the box.
9. If correct she gets to be 'Mum' next time.
10. If not she has to go on doing jobs!

75

Activity 3   Renovating a house

A co-operative game for 4 children. Its purpose is to practise the skills developed in activities 1 and 2 in another play situation.

Materials
- Game board, see figure 2.
- On cards:
    house
    chimney
    windows
    doors, see photomaster.
- Tens die, numbered 1 and 2 only.
- Units die, numbered 0 to 9.
- Play money: £10, £5, £1 coins.
- Slips of paper, pencils.

It is a good idea to introduce the game with costs in round numbers, e.g. window £30, door £50, and progress to harder numbers as shown. For this two houses will be needed or adhesive labels used, after laminating, on which there are various sets of prices.

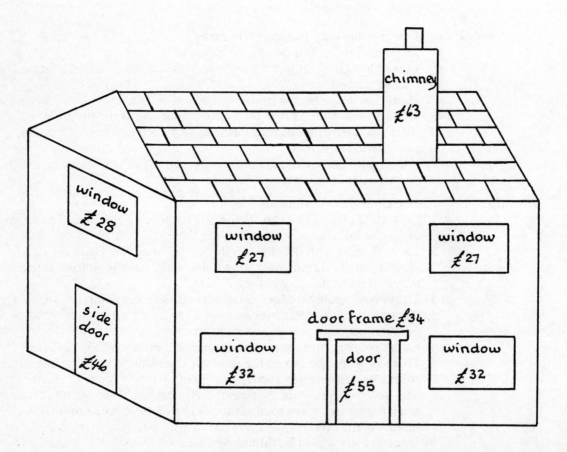

Figure 2   Renovating a house.

What they do

1. One child acts as banker, one as builder's merchant, and two as a young couple who are saving what they can each week and putting the money towards parts for their house. This is an old house which they have bought cheaply and are renovating.
2. Each of the couple throws the dice to determine how much they have saved from their earnings that month.
3. They record these amounts on a slip of paper, and add them together.

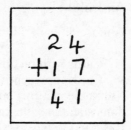

4. They take their slip to the banker, who checks their total and gives them cash in exchange, keeping the slip.
5. When they have enough, they go to the builder's merchant and buy a door, window, or chimney. The banker may be asked to exchange large notes for smaller.
6. When the house is built, they may play another game, exchanging roles.

Activity 4 Planning our purchases

For a small group. This activity uses the same mathematics for a situation which is the reverse of activity 2. Instead of accumulating money for a predetermined single target (which may be exceeded), they have a given amount of money which they plan to spend on a variety of purchases, keeping to a total cost within the given amount.

Materials

- A variety of labelled articles for the shop.*
- Slips of paper or card.**
- Plastic money.
- Pieces of paper and pencils for each child.

* Varied prices ranging from 48p, 19p, 7p and a few penny objects.
** On these are varying sums from 50p to 90p, in tens.

What they do

1. One child acts first as banker, and has charge of the money; then as shop keeper.
2. The other players draw slips of paper to discover how much they have to spend.
3. Each child takes her slip to the banker to get cash.
4. She then makes a shopping list which she totals.
5. When ready, she goes to the shop with her money and shopping list.
6. The shopkeeper then sells her the goods, naturally making sure that she receives the correct payment.

As described above, shoppers can use penny and twopenny objects to make up an exact amount, thereby avoiding the necessity for giving change. Children could also ask the banker to change a 10p coin into 5p and/or single pennies, which is good practice for mentally changing between tens and singles. Receiving change is however something the children will already have experienced outside school, so you may prefer to leave out the penny and twopenny objects and let the shopkeeper give change instead.

Activity 5   Air freight

A more difficult addition activity, for children playing in pairs.

Materials
- Cards with pictures of objects together with their weights.*
- Cards representing containers.

* Suitable pictures might be bags, suitcases, small items of furniture, domestic items like tape recorders, televisions etc.

It is good to have several assorted sets of these. We are using a set having 19 cards, each with a picture from a mail order catalogue, marked with the following weights:

$$64kg, \quad 54kg, \quad 52kg, \quad 48kg, \quad 46kg, \quad 42kg,$$
$$39kg, \quad 38kg, \quad 35kg, \quad 31kg, \quad 28kg, \quad 22kg,$$
$$20kg, \quad 19kg, \quad 17kg, \quad 15kg, \quad 12kg, \quad 9kg, \quad 8kg$$

This makes a total of 599kg, which it is possible to pack into 6 containers (5 holding 100kg each, and 1 holding 99kg). You could use other combinations of weight. It is probably easiest to choose them by breaking down 100kg's initially.

e.g 62,   27,   11.
53,   17,   22,   8.
49,   33,   18.
35,   31,   19,   10,   5 etc.

What they do
1. The aim is to pack all the objects into the smallest possible number of containers. No single container must weigh more than 100 kilograms.
2. They may work however they choose. One way is for one to act as packer, and the other as checker who makes sure that no container exceeds 100 kg.
3. If there are several pairs doing this activity at the same time, they may compare results to see which pair is the best at packing the containers.

Discussion of activities

These involve the extrapolation of techniques already learnt to larger numbers, and the combining of concepts already formed. So the schema building involved in this topic is a good example of mode 3: creativity. Grouping and re-grouping in tens from Org 1, adding past ten from Num 3.6, and notations for tens and units from Num 2, are the chief concepts to be synthesised.

In Activity 1, stage (a) renews the connection between written addition and its meaning as embodied in place-value notation. Stage (b) is transitional to addition using place-value notation in stage (c). In all these stages, place-value notation sometimes occurs in combination with headed columns. This hybrid was only adopted after careful analysis and discussion with teachers. It is implicit in the conventional notation, when small 'carrying' figures are used; so is it not better to show clearly what we are doing, especially since it represents such an important part of the calculation? The layout suggested is very little slower than the traditional one. If speed is the main object, then calculators are the best means to achieve it.

Activity 2 has been devised in the form shown to introduce a predictive element – checking the total on paper against coins in the money box. This you will recognise as an example of mode 1 testing.

Activities 2, 4 and 5 introduce multiple addends. In activity 2, this is done by stages, each total being recorded before the next one is added. This is how we add mentally, so it is a good preparation for activity 4 where the running totals need not be recorded unless children find it helpful. Activity 3, and the more difficult activity 5, have been included to give a further choice of activities in this section, since it is good for children to get plenty of assorted practice at addition with re-grouping.

OBSERVE AND LISTEN   **REFLECT**   **DISCUSS**

Num 3.9   ADDING, RESULTS BEYOND 100

Concept   Adding when the results are from 100 to 999.

Ability   To add 2 or 3 digit numbers, results in the above range.

Discussion of concept	As in Num 3.8, what we are concerned with in this topic is the further extension of their existing abilities in addition.

Activity 1   **Start, Action, Result beyond 100**

This repeats activity 1 of the last topic with hundreds, tens and units. Its familiarity should give children confidence in tackling these larger numbers before they use them in the new activities which follow.

Materials
• SAR board as for Num 3.8 but with an extra column for hundreds.
• Start and Action cards with assorted numbers between 1 and 499.
• Base 10 material, hundreds, tens and units.
• Pencil and paper for each child.

Stages (a), (b), (c)   These are the same as for Num 3.8/1 except for the larger numbers.

Activity 2   **Cycle camping**

A board game for 2 or more. Its purpose is to exercise children's skills in addition, relating this to what they have learnt on the number line.

Materials
- Board (see photomaster in Vol. 2a).
- Markers in the form of tents.
- Die marked 1-6.
- Die marked 0-9.
- Shaker.

What they do
1. The board represents a long and winding road through beautiful countryside.
2. The players begin at 0, and in turn throw the dice to determine their day's mileage.
3. The 1-6 die gives the tens, and the 0-9 die gives the units. The result is a variable daily mileage from 10 to 69. Children may use their imaginations to explain these.
4. Adding is done by counting on separately in tens and in units, a decade at a time for the tens.
5. Before moving, a cyclist points to where he thinks the day's mileage will take him.
6. The others check and say 'Agree' or 'Disagree'. If the cyclist's prediction is incorrect, he has a puncture that day and cannot move.
7. To finish, in this game the exact number need not be thrown. Any mileage equal to or greater than the remaining distance will do.

Activity 3 **One tonne van drivers**

A board game for up to four players. Their roles as van drivers give them plenty of practice in addition of numbers with sums up to one thousand.

Materials
- Game board, see figure 3.
- Cards representing vans, one for each player.
- Cards representing loads.*
- A calculator.
- Pencil and paper for each player.
- Paper clips, one for each player.

* The choice of loads affects both the length and the difficulty of the game. As a start I suggest you try the following:

6 large: 509, 576, 624, 697, 718, 745.
8 medium: 132, 194, 246, 287, 355, 369, 424, 431.
12 small: 12, 17, 21, 25, 34, 39, 40, 46, 65, 78, 89, 96.

What they do
1. One player acts as foreman, the others are van drivers.
2. The foreman has a calculator, the drivers do not.
3. The load cards are piled face down at the depots, which have respectively large, medium, and small packages.
4. The drivers have cards representing vans of 1 tonne (1000 kg) capacity. They drive these to the depots, and bring back a load to the warehouse. The load cards are kept on the vans by paper clips.
5. Players start at the warehouse, and move in turn. In a single move they may do any one of the following.
   (a) Drive to any depot and take what is offered (the top card).
   (b) Stay where they are and take another item.

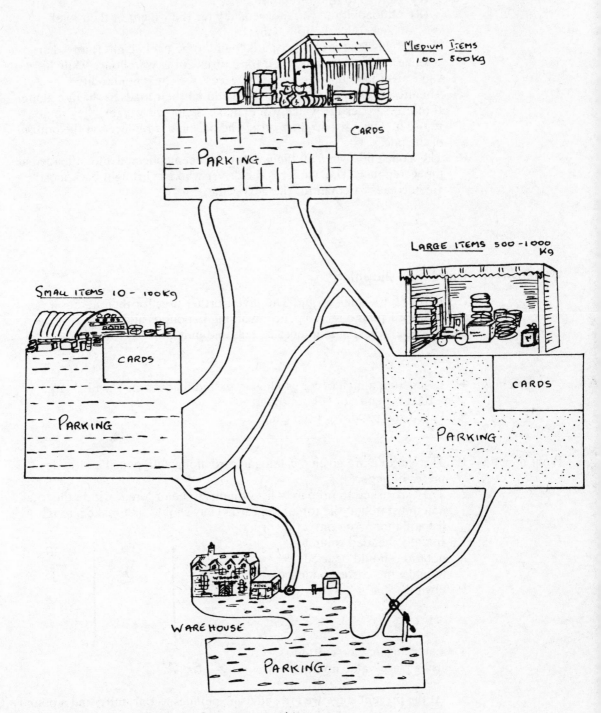

Figure 3 One tonne van drivers

  (c) Return to the warehouse.

  (d) Offload at the warehouse and have the weight of their load checked by the foreman.

6. If, when his load is checked, it is found to be overweight (more than 1 tonne), the driver must wait for 2 turns at the warehouse while his van is overhauled and tested. The excess weight is not credited.

7. The drivers use pencil and paper to add up their loads as they go along. If offered a package which would make them overweight, they should refuse it. This uses up their turn. The package is replaced at the bottom of the pile.

8. The game ends when all the goods have been collected and offloaded at the warehouse. The winner is the driver who has brought back most. He becomes foreman for the next game.

Activity 4 Catalogue shopping*

An activity for a small group. This gives further uses for their addition skills. Since 1 pound = 100 pence, working in pounds and pence is equivalent to working in hundreds, tens and units.

Materials
- Pages from a mail order catalogue, pasted on card and headed, e.g. '£100 to spend'. or '£25 to spend'.
- Pencil and paper for each child.

What they do

1. The children are given a catalogue card along with pencil and some pieces of paper.

2. They are asked to prepare a list of items to be ordered, within the total amount stated at the top of the card. They should first make a rough list and then write out a tidy order.

3. Initially, headed column notation should be used to make the correspondence obvious.

Hp	Tp	Up
5	2	7

4. Later this may be written as using place-value notation.

  £ 5. 27

5. At the present stage we are still using pennies as our units, and a pound is just another name for 100 of these. Later, when the pound is taken as the unit, the full stop becomes a decimal point and the next two digits represent tenths and hundredths. Decimal fractions are still in the future, but this transitional notation is excellent preparation.

* For this activity I am indebted to Mrs A. Cole, Headteacher of Loveston County Primary School, Dyfed.

Discussion of activities	We begin with the familiar 'Start, Action, Result' in the same three stages as before. This picks up the group of related concepts which are by now well established, and which we want them to extrapolate further. 'Cycle camping' (activity 2) uses a number line, in the form of a game, as another way of adding. Though the results go past 100, the new numbers to be added on do not. With this grounding in the expanded technique, children should be ready for activities 3 ('One tonne van drivers') and 4 ('Catalogue shopping'). The first of these is a little like 'Air freight' from the previous topic, but it also involves comparing possible outcomes of the moves they might make. The other is a budgeting activity. In adult life, planning the use of money and other resources – time, labour – is one of the major uses of arithmetic. This is one of the reasons I have introduced games of this kind.

OBSERVE AND LISTEN   **REFLECT**   **DISCUSS**

SUBTRACTION
Taking away, Comparision, Complement,
Giving change

Num 4.7 GIVING CHANGE

Concept Paying a required amount by giving more and getting change.

Abilities (i) To give the correct change.
(ii) To check that one received the correct change.

Discussion of concept

This is another contributor to the comparison aspect of subtraction. In this case, the larger number is the amount tendered, the smaller number is the cost of the purchase, and the difference is the change.

Activity 1 **Change by exchange**

An activity for 3 or 4 children (not more). Its purpose is to 'spell out' with the coins themselves what is happening when we give or receive change.

Materials
● Play money.
● A 'till' (tray with partitions).
● Pictures on cards representing objects for sale, with prices marked, all less than 10p.

What they do
1. One child acts as shopkeeper, the rest as customers.
2. The customers start with 30p, made up of two 10p, one 5p, two 2p, one 1p. The shopkeeper has plenty of 1p, 2p, 5p coins.
3. The shopkeeper sets out her wares. If there is not enough table space for all the goods, some may be kept 'in the stock room' and put out later.
4. The customers in turn make their purchases one at a time.
5. To start with, they pay with exact money. When they no longer have the exact money for their purchases, they pay by giving more and getting change.
6. Suppose that a customer asks for a 6p apple, and hands a 10p coin to the shopkeeper.
7. The shopkeeper says 'I have to take 6p out of this, so I need to exchange it.' She puts the 10p coin into her till and takes out 10 pennies. (With experience, a combination of 5p, 2p, and 1p coins will be used.)
8. Spreading these smaller coins out, she then says 'I'm taking this 6p for your apple' and does so. 'The rest is your change: 4 pence.'
9. The shopkeeper gives the apple and the 4p change to the customer, who checks that she has received the right change.

Activity 2   Change by counting on

A continuation from activity 1, for 3 to 6 children. (May be included or by-passed, at your discretion.) Its purpose is to relate the method of giving change which children will often have encountered in shops to its mathematical meaning, by putting it between activities 1 and 3.

Materials   The same as for activity 1.

What they do   1, 2, 3, 4 are the same as in activity 1.
5.   The method of giving change is now different. Assume as before that the customer has handed a 10p coin to the shopkeeper for a 6p apple. The shopkeeper goes to the till and picks up coins to make the total up to 10p, saying to herself '7, 8, 9, 10'. These coins may be single pennies, or any combination of 2p and 1p coins.
6.   She says to the customer '6p for your apple,' and then while counting the change into the customer's hand '7, 8, 9, 10'.
Note that with this method, the amount of the change is not explicity stated or written.

Activity 3   Till receipts

A continuation from activity 2, for 3 to 6 children. Its purpose is to relate the kind of subtraction involved in giving change (comparison) to the conventional notation for subtraction.

Materials   The same as for activities 1 and 2, and also
●   A pad of till receipts. (See illustration below.)

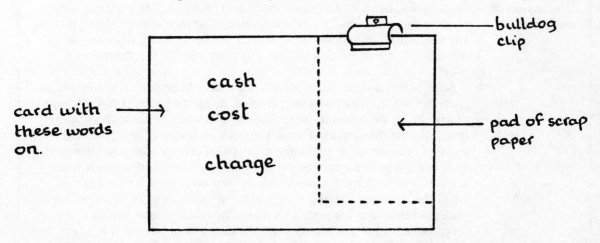

What they do   1, 2, 3, 4 are as in activity 1.
5.   Having arrived at the right change by any means she likes, the shopkeeper then writes for the customer a till receipt as overleaf.

6. She shows it to the customer like this, before removing it from the pad and handing it to the customer.

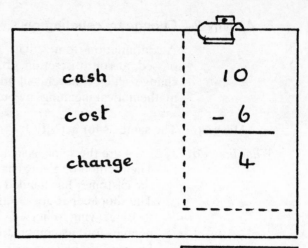

cash	10
cost	− 6
change	4

7. This is what the customer receives, together with her purchase and change.

$$10 - 6 = 4$$

Discussion of activities

Once again, there is more here than meets the eye. The counting on method for giving change, as usually practised in shops, produces the correct change and allows the customer to check. But it does not say in advance what amount this will be, nor does it lead to subtraction on paper.

So in activities 1, 2, 3, we have a sequence. In activity 1, the emphasis is on the concept itself of giving change, using the simplest possible way of arriving at the amount. Note that the customers begin with assorted coins, so that the activity does not begin with giving change, but with paying in the direct way. Giving more and receiving change is then seen as another way of paying the correct amount. We found that when this approach was not used, some children continued to give change even when the customer, having collected the right coins by receiving change, then paid the exact amount! This shows how easily habit learning can creep in instead of understanding, and also how important it is to get the details right in these activities. Activity 2 uses counting on as a method for first producing the correct change, and then allowing the customer to check. Finally, activity 3 transfers this to paper and makes explicit the amount of change which the customer should receive. It also relates this new aspect of subtraction to the notation with which children are already familiar. This helps to relate it to the overall concept of subtraction.

OBSERVE AND LISTEN   **REFLECT**   **DISCUSS**

Num 4.8   SUBTRACTION WITH ALL ITS MEANINGS

Concept   Subtraction as a single mathematical operation with four different aspects.

Ability   To relate the overall concept of subtraction to any of its embodiments.

Discussion of concept

In this topic we are concerned with re-capitulating the four earlier aspects of subtraction: taking away, comparison, complement, and change. Finally in activity 5, these are fused together into a concept of subtraction from which can be extracted all of these particular varieties.

Activity 1   Using set diagrams for taking away

A teacher-led discussion for a small group. Its purpose is to relate the take-away aspect of subtraction to set diagrams.

Materials   •   Pencil and paper for all.

Suggested sequence for the discussion

1. Write on the left of the paper: $-\begin{array}{r}8\\5\end{array}$

2. Say and draw (pointing first to the 8, then the 5):

   'This says we start with 8.'

   'This says we take away 5.'
   Cross out the 5 to be taken away.

3. Write the result, 3.
4. Review the correspondences between the number sentence and the starting set, the action (crossing out), and the result.

   $\begin{array}{r}8\\-\ 5\\\hline 3\end{array}$

5. Let the children repeat steps 1 to 4 with another example. Use vertical notation, as above.
6. Give further practice if needed.

Activity 2   Using set diagrams for comparison

A teacher-led discussion for a small group. Its purpose is to relate the comparison aspect of subtraction to set diagrams, and thereby to what they have just done.

Materials   •   Pencil and paper for all.

Suggested sequence for the discussion

1. Write as before.

2. Say, 'This subtraction can have another meaning, besides taking away.' Here we have two numbers, the larger one above.

3. Draw these on the right of the subtraction sentence.

4. Ask (pointing): 'How many more are there in this set, than this?'

5. If they answer correctly, say 'Let's check.' Draw lines like this and say (pointing) 'These 5 lines show where the sets are alike, so these 3 without lines show where they are different.

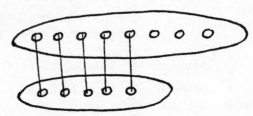

6. If they do not answer correctly, use step 5 to show how they can find the result.

7. Either way, write the result in the subtraction sentence.

8. Review the correspondences between the number sentence, the two sets, the action (comparison), and the result.

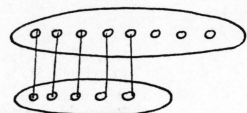

9. Explain: 'We've not been taking away, so we shouldn't read the number sentence as 'take away'. We say '8, subtract 5, result 3'.

10. Give further practice, as required. Use vertical notation only.

11. Say, 'Now we have 2 meanings for this subtraction sentence.' Review these.

Activity 3 Using set diagrams for finding complements

A teacher-led discussion for a small group. Its purpose is to relate the complement aspect of subtraction to set diagrams, and thereby to what they did in activities 1 and 2.

Materials
- Pencil and paper for all.
- Red and blue felt tips.

Suggested sequence for the discussion

1. Write, and draw in pencil.

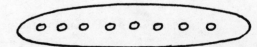

2. Say, 'Here is another meaning. We're told that these are all to be coloured red or blue. If 5 are coloured red, how many blue?'
3. If (as we hope) they say 'Three', check by colouring. If not, demonstrate.
4. Say, 'If we didn't have red and blue felt-tips, what could we do instead?'
5. Accept any sensible answers, and contribute the suggestion below. Tell them that they may continue to use their own way if they like.

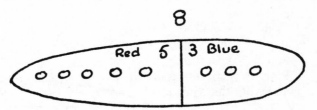

6. Invite other meanings, e.g. 8 children, 5 girls, how many boys?
7. Review the correspondences between the number sentence, the whole set, and the two parts of the set.

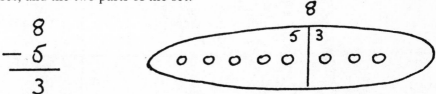

8. Remind them that the larger number has to be above. This time the larger number is the whole set, the next number is one part, and the last number is the other part.
9. Give further practice, as required. Use vertical notation only.
10. They now have 3 meanings for the subtraction sentence. Review these.

Activity 4   Using set diagrams for giving change

A teacher-led discussion for a small group. Its purpose is to relate the 'cash, cost, change' aspect of subtraction to set diagrams, and thereby to what they did in activities 1, 2, and 3.

Materials   • Pencil and paper for all.

Suggested   1.   Write, on the
sequence for the   left of the
discussion   paper:

$$\begin{array}{r} 8 \\ -\,5 \\ \hline \end{array}$$

2.   Say, 'There's just one more meaning we can give this. Suppose you are a shopkeeper, and a customer gives you 8p for an apple. But the apple only costs 5p. What money will you give him back?'
3.   Assuming that they answer correctly, say, 'Yes. Now let's check.'
4.   Draw.

8

5. Say, 'these are the 5 pennies for the apple,' and draw the partition line. Write the 5 inside.

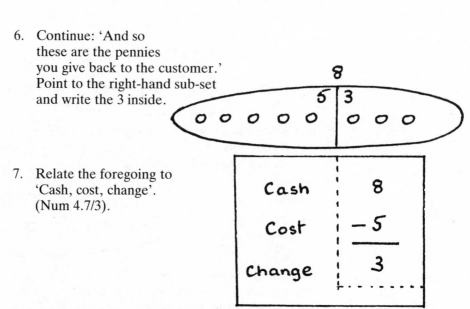

6. Continue: 'And so these are the pennies you give back to the customer.' Point to the right-hand sub-set and write the 3 inside.

7. Relate the foregoing to 'Cash, cost, change'. (Num 4.7/3).

Cash	8
Cost	−5
Change	3

8. Give further practice, as required.
9. Review all 4 of the meanings they now have for subtraction.

Activity 5 Unpacking the parcel

A game for up to 6 children. Its purpose is to consolidate children's understanding of the 4 different aspects of subtraction.

Materials
- Parcel cards, of two kinds:
  as illustrated in step 1
  as illustrated in step 6.
- A bowl of counters.

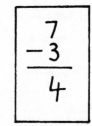

Rules of the game
1. The first set of parcel cards is put face down, and the top one turned over. (Reminder: this is read as '7, subtract 3, result 4', NOT as '7, take away 3. . .'.)

2. Explain that this has a number of different meanings which can be 'taken out', one at a time, like unpacking a parcel.
3. The children take turns to give one meaning. If the others agree, he takes a counter.
4. There are four different mathematical meanings, as in activities 1, 2, 3, 4.

5. An unlimited number of situational meanings can also be found, and these can become repetitive, e.g. if someone says,
'7 boxes, 3 empty, so 4 have something in them,'
and someone else then says,
'7 cups, 3 empty, so 4 have something in them,'
this is so little different as to be hardly worth saying. If the rest of the group unanimously think that an example is of this kind, they might reject it even though correct. This might lead to discussion as to what is acceptable as a genuinely different meaning.

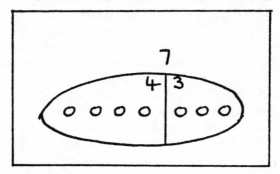

6. 'Parcels' like this one have even more possible meanings, e.g.

$$+\ \frac{\begin{array}{r}4\\3\end{array}}{7} \qquad -\ \frac{\begin{array}{r}7\\4\end{array}}{3} \qquad -\ \frac{\begin{array}{r}7\\3\end{array}}{4}$$

with 4 different meanings for each of the subtractions.

7. This activity involves much concentration of mathematical meaning, and children should return to it at intervals until all four aspects are mastered. Children find the part-whole relationships harder than the take-away and comparison aspects of subtraction.

<table>
<tr><td>**Discussion of activities**</td><td>In this topic we have a good example of the highly abstract and concentrated nature of mathematical ideas. Hence its power, but hence also the need for very careful teaching.

In the four topics which lead up to this one, the four different aspects of subtraction are introduced separately, with the use of materials to provide a less abstract approach. In the present topic these are brought together by using set diagrams, which again provide a less abstract symbolism than the purely numerical symbols whose use, with full understanding, is the final learning goal.

In activity 5, the children are learning explicitly something about the nature of mathematics, namely its concentration of information. We ourselves have been taking notice of this from the beginning.</td></tr>
</table>

OBSERVE AND LISTEN   **REFLECT**   **DISCUSS**

Num 4.9   SUBTRACTION OF NUMBERS UP TO 20, INCLUDING CROSSING THE 10 BOUNDARY

Concept Expansion of the subtraction concept to include larger numbers.

Ability To subtract numbers up to 20, including examples which involve crossing the 10 boundary.

Discussion of concept	'Crossing the ten boundary' means calculations like $12 - 3$, $14 - 6$, $17 - 9$. All subsequent examples which involve regrouping, such as $52 - 4$, $82 - 36$, $318 - 189$, depend on this.

Over the years there has been much discussion whether children should be taught to subtract by decomposition or complementary addition. The argument for decomposition has been that it can be demonstrated with physical materials, and so is better for teaching with understanding. For complementary addition, it has been claimed that it is easier to do, and makes for faster and more accurate calculations. The latter can also be justified sensibly, though it seldom is: 'borrowing' and 'paying back' is a nonsensical explanation.

The present approach is based on the physical regroupings which the children have learnt in Org 1, and the concept of canonical form which comes in both Org 1 and Num 2. It has several advantages:

(i) It is mathematically sound.

(ii) It allows children to use whichever technique they find easier: counting back, corresponding to the take-away aspect of subtraction, or counting on, corresponding to complementation. Both of these they have already experienced with physical materials. Taking away across the ten boundary involves decomposing one larger group into 10 smaller groups; complementing involves putting together 10 smaller groups into one larger group. Either way, re-grouping and canonical form are the key concepts.

(iii) the same technique (changing out of or into canonical form) is also good for adding, multiplying, and dividing.

The present topic is preparatory to the full technique, which follows in Num 4.10. It teaches what we do after changing out of canonical form.

Activity 1   Subtracting from teens: choose your method

A teacher-led activity for up to 6 children. Its purpose is to show them two ways of subtracting across the tens boundary, help them to see that these are equivalent, and choose which method they prefer.

Materials • Two sets of number cards, in different colours. One set is from 10-19, the other is from 0 to 9.
  • Subtraction board, as illustrated opposite.

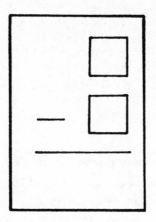

What they do 1. Before starting, they should revise finger counting, including 'Ten in my head'. (See Num 1.5/1 and Num 1.7/1.)

2. The subtraction board is put where all the children can see it the same way up. Both sets of cards are shuffled and put face down, near the board, with the teens set on the left.

3. The top card from each pack is turned over, and put, one in each space on the board, to give (e.g.).

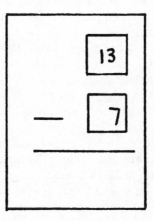

4. Demonstrate the two ways of doing this using finger counting.
(a) Counting back. 'We start at 13 and count back to 7, putting down one finger each time. 12 (one finger down), 11, 10, 9, 8, 7 (six fingers down). The difference is 6.' They all do this.
(b) Counting on. 'We start at 7 and count on to 13, putting down one finger each time. 8 (one finger down), 9, 10, 11, 12, 13 (six fingers down). The difference is 6.' They all do this.

5. Note that
(i) we use the word 'difference' in both cases to link with this aspect of subtraction.
(ii) We do *not* put down a finger for the starting number.
(iii) This method gives (as intended) a mixture of examples in which some do and some do not involve crossing the tens boundary.

6. With another pair of numbers, half the children arrive at the difference by counting back, and half by counting on. They should all have down the same number of fingers.
7. Step 5 is repeated until the children are proficient.
8. Tell them that having tried both, they may use whichever method they prefer from now on. They may like to discuss the reasons for their preference.

Activity 2 Subtracting from teens: 'Check!'

A game for 4 or 6 children, playing in teams of 2. Its purpose is to give them fluency in subtracting across the tens boundary.

Materials
- Number cards 10-19 and 0-9.*
- Subtraction boards.*
- A bowl of counters.

* The same as for activity 1.

What they do
1. Subtraction board 1 is put where all can see it the same way up. Both sets of cards are shuffled and put near the board, with the teens set on the left.
2. In the first team, each player turns over the top card from one of the packs and puts it on the board, the teens card being on the left.
3. The two players then do the subtraction independently by any method they like.
4. Another player says, 'Ready? Check!'
5. On the word 'Check', both players immediately put fingers on the table to show their results. No alteration is allowed.
6. In some cases the result will be over 10. Example: $15 - 2$. Both players should now put down 3 fingers, saying '10 in my head'. (See Num 1.7/1.)
7. The other players check, and if both have the same number of fingers on the table (and the others agree that this is the correct answer), this team takes a counter.
8. Steps 2 to 6 are repeated by the next team.
9. The game continues as long as desired, the number cards being shuffled and replaced when necessary. All teams should have the same number of tries.
10. The winners are those with the most counters.

Activity 3 Till receipts up to 20p

A continuation from Num 4.7/3, for 3 to 7 children. Its purpose is to consolidate their new skill in a familiar activity.

Materials
- Play money. The customers each have 40p in 10s and 20s, also one 5p, two 2p, and one 1p. The shopkeeper has a good assortment of all coins.
- A tray with partitions, used as a till.
- Pictures on cards representing objects for sale with prices marked, ranging from (say) 3p to 19p.

- Base 10 material, units and ten-rods.

What they do
1. to 7. the same as in the earlier version of 'Till receipts' (Num 4.7/3), except that the prices range all the way up to 19p.
8. Customers may now purchase several objects at a time, provided only that the total is below 20p. They may also give a 20p coin to pay for (e.g.) an object costing only 4p.
9. At any time when children have difficulty in writing the till receipts or checking them, they should help themselves by using base 10 material as in activity 1. They may also use the counting on method of Num 4.7/2.

Activity 4 Gift shop

A game, continuing on from the previous activity, for 3 to 6 children.

Materials The same as for activity 3, together with a notice as illustrated in step 9. Its purpose is further to consolidate their new skills, and extend these to subtraction other than from multiples of 10.

Rules of play
1. to 8. The same as in activity 3.
9. However, the shopkeeper also displays a notice:

```
┌─────────────────────────────────┐
│                                 │
│   YOUR PURCHASE FREE            │
│                                 │
│  if I give the wrong change.    │
│                                 │
└─────────────────────────────────┘
```

10. If a customer thinks she has received incorrect change, the other customers also check. If it is argued that the change was incorrect, the shopkeeper must give the customer her purchase free. The cash is returned to the customer, and the change to the shopkeeper.
11. If this happens 5 times the shopkeeper goes broke, and someone else takes over the shop. (The number of mistakes allowed to the shopkeeper should be adjusted to the children's ability.)
12. To make things more difficult for the shopkeeper, customers may pay with whatever amounts they like. E.g., they could hand over 17p for an object costing 9p. (This rule should not be introduced until the children have learnt the rest of the game.)

Discussion of activities
It will be noticed that the activities of this topic do not begin with the use of physical materials, in spite of the importance which in general we attach to these. Base 10 material is good for teaching the exchange of 1 ten for 10 units, but they already have plenty of experience of this. It is also good for teaching conversion into and out of canonical form, and

this too is done in earlier contributors to the present topic. It lends itself well to teaching subtraction in its 'take-away' form, but not nearly so easily to the comparison and complementation forms. The latter are easier to do mentally, since counting forward is easier than counting back. So the approach in this topic relies on the foundations laid by Mode 1 schema-building in earlier topics, and uses finger counting as a transitional technique which applies equally well to either aspect of subtraction. This will fall into disuse as children gradually learn, and use for subtraction, their addition facts.

These are followed by the application of these new techniques in familiar activities. The last activity, 'Gift shop', introduces a penalty for the shopkeeper if he makes too many mistakes, and a reward for the customer who detects a mistake. It is not only in this game that a shopkeeper who cannot do his arithmetic finds himself in difficulties!

OBSERVE AND LISTEN   **REFLECT**   **DISCUSS**

Num 4.10   SUBTRACTION UP TO 99

Concept   Their existing concept of subtraction, expanded to include subtraction of two-digit numbers.

Abilities   (i)   To subtract two-digit numbers.
(ii)   To apply this to a variety of situations.

Discussion of concept

So far as the concept itself is concerned, all that is new is the size of the numbers to which the operation is applied. However this requires the introduction of new techniques, and it is important that the manipulations of symbols which children learn at this stage should be meaningful in terms of the underlying mathematics.

The method we recommend has been reached by much thought, discussion, and field trials with children. It begins in Num 4.9, and continues here. However, rather than split the discussion, the whole of it was given at the beginning of Num 4.9. It would therefore be useful to re-read this.

Before embarking on this, we need to guard against the common error of subtracting the wrong way round, e.g.,

$$\begin{array}{r} 32 \\ -\ 17 \\ \hline 25 \end{array}$$

This gives the wrong result because subtraction is non-commutative. It contrasts with addition, which is commutative. The result of these two additions is the same if we interchange the numbers:

$$\begin{array}{r} 7 \\ + \ 2 \\ \hline 9 \end{array} \qquad \begin{array}{r} 2 \\ + \ 7 \\ \hline 9 \end{array}$$

Not so for these two subtractions:

$$\begin{array}{r} 7 \\ - \ 2 \\ \hline 5 \end{array} \qquad \begin{array}{r} 2 \\ - \ 7 \\ \hline \end{array}$$

cannot be done, with the
numbers they know about
so far.

I leave it to your own judgment relative to the children you teach,
whether or not to introduce the terms 'non-commutative' at this stage.
The important practical result is what activity 1 is about.

Activity 1   'Can we subtract?'

A teacher-led discussion for a small group, or for the class as a whole. Its
purpose is to emphasise that one can only subtract when the first number of
the pair is greater than or equal to the second. In vertical notation, the
upper number must be greater than or equal to the lower. (At this stage we
are not concerned with negative numbers.)

Materials   • Pencil and paper, or
              • Chalk and blackboard.

Suggested   1. Write a subtraction
sequence for the   in vertical notation, e.g.,
discussion

$$\begin{array}{r} 6 \\ - \ 2 \\ \hline \end{array}$$

2. Ask for the result.
3. Remind them of the first of the meanings for subtraction, taking away.
   (See Num 4.8).

$$\begin{array}{r} 6 \\ - \ 2 \\ \hline 4 \end{array}$$

4. Reverse the numbers, and ask 'Can we subtract this way round?'

$$\begin{array}{r} 2 \\ - \ 6 \\ \hline \end{array}$$

5. Depending on their responses, let them see that this would mean making a set with number 2 and crossing out 6.

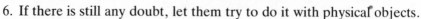

6. If there is still any doubt, let them try to do it with physical objects.
7. Repeat steps 1 to 6 with other examples. Include equal numbers, and also cases where one number is zero. Start sometimes with the not-possible case.
8. Continue, 'How about one of the other meanings of subtraction? Let's try it with case, cost, change.'
9. Clearly in this case you get change.

pence

cash   9

cost   − 5

change   4

10. But in this case, the shopkeeper would say, in effect, 'Can't be done.'

pence

cash   5

cost   − 9

11. Repeat steps 8 to 10 with one or more further examples.
12. Ask 'What have we learnt?' and obtain agreement on a suitable formulation, in their own words. It should mean the same as the learning goal described in the heading for this activity.

Activity 2   Subtracting two-digit numbers

A teacher-led activity for a small group. Its purpose is to teach subtraction of two-digit numbers, including cases which involve crossing the tens boundary. This now extends its meaning to include that between teens and twenties, twenties and thirties, etc.

Materials
- Subtraction board.*
- Two sets of number cards, in different colours. One set contains twenty cards bearing assorted numbers between 50 and 99, the other contains twenty cards with assorted numbers all less than 50.**

* Like that for Num 4.9/1.

** Suitable assortments are:

50 and over − 50, 53, 56, 59, 61, 67, 68, 72, 74, 75, 78, 79, 80, 82, 84, 87, 91, 93, 96, 99.

Under 50 −   8, 9, 12, 14, 17, 18, 21, 23, 26, 29, 30, 33, 36, 39, 41, 42, 44, 45, 47, 48.

Suggested sequence for the discussion

1. Put out the subtraction board and number cards as in Num 4.9/1. Explain that this is like the earlier activity, but they are going to learn how to do subtraction of larger numbers.

2. Begin with an example
such as this, in which both
the upper digits are
larger than the digits
below them.

$$\begin{array}{r} 68 \\ - \ 21 \\ \hline \end{array}$$

3. Explain: 'We subtract
a column at a time,
units from units, tens
from tens.'

$$\begin{array}{r} 68 \\ - \ 23 \\ \hline 45 \end{array}$$

4. Let them practise a few examples of this kind.

5. Next, introduce an example
for which this is not so.

$$\begin{array}{r} 74 \\ - \ 26 \\ \hline \end{array}$$

6. 'Can we do 4 subtract 6?
(No.) 'So this is what we
do. First, we write it
in headed columns.'

T	U
7	4
− 2	6

7. 'Next, we write the upper
number differently.'
(This is changing into a non-canonical
form.)

T	U
6	14
− 2	6

8. 'Now we can subtract
a column at a time,
as before.'

T	U
6	14
− 2	6
4	8

9. This is the answer in place-value notation.

$$\begin{array}{r} 74 \\ - \ 26 \\ \hline 48 \end{array}$$

10. The whole process may be set out as below. (The sign ⇔ means 'is
equivalent to'. Its use is optional.)

$$\begin{array}{r} 74 \\ - \ 26 \\ \hline 48 \end{array} \quad \Longleftrightarrow \quad \begin{array}{c|c} T & U \\ \hline 7 & 4 \\ - \ 2 & 6 \\ \hline & \end{array} \quad \Longleftrightarrow \quad \begin{array}{c|c} T & U \\ \hline 6 & 14 \\ - \ 2 & 6 \\ \hline 4 & 8 \end{array}$$

This 48 is written last.

11. The middle step may soon be done mentally.

$$74 - 26 = 48 \iff \begin{array}{c|c} T & U \\ 6 & 14 \\ -2 & 6 \\ \hline 4 & 8 \end{array}$$

12. Now let the children use the subtraction board as in Num 4.9/1, to give assorted examples. That is, the two piles of number cards are shuffled and put face down, and the top card from each pile is turned over and put on the board. The children copy what is there onto their papers, calculate the results, and check.

Notes (i) If step 7 is not understood, use base 10 material to demonstrate the exchange of 1 ten-rod for 10 unit cubes. The rest of the calculation is more easily dealt with symbolically, with the help of finger counting if necessary. This allows either the use of counting forward from the smaller number (the complement aspect of subtraction), or counting back from the larger number (the take-away aspect of subtraction): see Num 4.9/1 – 'choose your method.' Many children find complementation the easier method.
(ii) Eventually, the right-hand step may be done mentally, but this should not be done until the children have had a lot of practice in the written form.

Activity 3 Front window, rear window

A game for two. Its purpose is to practise subtraction of two-digit numbers.

Materials
- Game board (see Vol. 2a).
- 'Motor car' as illustrated below.
- Pencil and paper for each player

The motor car,
in coloured cardboard.
The windows (shaded areas)
are cut out as holes.
The arrow shows the
direction of travel

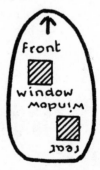

What they do
1. This game is based on the fact that the road signs we see looking backward tell us distances of places we have left behind.
2. The players sit opposite each other with the board between them.
3. The car is put at the starting town (bottom left), with the arrows pointing in the direction of movement. The players find out which window they look through from the writing they see right way up.
4. The car moves to the first road sign and each writes the number he sees.
5. The car moves on to the next road sign and each again writes the number he sees.
6. Each has now recorded two distances. By subtraction, each finds the

distance they have travelled between the road signs. Though the numbers are different, the distances are of course the same, so each passenger should get the same result. For the first two signs in the example opposite, the subtractions are

$$\begin{array}{r} 87 \\ -\ 68 \\ \hline 19 \end{array} \quad \text{and} \quad \begin{array}{r} 46 \\ -\ 27 \\ \hline 19 \end{array}$$

7. The car moves on to the next road sign and steps 5 and 6 are repeated with the two latest numbers.
8. This continues to the end of the journey. At the intermediate towns the car begins to travel in the opposite direction, so the passengers change the windows they look through.
9. By turning the board round, the passengers can get a different lot of calculations.
10. Further practice may be given by using other figures, either by making other boards or putting stickers on the existing board.
   Here is another suitable set.

Road section	Road length					
1	113	Front window	100	79	52	33
		Rear window	13	34	61	80
2	125	Front window	99	76	51	36
		Rear window	26	49	74	89
3	110	Front window	81	55	25	16
		Rear window	29	55	85	94
4	100	Front window	78	57	38	19
		Rear window	22	43	62	81

Activity 4   Front window, rear window – make your own

An activity and game for two. It is an extension of Activity 3 'Front window, rear window', in which the children work out their own road signs. This is appreciably harder than activity 3.

Materials
- A board similar to that for activity 3, without the numbers written in, but with the lines showing locations of the road signs. This board must be covered in transparent film.
- Car, as for activity 2.
- 2 dice, one marked 0-2 for tens, 1-6 for units.
- A washable OHP marker, and a damp rag.

What they do
1. They first decide on the distance between the first two towns. This must be between 105 and 130 miles (or kilometres). They both write this number down.
2. They throw both dice, to obtain the distance travelled from the start.
3. One player marks in this distance for the 'rear window', the other subtracts from the total distance to get the 'front window' number and marks this on the board.

4. They throw the dice again for the next distance travelled.
5. They each work out their own number, and mark it on the board.
6. Steps 4 and 5 are then repeated twice more to complete the first stage of the journey.
7. They then repeat steps 1 to 6 for the remaining stages of the journey, choosing a different distance between each pair of towns.
8. They should then play as in activity 2 to check their calculations, or swap boards with another pair to do this. At first they might prefer to check at the end of each stage of the journey.

Discussion of activities	Activity 1 is intended to prevent the error of subtracting the wrong way round, discussed first in the 'Discussion of concepts' for this topic. Activity 2 then shows children how to subtract two-digit numbers. Since children should already be familiar with moving into and out of canonical form from the addition network, the suggestion is that they work at this level rather than go back to physical embodiments in base 10 material. This avoids going right back to the take-away aspect of subtraction, whereas the concept now includes important other components. Help from the latter may however be used to demonstrate the change from canonical form, also (correctly) called decomposition and (incorrectly) called borrowing, without detriment to the foregoing.
	Activities 3 and 4 are more sophisticated applications of the concept of subtraction than they have encountered so far, using the new technique which they have learnt.

OBSERVE AND LISTEN   **REFLECT**   **DISCUSS**

Num 4.11 SUBTRACTION UP TO 999

Concept   The existing concept of subtraction, extrapolated to numbers up to 999.

Abilities   (i)   To subtract numbers up to 999.
          (ii)   To apply this to situations involving any of the four aspects of subtraction already encountered.

Discussion of concept	Although all that is new here is (as in the previous topic) an expansion of the size of numbers to which the operation of subtraction is applied, this results in a substantial increase in the amount of information to be handled. This makes necessary careful organising, with the help of symbols on paper.

Activity 1   **Race from 500 to 0**

An activity for 2 children. Its purpose is to make sure that the relation between larger numbers and physical materials, and the process of exchanging, are kept active before the children embark on the symbolic work of activity 2.

Materials
- Base 10 materials in box:
  5 ten-squares
  at least 20 ten-rods
  at least 20 unit cubes.
- 2 dice 1-6.
- Two hundreds, tens, units boards, as illustrated below, one for each player.

HUNDREDS	TENS	UNITS

Rules of the game
1. Each player starts with 5 ten-squares, representing 500. These are put in the hundreds space on his board.
2. They throw the two dice alternately, and these determine the number to be subtracted. If the numbers thrown are (e.g.) 2 and 6, the player may choose to subtract either 2 tens and 6 units, or 6 tens and 2 units.
3. They physically take away that number in the base 10 material, exchanging with the material in the box where necessary.
4. It is important to return material not in use to the box, or confusion results.
5. The player who first reaches zero is the winner.
6. Zero must be reached exactly. To do this, players may add or subtract the numbers thrown. Both must be used, e.g., a player throwing 5 and 2 could subtract either 7 or 3, but not 5 or 2.
7. Either player may delay taking his turn in order to check what his opponent is doing.

Activity 2 Subtracting three-digit numbers

A teacher-led activity for a small group. It follows on from Num 4.10/2, and its purpose is to extend the children's ability to subtract to three digit numbers.

Materials
- Subtraction board.*
- Two sets of number cards, in different colours. One set contains twenty

cards bearing assorted numbers between 500 and 999, the other contains twenty cards bearing numbers all less than 500.**

* Like that for Num 4.9/1.

** Suitable assortments are:

Over five hundred: 514, 533, 576, 587, 606, 641, 652, 688, 751, 727, 765, 790, 825, 843, 879, 890, 900, 914, 939, 968.

Under five hundred: 36, 54, 60, 71, 115, 142, 179, 187, 200, 241, 254, 298, 323, 332, 387, 399, 406, 415, 423, 468.

Suggested sequence for the discussion

1. Put out the subtraction board and number cards as in Num 4.9/1 and 4.10/2. Explain that they are now going to continue their learning of subtraction to hundreds, tens and units.
2. As before, the top card from each pile is turned over and put on the subtraction board. The children copy onto their paper.
3. The method is a direct continuation of that already learnt, so you may invite their own suggestions as to how to deal with these new examples.
4. Changing out of non-canonical form may now involve one column, or two.

Example: one column involved.

This 584 is written last

Example: two columns involved

This 616 is written last

Not all examples will be as hard as the second; but even with this kind, and the one opposite, this technique keeps thinking under control. It reduces the amount which has to be dealt with to one step at a time, and still allows children to do these mentally when they feel ready.
Example: two zeros.

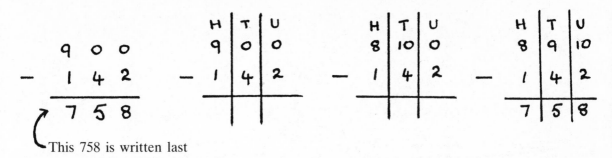

This 758 is written last

5. If one of the harder kinds comes up before the children are able to deal with it, it may be by-passed so that children build up confidence with easier examples.
6. If children still have difficulty, they probably need more practice changing from canonical form with the use of physical materials. (See Num 2.11.)
7. Steps 2 to 4 are now repeated. Each child copies from the board onto his paper, and does the subtraction. They then compare results with those sitting next to them. They should continue practising on their own until all are proficient.

Activity 3   Airliner

A game for two children. Its purpose is to illustrate the practical use of subtraction, and give practice in the subtraction of three-digit numbers.

Materials
- Airliner board, see figure 4.
- Three packs of 0-9 number cards.
- Pencil and paper for each player.

What they do
1. One player acts as flight engineer, the other as fuel operator.
2. They sit opposite each other with the board in between, facing the flight engineer. Some kind of screen is arranged so that only the flight engineer can see the aircraft's fuel gauges (as would be the case in the actual situation).
3. The number packs are put together and shuffled.
4. The 6 top cards are put in the 6 spaces. This gives a simulation of the readings on the fuel gauges when the aircraft lands.
5. The flight engineer wants to take on board the exact amount of fuel to equalise her port and starboard tanks. Suppose that these are the readings.

PORT TANK	STARBOARD TANK
724	419

She calculates that she wants 305 gallons in her starboard tank, and asks the fuel operator to put this in.
6. The fuel operator asks, 'What is your present reading, please?' The flight engineer tells her.
7. The fuel operator calculates what the reading should be when she has

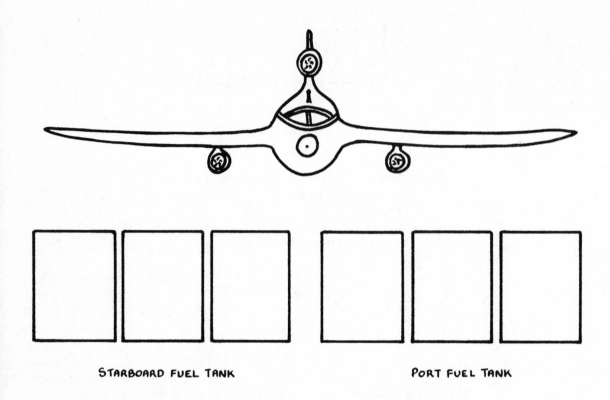

STARBOARD FUEL TANK   PORT FUEL TANK

Figure 4 Airliners

pumped in 305 gallons (in the present case). This of course is 724, the reading on the port tank gauge which she cannot see.

8. The fuel operator says, 'Check, please. I have put in 305 gallons according to my own gauge, so yours should now read 724'.

9. If both calculations are correct, this figure will be the same as the reading on the port tank gauge (which the fuel operator cannot see). If not they look for the mistakes in their calculations.

10. Steps 4 to 9 are repeated, simulating another flight.

11. After a few flights, the players change roles.

Activity 4   Sweet shop: selling and stocktaking

An activity for 4 to 6 children. Its purpose is to consolidate their new abilities in a game which links it back again with physical embodiments.

Materials
- 'Sweets.' Whatever sweet-sized objects you can obtain.
- Small self-sealing plastic bags.
- Cardboard boxes to hold ten bags.
- A pack of 30 spending cards on which are written sums of money varying between 4p and 25p.
- Play money.
- Pencil and notebook for each child.

• Shallow money containers, one for each player (useful but not essential).

What they do

1. One acts as shop owner, one as shop assistant, and the rest as customers.
2. Before opening the shop, the shop owner and shop assistant pack the sweets into bags of 10. They also pack boxes containing 10 bags.
3. The players begin with about 100p each, and the shop has about 200p: not these exact amounts, however.
4. Before the shop opens, the shop owner checks and records her stock and cash: e.g. stock 347 sweets, cash 185p.
5. Likewise each customer notes how much money she starts with.
6. Shopping now begins. Each sweet costs 1p. The customers find it hard to decide how much to spend on sweets, so each in turn takes the top card from the pile of spending cards which is put face down on the table.
7. Having taken a card, the customer spends that amount on sweets, keeping the card as a record of what she has spent.
8. The shop assistant does the selling. She breaks bulk as may be necessary to give customers the number of sweets they ask for. She also gives change if required.
9. This continues until each customer has made (say) 3 purchases. With 4 customers, this will make 12 transactions.
10. At closing time, the shop owner checks stock and cash. The total value of the sweets still in stock, added to the money taken, should be equal to the stock at the beginning of the day.
11. Meanwhile the customers also check. The total of their spending cards should be equal to the value of their sweets. Also, the money they have spent subtracted from what they started with should be equal to the amount they have left.
12. Another pair then takes over as shop owner and shop assistant. Everyone helps in restoring all the materials to their starting positions, and another day's shopping can begin.

Note

When children are proficient at this, the price per sweet may be varied. This complicates matters considerably. It might be a good activity for use with calculators.

Discussion of activities

Activity 1 returns to the use of mode 1 schema building, to make sure that the symbolic manipulations do not lose their connections with their underlying concepts. Base 10 material embodies grouping and exchanging particularly well, so we use it once again here.

Activity 2 extends the pencil-and-paper technique for subtraction, already learnt for numbers up to 99, into the domain of three-digit numbers. This is a simple form of mode 3 building – extrapolating ideas and skills they already have into new situations. It is simple, because no new concepts are involved.

Activity 3 is an easy game in which the players have a good reason for checking each other's calculations.

Activity 4 is a fairly ambitious one which brings together all the aspects of subtraction described earlier in this network. There is taking away, since the sweets sold are taken from those in the shop. At any time, the value of the sweets in stock and the money taken are complementary, the total being the starting value of the stock before any is sold and before any money is taken. This is also true for the sweets in stock and the money in the till. Giving change is also involved, and the change due is the difference between the cost of the goods and the cash tendered. The predictions are made and tested, in the checking of stock and takings, money spent and sweets acquired. And it is likely that at some stage of the activity children will decide to use recording to help them in what they are doing. There is a lot in this package, so it will be worthwhile letting children repeat it for as many times as they still enjoy it, so that they may have time to consolidate the many relationships which are embodied.

OBSERVE AND LISTEN   **REFLECT**   **DISCUSS**

MULTIPLICATION
Combining two operations

Num 5.4   NUMBER STORIES: ABSTRACTING NUMBER SENTENCES

Concepts   Number and numerical operations as models for actual happenings, or for verbal descriptions of these.

Abilities   (i)   To produce numerical models in physical materials corresponding to given number stories, to manipulate these appropriately, and to interpret the result in the context of the number story: first verbally, then recording in the form of a number sentence.
(ii)   To use number sentences predictively to solve verbally given problems.

Discussion of concepts

The concept is that already discussed in Num 3.4 (Vol 1, page 110). In Num 4.4 it was expanded to include subtraction, and here we expand it further to include multiplication.

In some applications of multiplication, we need to place less emphasis on the first action and the second action, and more on their results: namely a small set (of single objects) and a large set (a set of these sets). The use of small set ovals and a large set loop from the beginning provides continuity here.

Activity 1   Number stories

An activity for 2 to 6 children. Its purpose is to connect simple verbal problems with physical events, linked with the idea that we can use objects to represent other objects.

Materials   • Number stories on cards, of the kind shown in step 5. Some of these should be personalised, as in Num 3.4/1, but now there should also be some which do not relate to the children, more like the kind they will meet in textbooks. Also, about half of these should have the number corresponding to the small set coming first, and about half the other way about.
• Name cards for use with the personalised number stories.
• Number cards 2 to 6.
• 30 small objects to manipulate: e.g. bottle tops, shells, counters.
• 6 small set ovals.*
• A large set loop.
• Slips of blank paper.
* Oval cards, about 6cm by 7.5cm.

What they do   (*apportioned according to how many children there are*)
1. A number story is chosen. The name, cards and number cards are shuffled and put face down.
2. If it is a personalised number story; the top name card is turned over and put in the number story. Otherwise, explain 'Some of these stories are about you, and some are about imaginary people'.
3. The top number card is turned over and put in the first blank space on the story card.
4. The next number card is turned over and put in the second blank space.
5. The number story now looks like this.

There are 3 children in each rowing boat and 4 rowing boats on the lake. So altogether ⬜ children are boating on the lake.

6. Using their small objects (e.g. shells) to represent children, the oval cards for boats, and the set loop for the lake, the children together make a physical representation of the number story. If it is a personalised number story, this should be done by the named child.
7. The total number of shells is counted, and the result written on a slip of paper. This is put in the space on the card to complete the story.
8. While this is being done, one of the children then says aloud what they are doing. E.g. 'We haven't any boats, so we'll pretend these cards are boats, and put shells on them for children. We need 3 children in each boat, and 4 boats inside this loop which we're using for the lake. Counting the shells, we have 12 children boating on the lake.'
9. The materials are restored to their starting positions, and steps 1 to 8 are repeated.

Activity 2   Abstracting number sentences

An extension to activity 1 which may be included fairly soon. Its purpose is to teach children to abstract a number sentence from a verbal description.

Materials   • As for activity 1, and also:
• Pencil and paper for each child.

What they do   As for activity 1, up to step 8.

9. Each child then writes a number sentence, as in step 7 of activity 3. They read their number sentences aloud.
10. The materials are restored to their starting positions, and steps 1 to 8 are repeated.

Activity 3   Number stories, and predicting from number sentences

An activity for 2 to 6 children. It combines activities 1 and 2, but in this case completing the number sentence is used to make a prediction.

Materials
- Number stories asking for predictions.
- Name cards for use with the personalised number stories.*
- Two sets of number cards 2 to 6.*
- 30 objects to manipulate.*
- 6 oval small-set cards.*
- A set loop.*
- Pencil and paper for each child.*

* As for activity 1.

What they do   *(apportioned according to how many children there are)*

1. A number story is chosen. The name cards and number cards are shuffled and put face down.
2. If it is a personalised number story, the top name card is turned over and put in the number story. Otherwise, explain 'some of these stories are about you, and some are about imaginary people'.
3. Two more children turn over the top two number cards, and put these in the first two spaces on the story card.
4. The number story now looks something like this.

Giles is collecting fir cones in a wood.

He gets 5 cones into each pocket.

and he has 6 pockets.

When he gets home and empties his pockets, how many fir cones will he have?

---

5. The named child (if there is one) then puts out an appropriate number of small-set cards, and a number card from the second pack, to represent the situation. (This corresponds to step 6 of activity 1.) For the present example, this is what he should put.

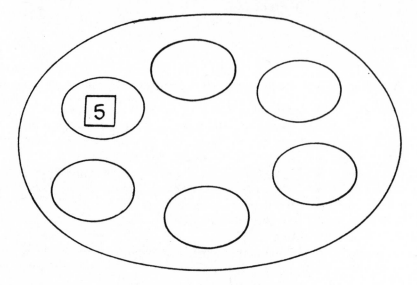

6. He explains, using his own words and pointing: 'These 6 ovals represent my 6 pockets, and this 5 is the number of fir cones I have in each.' (This verbalisation is an important part of the activity.)
7. All the children then write and complete number sentences, as in activity 2. For the present example, these would be

either $6(5) = 30$
        'six fives make 30'

or $5 \times 6 = 30$
        'five, six times, equal 30'

They read these aloud.
8. Another child then tests their predictions by putting the appropriate number of objects in each small-set oval. The number sentences are corrected if necessary.
9. They then write their answers to the question as complete sentences. E.g. (in this case) 'Giles will have 30 fir cones'.
10. The materials are returned to their starting positions, and steps 1 to 8 are repeated using a different number story and numbers.

Discussion of activities

The activities in this topic parallel those in Num 3.4 (addition) and Num 5.4 (subtraction), and in view of their importance it will be worth re-reading the discussion of these.

Solving verbally stated problems is one of the things which children find most difficult, as usually taught. This is because they try to go directly from the words to the mathematical symbols. In the early stages, it is of great importance that the connection is made via the use of physical materials, since these correspond well both to the imaginary events in the verbally-stated problem, and to the mathematical schemas required to solve the problem. The route shown below may look longer, but the connections are much easier to make at the present stage of learning.

Since these physical materials have already been used in the earlier stages for schema building, they lead naturally to the appropriate mathematical operations. Side by side with this, they learn the mathematical symbolism which will in due course take the place of the physical materials.

OBSERVE AND LISTEN   **REFLECT**   **DISCUSS**

Num 5.5   MULTIPLICATION IS COMMUTATIVE: ALTERNATIVE NOTATIONS: BINARY MULTIPLICATION

Concepts
(i) The commutative property of multiplication.
(ii) Alternative notations for multiplication.
(iii) Multiplication as a binary operation.

Abilities
(i) To understand why the result is still the same if the two numbers in a multiplication sentence are interchanged.
(ii) To recognise and write multiplication statements in different notations with the same meanings.
(iii) To multiply a pair of numbers.

Discussion of concepts

(i) Particularly when considered in a physical embodiment, the commutative property of multiplication is interesting, and surprising if we come to it with fresh eyes. Why should 5 cars with 3 passengers in each convey the same number of persons as 3 cars with 5 passengers in each? And likewise whatever the numbers? If you think that the answers are obvious, try to explain both of these before reading further. I have tried to introduce this element of surprise in the first two activities.
(ii) So far the children may have used only one notation, for multiplication but there are several in common use.

5(3)   which may be read as 'Five times three' or 'Five threes'.

3 ×5   read as 'Three, five times'.

3 × 5   (note the equal spacing)
          which may be taken either to mean the same as the one
          above, or as representing binary multiplication.

$3 \xrightarrow{\times 5}$ read as 'Three multiplied by five'.

There is also this   3
vertical notation   ×5
                       ―

which will be needed
later for calculations   473
like this   ×5
                       ―

We are more likely to read the lower one as 'five threes . . . five sevens . . . five fours . . .' than as 'three, five times . . . seven, five times . . . four, five times'. So here is an inconsistency.

This inconsistency is neatly removed by using the notation for binary multiplication, which is explained in the next section.

(iii) These are 3 different multiplications, shown in 2 notations.

5(3) $3 \xrightarrow{\times 5}$

6(3) $3 \xrightarrow{\times 6}$

7(3) $3 \xrightarrow{\times 7}$

The operand in every case is 3, but there are three different operations. These are, unary multiplication by 5, by 6, and by 7.

In contrast, binary multiplication has a *pair* of numbers as operand; and there is just one operation, multiply, for all pairs of numbers.

In some school textbooks, binary multiplication is represented like this.

(3,5) $\xrightarrow{\times}$

(3,6) $\xrightarrow{\times}$

(3,7) $\xrightarrow{\times}$

The above is correct mathematically, but I think it is difficult and inconvenient for children.

All the foregoing can be taken care of at a single stroke, by introducing computer notation for multiplication.

3 ∗ 5 = 15   read as 'Three star five equals fifteen'

means the binary product of 3 and 5. Because multiplication is commutative (see activity 2), it includes and replaces all the following:

$$5(3) = 15 \qquad 3 \times 5 = 15$$
$$3(5) = 15 \qquad 5 \times 3 = 15$$

$$3 \xrightarrow{\times 5} 15 \qquad \begin{array}{cc} 3 & 5 \\ \times 5 & \times 3 \\ \hline 15 & 15 \end{array}$$

$$5 \xrightarrow{\times 3} 15$$

$$(3,5) \xrightarrow{\times} 15$$

$$(5,3) \xrightarrow{\times} 15$$

This seems good value to me, particularly since children need to learn computer notation anyway. The computer books do not specifically mention binary multiplication: I am including this meaning as a bonus.

All the above will become clearer as you work through the activities in this topic.

Activity 1 Big Giant and Little Giant

An activity for up to 6 children. It is a sequel to 'Giant strides on a number track' (Num 5.1/3), and its purpose is to introduce the commutative property of multiplication in a way which does not make it seem obvious (which it is not).

Materials
- Activity board, see figure 5.
- Two sets of number cards 6 to 9 (single).*
- One set of number cards 2 to 5 (double).*
- Double width number track 1 to 50. (Card, 1 cm squares.**)
- Blu-Tack.

* To fit the spaces in the activities board. See illustration below.
** These need to be accurate in size, since the track will also be used with 1 cm cubes in activity 2.

Number cards

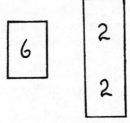

What they do
1. Two children act the parts of Big Giant and Little Giant, respectively. Big Giant is large and stupid, Little Giant is smaller and cleverer.
2. Big Giant has the set of double number cards and one of the sets of single number cards. Little Giant has the other set of single cards.
3. Big Giant turns over the top cards in each of his packs, and puts these face up in their respective spaces on the activity board.
4. Big Giant puts into action the statement which he has completed. He

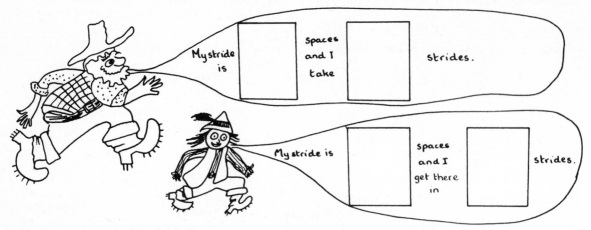

Figure 5   Big Giant and Little Giant.

does this by putting footprints (small blobs of Blu-Tack) on the number track, one for each stride of the given length. He uses the upper part of the number track.

5. Little Giant's stride is of a different length. He has to find out how many of these strides he must take to arrive at the same place as Big Giant. He does this in the same way as Big Giant, using the lower part of the number track.

6. He then puts the appropriate number card in his second space to complete his own statement.

7. The children then read aloud from the board what they have done.

8. Steps 3 to 6 are now repeated, with other children taking the parts of Big Giant and Little Giant. Say to Little Giant: 'If you think you know how many strides you need, to get to the same place as Big Giant, put the number in the space first and then see if you were right. If you don't know, find out first and then put in the number.'

9. Eventually one of the children acting as Little Giant will realise that his own numbers are always the same as Big Giant's the other way round. He will then be able to predict successfully every time. He keeps this discovery to himself for the time being.

10. This continues, with children taking turns at Little Giant, until all have discovered *how* to predict, though probably not yet *why*.

11. When this stage is reached, ask: 'But can you explain *why* your method always works?'

12. If any Little Giant can give a good explanation before having done activity 2, then he is really clever!

Activity 2   Little Giant explains why

A teacher-led discussion for up to 6 children. Its purpose is to provide the explanation asked for in step 9 of activity 1. For this, it may be necessary for you to take the part of Little Giant.

Materials   • The same as for activity 1, and also
   • Squared paper and pencil for each child.
   • 100 1 cm cubes, if possible 20 each in 5 different colours.

What they do

1. Start with a set of cards in position on the activity board, as in steps 3, 4, 5 of activity 1. This time, Little Giant's card should also be face up. So the board will read (e.g.)
Big Giant: 'My stride is 7 spaces and I shall take 3 strides.'
Little Giant: 'My stride is 3 spaces and I shall get there in 7 strides.'

2. Instead of footmarks on the number track, the giants represent their strides by rods. So in this example, Big Giant uses a 7-rod to represent one of his strides, and puts together 3 of these on the number track. Little Giant uses a 3-rod for one of his strides, and joins together 7 of these alongside those of Big Giant. Adjacent strides should be of different colours, to keep them distinguishable.

3. At this stage it is still not obvious why both are of the same length, since the two journeys look different.

4. 'Now,' says Little Giant, 'we arrange the rods like this.' The long rods are then separated again into single strides, and arranged in rectangles as shown below.

Big Giant.

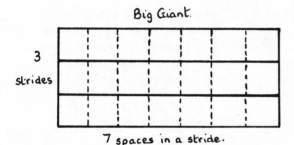

3 strides

7 spaces in a stride.

Little Giant.

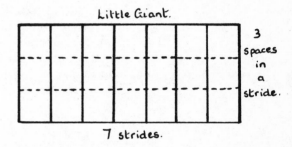

3 spaces in a stride.

7 strides.

5. From this it can be seen why the two journeys are of the same length. 3 strides, each of 7 spaces makes the same rectangle as 7 strides, each of 3 spaces. Both rectangles have the same number of cubes.

6. Big Giant asks, 'Will it always happen like this, whatever the numbers?'

7. The group as a whole discusses this. One or two other examples might be done using the cubes.

8. This should now be continued as a pencil and paper activity, using squared paper, as follows.

9. Two more numbers are shown on the activity board: e.g. 6 and 4.

10. All the children draw rectangles 6 squares long and 4 squares wide.

11. The children make these into diagrams for the two different ways of getting to the same place, as shown in step 4. About half the children make diagrams representing Big Giant's journey (6 spaces in a stride, 4 strides), and the rest make diagrams representing Little Giant's journey (4 spaces in a stride, 6 strides).

12. They interchange, and check each other's diagrams.

13. Finally, Little Giant tells the others: 'There is a word for what we have just learnt. Multiplication is *commutative*. It means that if we change the two numbers round, we still get the same result. Always.'

Activity 3   Binary multiplication

Continuing the discussion in activity 2.

Materials   • Pencil and squared paper.

Suggested sequence for the discussion

1. Draw a rectangle, say 5 squares by 3 squares.

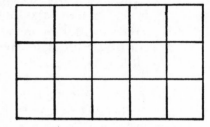

2. Ask the children how many different multiplication sentences they can write based on this diagram. Collect these in two groups, those meaning 5 sets of 3 and those meaning 3 sets of 5. (See 'Discussion of concepts'.)
3. Now that they have learnt that multiplication is commutative, all the notations in both groups are different ways of writing and thinking about the same thing. So it would be sensible to have just one way of writing all these, not 6 different ways (or however many you have collected).
4. Computer notation provides just what we need.

$$3 * 5$$

combines all the above in just one notation. So we shall use this from now on, unless there is a particular reason for using one of the others.
5. (This part of the discussion is optional.) It follows that $5 * 3$ and $3 * 5$ mean the same thing as each other. It would be nice to have a notation in which neither number was written before the other, but it is hard to think how this could be done. The nearest representation we can get to this is the rectangle 3 squares by 5 squares, shown in step 1. Here, there is no distinction between rows and columns; i.e. no distinction between the 3 and the 5.

Activity 4   Unpacking the parcel (binary multiplication)
Alternative notations

A game for up to 6 children. Its purpose is to consolidate the connections between the notation just learnt, and its various possible meanings. Also, to show what a great amount of information is contained in a single statement.

Materials   • About 10 cards on which are written an assortment of number sentences like $3 * 5 = 15, 6 * 4 = 24$.
• Pencil, plain and squared paper for each child.
• Number track.
• A bowl of counters.

What they do

1. The cards are shuffled and put face down.
2. The top card is turned over: e.g. 2 * 7 = 14.
3. The players in turn 'unpack the parcel', by giving some of the various meanings contained in this number sentence. They may use drawings, or appropriate number sentences.
   E.g. (drawing)
   'Make a set of 2.
   Make it 7 times.
   Combined result, 14'

   writes: 2 ×7 = 14

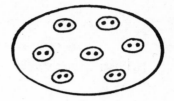

4. The next player might draw this, and say
   'Rectangle 2 by 7,
   14 squares. The notation for
   this is the one on the card'.

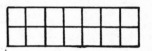

5. The next players might use the same rectangle, first as 7 2-rods, then as 2 7-rods, writing these respectively as 7(2) = 14 and 2(7) = 14.
6. Points may also be scored by writing a number sentence in a different notation, which has the same meaning as that which another player has just given. This may be done only once for each example.
7. Others might use the number track, in the ways already learnt.
8. Each time a player gives a meaning, the others say 'Agree' if they think he is correct, and he takes a counter. If they do not agree, they explain why not and if necessary discuss.
9. When all have made a statement about this card, or when players run out of ideas, the next card is turned, and steps 2 to 6 are repeated.
10. The player with the most counters at the end of play is the winner.

Discussion of activities

In this topic, the children are introduced to some more ways of symbolising multiplication. For their future work they will need to know all of these, except perhaps the arrow notation.

To minimise the likelihood of confusion and maximise the advantages described, the important thing is to continue to strengthen the connections between the symbols and the concepts, rather than between symbols and each other.

Not this:

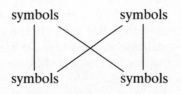

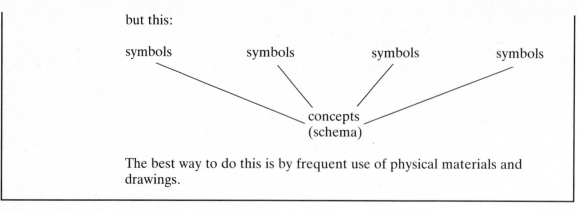

but this:

The best way to do this is by frequent use of physical materials and drawings.

OBSERVE AND LISTEN   REFLECT   DISCUSS

Num 5.6   BUILDING PRODUCT TABLES: READY-FOR-USE RESULTS

Concepts   (i)   Product tables, as an organised collection of ready-for-use results.
(ii)   The complete set of products, up to 10 $*$ 10.

Abilities   (i)   To recall easily and accurately whatever results are needed for a particular job.
(ii)   To build new results from those which are already known.

Discussion of concepts	In view of the strong emphasis throughout this book on concepts, schemas, and understanding, it may come as a surprise that I believe firmly in the importance of children's 'knowing their tables', even in these days of inexpensive calculators. But there is no inconsistency.

To put our knowledge to good use, which includes using it to extend its own boundaries, we must have readily available all the results which we need for frequent use. Just as our writing would be very slow if we had not memorised the correct spelling of a large number of words, so our arithmetic would be very slow if we had not learnt our addition facts and product tables. (Note that the result of an addition is called a sum, and that the result of a multiplication is called a product.)

However, we would hardly think it sensible to make children memorise the spelling of words which to them were meaningless. Yet until recently, and perhaps even now, children are required to memorise multiplication tables while their concept of multiplication is so weak that they still have to ask, 'Please, Miss, is it an add or a multiply?'

Understanding of the relationship between multiplication and physical events, both with actual objects and events as described in number stories, has been carefully developed in preceding topics. In the present topic, although the activities are intended to help children acquire a repertoire of ready-for-use results, you will see that this is done in such a way that many of these are built up from results already known. So children are learning, not a collection of isolated facts but a system of inter-related results.

Activity 1 also uses an important property of multiplication, called by mathematicians the distributive property: 'multiplication is distributive over addition'. E.g.

$$4 * 8 = 4 * (5 + 3) = 4 * 5 + 4 * 3$$

The use of the product patterns shows this clearly, and at this stage of children's learning this intuitive and pictorial understanding is enough. A statement like the above would only confuse.

Later, we shall use this same property to multiply by numbers greater than 10. E.g. to multiply by 58, we multiply by 50 and by 8 and add the results.

Still later, this property will be much used in algebra.

$$a * (y + z) = a * y + a * z$$

Activity 1 Building sets of products

An activity for children in pairs. Its purpose is to help children build sets of product results; and to know these, ready for use. Stages 2 and 3 also give practice in mental addition.

Materials
- 4 sets of product patterns, for the products of 2, 3, 4, 5 respectively.*
- 4 corresponding sets of symbol cards.*

* See example in step 3 below. A full set is provided in Vol. 2a.

What they do *Stage (a) Products to 5*
1. Each pair uses one set of product patterns, and the first half (* 1 to * 5) of the corresponding set of symbol cards. We will suppose that they are using the sets of products of 4, so the symbol cards will be those from 4 * 1 to 4 * 5 inclusive.
2. The product patterns are laid face up in order, and the symbol cards are shuffled and put face down.
3. Each child in turn turns over the top symbol card, puts it below the corresponding product pattern, and says what this product is. (That is, the total number of dots in the rectangle.) E.g., she picks up 4 * 3, puts it as shown below,

Set of products of 4

 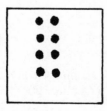 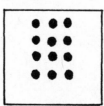 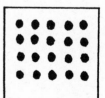

| 4 * 3 |

symbol card

and says '4 star 3 is 12'.

4. She may obtain this result either by counting the dots, or by recalling it from memory.
5. The other player then says either 'Agree' or 'Disagree'. If 'Disagree', they check by counting the dots.
6. The symbol card is then replaced in the pack, face down as before.
7. It is important that steps 3 to 6 are repeated until the children can recall all the results from memory before they continue to stage 2.

Stage (b)   Products to 10

1. A set of product patterns is put in a row, each with its symbol card just below. (See illustration for step 3)
2. The other half of the symbol cards is now used. As before they are shuffled and put face down, and the top one is turned over. Suppose that it is 4 * 8.
3. To deal with this, the product patterns for 4 * 3 and 4 * 5 are put together, each with its symbol card, as shown here.

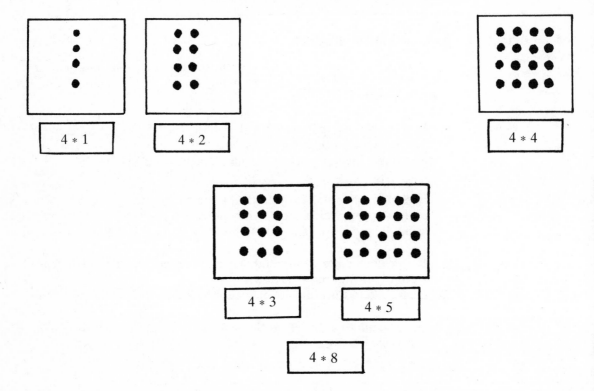

4. The player then says:

'4 * 8 is 4 * 3 plus 4 * 5
                    12   plus   20
4 * 8 is   32'

5. The symbol card is put on one side, and the product rectangles put back in line.
6. This is continued until all the symbol cards have been used. This activity is repeated until the children are fluent.

Notes

(i) Stage (b) is best introduced with even sets of products, 2 * and 4 *. These give multiples of 10 for the products 2 * 5 and 4 * 5.

(ii) The products with 10 should come late in the sequence. Let children devise their own responses. Some double the product with 5, some put together 3 product patterns, some already know the result without a product pattern.

Activity 2 'I know another way'

An activity for children in pairs. Its purpose is to consolidate results already known, to make further connections between these, and to extend their use of the distributive property of multiplication over addition. (This activity often arises spontaneously during activity 1, stage b.)

Materials   • A double set of product patterns.*
          • Symbol cards, full sets.*
          * As used in activity 1, stage 2.

Rules of the game   1, 2, 3. As in steps 1, 2, 3 of activity 1, stage (b). In this case there are two similar rows of product rectangles. Note that in step 2, the beginning player may now use either a single product rectangle if available (e.g. for 4 * 3) or two of these (e.g. 4 * 2 + 4 * 1).

4. If the other player agrees, she says 'Agree'.

5. She then says 'I know another way'. Using again the example given in activity 1, stage (b), step 3, and following on from there, she might put together product rectangles like this

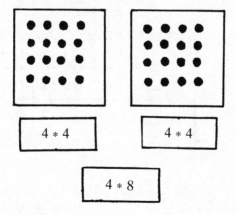

and says

'4 * 8 is 4 * 4 plus 4 * 4
       16 plus 16
          32
as before.'

6. If the first player agrees, she says 'Agree'.

7. The cards are replaced, and steps 1 to 6 are repeated.

8. As the players progress, they may use 3 product rectangles if they wish.

Activity 3 Completing the products table

An investigative activity for up to 6 children. The amount of help needed from their teacher will depend on the ability of the children.

Materials   For each child:
- A partly-completed product square, from 1 to 50.*
- An L-card, see figure below.
- Pencil.

* A full size one is provided in Vol. 2a.

What they are asked to find out   *Stage (a)*

What is the connection between the numbers in the squares, and the product patterns and results they have learnt so far? (The answer is shown, in brief, in the illustration.)

The lower right-hand number gives the number of squares in the rectangle, which is the same as the number of dots in the corresponding product pattern.

Here we have

$4 * 4 = 28$

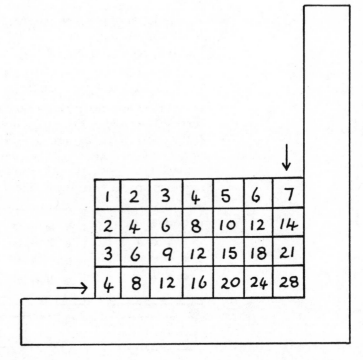

Stage (b)

How can they complete the product table by filling in the blank squares? (The left hand column, of course, continues from 6 to 10). We then want all the products of 6, of 7, of 8, of 9, and of 10. One way would be by laying down the L shape for each product, and counting squares. This is not as bad as it sounds, since it only involves counting the squares additional to those already numbered. But there are better ways.

(i) The first column, of course, continues to 10.

(ii) The next four columns can be completed by using their knowledge that multiplication is commutative. So $6 * 2 = 2 * 6$ which is already known, and so on.

(iii) Row 6 can now be completed by adding 6 each time. This is in fact another use of the distributive property.

$$6 * 6 = 6 * 5 + 6 * 1$$
$$= 30 \quad + \quad 6$$
$$= \quad 36$$

And so on.

(iv) The children should write all their new results lightly in pencil, until all their figures are checked with each others'. Then they should complete their product table as neatly as possible in ink (e.g. ball-point, thin fibre-tip) for their own future use. Tell them to keep these carefully.

Activity 4 Cards on the table

An activity for children to play in pairs, as many as you have materials for. They may with advantage make their own, and practise in odd times which might otherwise be wasted. Its purpose is to practise the recall of all their product results.

Materials
- 9 sets of symbol cards, each with 10 cards in each set, from $1 * 1$ to $10 * 10$.
- One product table and L-card for each pair.

What they do
1. In each pair, one child has in his hand a single pack of cards, shuffled and face down. The other has on the table his multiplication table and L-card.
2. Child A looks at the top card, say $3 * 8$, and tries to recall this result. Child B then checks by using his multiplication square and L-card.
3. If A's answer was correct, this card is put on the table. If incorrect, it is put at the bottom of the pile in his hand so that it will appear again later.
4. A continues until all the cards are on the table. This method gives extra practice with the cards she got wrong.
5. Steps 1 to 4 are repeated until A makes no mistake, and her hand is empty.
6. The children then change roles, and repeat steps 1 to 5.
7. Steps 1 to 5 are then, possibly at some other time, repeated with a different pack until all the packs are known.
8. The final stage is to mix all the packs together. Each child then takes from these a pack of 10 mixed cards, and repeats steps 1 to 5 with this pack.
9. Step 7 is then repeated with a different pack.
10. This activity should be continued over quite a long period: say, one new pack a week, with revision of earlier packs, including mixed packs.

Activity 5 Products practice

A game for up to 6 children. Its purpose is further to consolidate children's recall of multiplication results. This game may be introduced for variety before children have completed activity 4, using the packs which they have learnt so far.

Materials • Multiplication cards: all the packs which they have learnt, mixed together.
• A multiplication table and L-card.
• Products board, see figure 6.

PRODUCTS PRACTICE.	= 2	= 3	= 4	= 5	= 6
= 7	= 8	= 9	= 10	= 12	= 14
= 15	= 16	= 18	= 20	= 21	= 24
= 25	= 27	= 28	= 30	= 32	= 35
= 36	= 40	= 42	= 45	= 48	= 49
= 50	= 54	= 56	= 60	= 63	= 64
= 70	= 72	= 80	= 81	= 90	= 100

Figure 6

Rules of play 1. All, or nearly all, the cards are dealt to the players. Each should have the same number, so when the remaining cards are not enough for a complete round, they are put aside and not used for the game. The products board is put on the table between them.
2. The players hold their cards face down. In turn they look at their top card (e.g. 7 * 8) and put it in the appropriate space on the products board (in this case 56). It does not matter if there is a card in that space already – the new card is then put on top.
3. The others check. If it is wrong, they tell her the correct answer and she replaces the card at the bottom of her pack.
4. If she does not know, she asks and someone tells her. She then replaces the card at the bottom of her pack.
5. Any disagreements are settled by using the multiplication board.
6. Play continues until all have put down all their cards. If there are no mistakes, all will finish in the same round. Those who do make mistakes, or do not know, will be left with cards in their hands to put down in subsequent rounds.
7. If one player finishes a clear round ahead of the others, she is the winner.

Variation   If a stopwatch is available, this game may also be played as a race. To make a fair race, each player needs to be using the same pack. This suggests various forms, e.g.,

Form (a)   A single pack, of a table to be consolidated or revised.
Form (b)   Several packs mixed.
Form (c)   (For advanced players.) All packs from twos to tens, making 90 cards in all.

The rules for all forms are the same:
1.   One player acts as starter and timekeeper.
2.   The others in turn see how quickly and accurately they can put down all their cards.
3.   Those not otherwise involved check for accuracy, *after* all the cards have been put down.
4.   For each incorrect result, 5 seconds are added to the time. (This figure may be varied according to the skill of the players.)
5.   The winner is the player with the fastest time after correction for errors.

Activity 6   Multiples rummy

A popular game of the rummy family. Best for 2 to 5 players; 6 is possible. Its purpose is to consolidate their knowledge of multiplication facts.

Materials   • 2 packs of double-headed number cards, a beginners' pack and an advanced pack. The beginners' pack contains 2 each of all the numbers from 2 to 30, excluding primes greater than 20 (54 cards). The advanced pack contains one each of all the numbers from 2 to 100, excluding primes greater than 40 and even numbers greater than 20 (43 cards).

Rules of the game   1.   The pack is shuffled. Five cards are dealt to each player.
2.   The rest of the pack is put face down on the table, with the top card turned over to start a face upwards pile.
3.   The object is to get rid of one's cards by putting down sets of 3 multiples of the same number; e.g. 3, 15, 21; 2, 18, 20.
4.   Players begin by looking at their cards and putting down any trios they can. They check each others' trios.
5.   The first player then picks up a card from either the face down or the face up pile, whichever she prefers. If she now has a trio, she puts it down. Finally she discards one of her cards onto the face-up pile.
6.   In turn the other players pick up, put down if they can, discard. (This sequence should be memorised.)
7.   The winner is the first to put down all her cards. Play then ceases.
8.   The others score the total of the remaining cards in their hands. The lower the score the better, the winner scoring zero.
9.   Another round may then be played, and the scores added to those of the previous round. The overall winner is the one with the lowest total score.

Discussion of activities

The emphasis of this topic is to combine easy and accurate recall of multiplication results (products) with knowledge of many of their inter-relationships. This means that although there is memorising to be done, the facts which are thus learnt are related both to each other, and to their underlying numerical concepts. It also means that if a particular result if temporarily forgotten, the children know ways of reconstructing it for themselves.

Thus in activity 1, the products are related to patterns of dots which show both

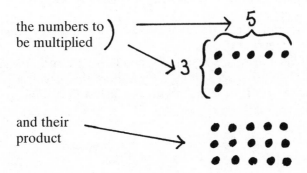

the numbers to be multiplied

and their product

Numerals are not written on the product pattern cards, so that children do not just match symbols to symbols in this activity. The number of rows and columns are however both small enough to be subitised – perceived without counting.

In stage (b), known products are used to construct new ones. This is mode 3 concept building, creativity. Here and in stage 3 they are also building up the interconnections mentioned above. Practice in mental addition is also provided – though you may allow them to use pencil and paper while gaining confidence.

Activity 2 further builds up the interconnections, and consolidates use of the distributive property.

Activity 3 is another constructive, extrapolative activity: mode 3 again.

Activities 4 and 5 are for developing effortless recall – 'facts at their fingertips'. But with such a strong relational beginning in activities 1, 2, 3, this should not become just rote learning. What we want children to acquire is fluency: easy recall without loss of meaning.

In activity 4, it is tempting to write the results on the back of the cards; e.g. to write 18 on the back of 6 * 3. I suggest that it is better not to do this, since it is a step in the direction of rote memory.

It strengthens this link

whereas we want this

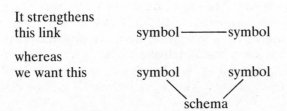

Eventually we   symbol — — — symbol
want all   \   /
three links   schema

and activity 5 promotes learning of the link shown in dashes. But the other two links, shown in continuous lines, are the most important.

Activity 6, 'multiples rummy', is a popular game which uses recall of relevant products to make the best decisions.

OBSERVE AND LISTEN   **REFLECT**   **DISCUSS**

Num 5.7 MULTIPLYING 2- OR 3-DIGIT NUMBERS BY SINGLE DIGIT NUMBERS

Concept Expansion of the multiplication concept to include examples in which the larger number has 2 or 3 digits, the smaller still having only 1 digit.

Ability To calculate any result of the kind described.

Discussion of concept

It is no small thing that once we know the multiplication facts from $1 * 1$ to $9 * 9$, we can use these to multiply numbers of any size, such as $5283 * 364$. Now that calculators are so widely available, it is quite unnecessary for children to achieve a high degree of proficiency in doing calculations of this kind, and there are some teachers who think that these should now be omitted altogether. My personal view is that this ability to make use of a relatively small number of multiplication facts (55, including products with 1 and 10) to multiply any two numbers we choose, without learning any more multiplication tables, is a fine example of extending our knowledge from within. Also, it depends on certain properties of multiplication and addition which, together with the idea of a variable, form the main foundations of algebra. So I continue here along the path towards long multiplication, in the belief that there are interesting things to be learnt on the way.

There are five of these properties altogether, of which two are important for this expansion of multiplication. They have been given technical names by mathematicians.

(i) Multiplication is distributive over addition.

$$\text{e.g. } 47 * 6 = (40 + 7) * 6 = (40 * 6) + (7 * 6)$$

If we think of 40 as 4 tens, we can calculate this because we know $4 * 6$. We already know $7 * 6$. The distributive property says we can get the correct result by adding these two products.

(ii) Multiplication is associative.

e.g. $2 * 3 * 4$ will give the same result whether the first two, or the second two, are multiplied first.

$$(2 * 3) * 4 = 6 * 4 = 24$$
$$2 * (3 * 4) = 2 * 12 = 24$$

You can easily check that this is not true for division. Its importance is that it allows us to multiply by one factor at a time. e.g.

$$38 * 40$$
$$= 38 * (10 * 4)$$
$$= (38 * 10) * 4$$
$$= 380 * 4$$

which we can calculate using the distributive property.
(Note that we have also used a short-cut for multiplying by 10, which needs to be justified.)
It is not easy to decide how much of this should be explained to the children. A full explanation is probably too much for most, but to teach just the methods is to teach instrumentally something which calculators can do much better.

So what I have done is to present the distributive property intuitively, as embodied in base 10 material; and the associative property explicitly, followed by a demonstration of its usefulness. In both cases I have replaced the technical names by simpler descriptions, but some of your children may like to know the former.

Activity 1   Using multiplication facts for larger numbers

An activity for any number of children working in pairs. Its purpose is to take the first steps in extending children's ability to multiply. Before they do this activity, it may be desirable to revise canonical form (Num 2.11).

Materials
- Base 10 material, tens and units.
- 6 small set ovals.
- Large set loop.
- Two dice 1 to 6 for each pair.
- Two dice 1 to 9 for each pair.
- Pencil and paper for each child.

What they do
1. The 1 to 6 dice are used to begin with. First two are thrown together, to give a two digit number. Then a single die is thrown to give a single digit number.
2. These are then written by each pair as a multiplication, in vertical notation, using headed columns. For example:

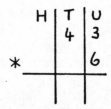

130

3. Base 10 material is put in one of the small set ovals to represent 43.

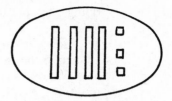

4. They then put more small set ovals to make six in all, and a set loop around them. (Base 10 material is only used in one of the small set ovals.)

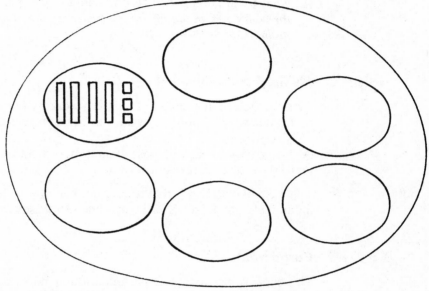

5. They think and write as follows. 'We have to make 6 sets like the one shown. 6 sets of 3 units is 18 units. 6 sets of 4 tens is 24 tens.

H	T	U
	4	3
		6
	24	18

*

6. Re-arrange in canonical form (working mentally from right to left), and there is our answer.

H	T	U
	4	3
		6
2	5	8

*

43 * 6 = 258

7. They compare their final answers. If these are different, they discuss.
8. Steps 1 to 6 are repeated.
9. The use of the base 10 material may be discontinued when you think that the children have well established the concept that what they are

doing on paper represents making many sets like the one in the set loop.

10. When the children are proficient with these smaller numbers, they may change to the two 1-9 dice.

11. The notation shown in steps 5-6 leads naturally to the conventional notation, in which step 5 is omitted and the re-arrangement into canonical form is done as we go along, with help from small 'carrying' figures. This conventional notation is quick and convenient, but it is also very condensed. The notation in step 5 shows much more clearly what we are doing, so I recommend using this to start with. *Note that the condensed notation will be needed by the time they reach long multiplication (Num 5.10).*

Activity 2   Multiplying 3-digit numbers

An activity for any number of children working in pairs. It follows directly on from activity 1, but the larger number now goes up to 999.

Materials   As for activity 1, but with base 10 materials in hundreds, tens, and units, and 3 dice for each pair of children.

What they do   This is so like activity 1 that it does not need to be described in detail. The method already learnt is easily extended to these larger numbers.

Activity 3   Cargo boats

This game is best for 2 or 3 players, though more could play. Its purpose is to give plenty of practice in multiplication.

Materials
- Game board, as illustrated opposite.
- Die 1-6 (for easier game), 1-9 (for harder game).
- Cargo boat for each player.
- Loading list for each player.
- Calculator.

The cargo boats are cut out of cardboard and look like this.

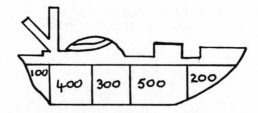

Rules of the game
1. Each player has a cargo boat, which he sails to each of 5 islands picking up cargo.
2. On each island there are packages of varying weight.
3. The first player sails his boat to the first island, and throws the die. This tells him the number of packages which he must take.
4. He may choose which packets he takes that number of. All packets of the same kind must go into the same hold. The capacity of these is shown both on the boat and on the loading list (see next step).

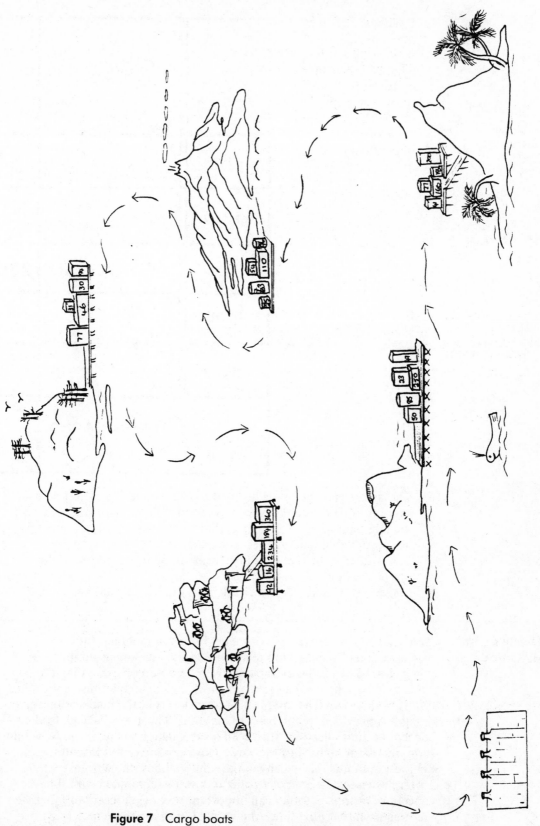

Figure 7 Cargo boats

5. Each player makes a loading list, on which he records what he takes on board. If he threw a five at the first island, his loading list might then look like this:

Compart-ment	PACKAGES		Load
	Number.	Weight.	
1 00			
2 00			
3 00	5 ✳ 50		250
4 00			
5 00			
	TOTAL CARGO		

6. The first player then sails his boat to the second island and repeats the process. Meanwhile the next player sails to the first island and starts loading; and so on. This means that by the third turn, all three players are occupied in making their calculations.

7. The winner is the player who returns to the home port with the heaviest cargo.

8. Players use a calculator to check each other's calculations.

Discussion of activities

Activity 1 is a good example of mode 3 schema building: the extrapolation of schema and technique to include larger numbers. In doing this, we want the extrapolation to be based on expanding the concept itself, and not just repeating a way of manipulating symbols in a different situation. The latter takes place too, but the justification for doing it is provided by the base 10 material. This takes us back to the concept of multiplication: start with a set, make it many times. Now our set has tens and units, but the way to make many of it is visually obvious. And it is this which lead to, and justifies, the written method.

Here as elsewhere, headed column notation combined with the concept of canonical form is an important way of representing what we are doing symbolically. Since the vertical lines are there to act as separators, there is no loss of meaning if we leave out the outside lines, on the left and right. And although I have still included the headings Th, H, T, S, I would see no objection to letting these gradually become, as it were, 'unwritten headings'.

The extension to hundreds, tens, units is so straightforward that I saw no reason for postponing it. Hence activity 2.

Activity 3 is another game like 'Air freight' and 'One tonne van drivers', for practising calculations in an interesting situation. You will easily be able to devise others. 'Catalogue shopping' also lends itself easily to purchasing several of a given article, and hence to price calculations which require multiplication.

I think that we should at this stage allow children to use a calculator for checking their work. In the present situation I see calculators as labour-saving devices, rather than as completely removing the need for children to learn to do these calculations themselves.

OBSERVE AND LISTEN   **REFLECT**   **DISCUSS**

Num 5.8   MULTIPLYING BY 10 AND 100

Concept   The mathematics behind the well-known shorthand.

Abilities   (i)   To multiply by 10 or 100, using the shorthand discussed below.
(ii)   To explain it in terms of place-value.

Discussion of concept

If asked 'How do you multiply by 10?', many children will say 'You add a nought'. This of course is not true. Adding zero to any number leaves it unchanged. Writing a zero after the last digit is a useful short-cut, but try using it to multiply 2.5 by 10 and it will give a wrong answer. Short-cuts can lead you astray if you don't know how they work.

Activity 1   **Multiplying by 10 or 100**

A teacher-led discussion for up to 6 children. Its purpose is to relate the 'shorthand' method of multiplying by 10 or 100 to its meaning.

Materials
- Two dice 1-9.
- Base 10 material.
- Base 10 Th H T U board.*
- Pencil and paper for each child.

* As illustrated below in step 3. This needs to be fairly large.

Suggested sequence for the discussion

1. Throw the two dice to give a random 2-digit number; say, 37.
2. Have them put out base 10 material on the board to represent this. In the present example,

Th	H	T	U

3. Ask them to show what this would look like if multiplied by 10, using additional base 10 material in the space below.

Th	H	T	U

*10

4. Ask them to record the result.

$$37 * 10 = 370$$

5. Repeat steps 1, 2, 3 using different numbers.
6. Repeat step 1, and ask if they can predict the result. If anyone talks about 'adding a nought (or a zero)', help them to see that this is incorrect by asking them what they get by adding (say) 3 + zero.
7. What we are really doing is to move every figure one place to the left, so that the units become the same number of tens, the tens become the same number of hundreds, and so on.

Activity 2 Explaining the shorthand

This is a teacher-led discussion for up to 6 children. It replaces activity 1 for children who already know the shorthand, but do not understand what is behind it.

Materials As for activity 1.

Suggested sequence for the discussion
1. Use the dice to give a random 2-digit number as before, and let them use their shorthand to multiply by 10.
2. Ask them to explain why this works, using the same explanation (that they are *not* adding a nought) as in Activity 1 step 6.
3. If they give an explanation like that in activity 1 step 7, or any other which is mathematically correct, good. Otherwise produce the base 10 Th H T U board, and take them through steps 2, 3, 7 of activity 1. Repeat if necessary, until you are satisfied that they understand what they are doing.

Activity 3 Multiplying by hundreds and thousands

A continuation of activity 1 or activity 2.
First revise Num 2.13/2, Naming big numbers, in the original form. Then repeat it using zeros to the right of a 2-digit number. Then, using zeros to the right of a 3-digit number.

Discussion of activities

This is a topic in which the use of the short cut without understanding is widespread. Activities 1 and 2 therefore use a combination of headed columns and base 10 materials to provide a sound conceptual foundation for what is undoubtedly a useful short-cut. Activity 3 parallels these at the symbolic level, emphasising the changes in meaning of each digit which result from their different positions.

OBSERVE AND LISTEN   **REFLECT**   **DISCUSS**

Num 5.9 MULTIPLYING BY 20 TO 90 AND BY 200 TO 900

Concept   The combination of their new knowledge of how to multiply by 10 and by 100 with their existing multiplication tables.

Abilities   To multiply any two or three digit number (later, more) by 20 to 90 and by 200 to 900.

Discussion of concept

The next step is easy. To multiply, say, 47 by 30 we multiply by 10 and by 3 in either order. What makes this true is the associative property, mentioned in Num 5.7. This tells us that

$$47 * 30 = 47 * (10 * 3) = (47 * 10) * 3 = 470 * 3$$

and for the last we only need to know our 3 times table.

Activity 1   **'How many cubes in this brick?' (Alternative paths)**

An activity for up to 6 children. Its purpose is to introduce children to the associative property.

Materials   ●   About 100 2 cm cubes.
           ●   Pencil and paper for each child.

What they do   1.   Some of the children make a solid 2 by 3 by 4 brick. (Call it a cuboid if you prefer.) Others make bricks of different dimensions, according to how many children and how many cubes there are.
           2.   Using the first brick, ask how many small cubes (or units) are there; and how they arrived at this result.
           3.   There are 3 possible paths, depending on which layer they calculate first.

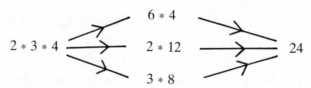

Elicit all three of these, and record them as above.
           4.   Repeat all three of these, and record them as above.
           5.   Discuss what this shows, namely that when multiplying three numbers together the result is the same whichever pair we combine (associate) first.
           6.   Help them to interpret these three results in relation to the brick. E.g. for the top path, 2 * 3 was calculated first. This corresponds to a layer, 2 cubes by 3 cubes, having 6 cubes in all. 6 * 4 means that there are 4 such layers.
           7.   Ask whether they think that this is always true, whatever the numbers. (It is: the number of cubes in a brick of any size can be calculated in all of these ways.)

Activity 2   Multiplying by n-ty and any hundred

An activity for up to 6 children. Its purpose is to combine the shorthand just learnt with the associative property, in order to multiply by 20, 30 . . . n-ty (where n is any number from 2 to 9); and likewise for 200, 300 . . . any hundred.

Materials
    Two dice 1-9.
- Pencil and paper for each child.

What they do   *Stage (a)*
1. Begin with numbers which do not give rise to special difficulties, such as extra zeros, e.g. 86 * 40.
2. Explain that by writing this as:

$$87 * 40 = 87 * 10 * 4$$

we can get the result without knowing our 40 times table, or our 8 times table. We just need to know how to multiply by 10, and then by 4. (Activity 1 tells us that we will get the same result this way. Think of a brick 8 by 10 by 4.)
3. The work may be set out as below. The final result at the end of the first line is written last.

$$87 * 40 = 87 * 10 * 4 = 3480$$

	Th	H	T	U
			8	7
* 10 =		8	7	0
* 4 =		32	28	0
=	3	4	8	0

4. Remind them that when converting into canonical form (last two lines) we work from right to left. When the new method is understood, the conventional notation may be re-introduced. (See Num 5.7/1, step 11.)
5. This is what we have now done.

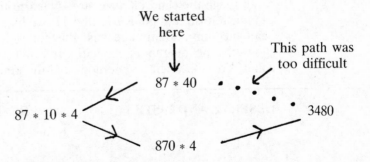

So we went the other way round, which was easier.
6. Even though this path is easier, there is a lot going on here, and it is important at this stage to consolidate these new ideas by discussion and by doing plenty of examples.
7. Steps 4 and 5 are repeated with other numbers.

8. When the children are confident at multiplying by numbers like 30, 80, let them extend the method to multiplying by numbers such as 300, 800.

Stage (b)

In preparation for long multiplication, they multiply simultaneously by 10 and by 4, as below. This may be taken in three steps.

1. $87 * 40 = 3480$

written last

	Th	H	T	U
			8	7
* 40 =		32	28	0
=	3	4	8	0

2. $86 * 40 = 3480$

	Th	H	T	U
			8	7
* 40 =	3	4	8	0

3.
```
   87
 * 40
 ----
 3480
```

Discussion of activities

We have now taken the first step into long multiplication, and this topic offers yet another example of how much is condensed into what on the surface looks like a simple process. I would not expect children necessarily to remember in detail all these reasons which they have been shown. What I think is important is for them to remember that there are reasons which they understood as they worked through them. They know that they did not learn rules without reasons, and that if necessary – possibly with a little help – they could remember why the new methods are correct.

Although the children have already learnt to change mentally into canonical form in topic 5.7/1, step 11, we back-track a little into the headed column notation because this notation is less condensed, and shows the meaning more explicitly. In other words, we are refreshing the connections between the methods and the underlying concepts.

OBSERVE AND LISTEN   **REFLECT**   **DISCUSS**

Num 5.10 LONG MULTIPLICATION

Concept   The use of just 55 known results (from $2 * 1$ to $10 * 10$) to calculate any desired product.

Ability To multiply 2 numbers in which the smaller has 2 or 3 digits, with understanding and accuracy but not necessarily with speed.

Discussion of concept

In the past, the main emphasis has usually been on the technique of long multiplication. The wide availability of inexpensive calculators has so changed the situation that if all that mattered was getting the answer, there would no longer be any good reason to teach this technique. This may well be the case for less able children. And I think that calculators should be freely used by all children in cases where the result is what is important, or when the figures are difficult.

However, the validity of the technique of long multiplication depends on several important mathematical principles, which have already been mentioned and which continue to be important in later mathematics. Two of these have already been specifically dealt with, in topic 5 (multiplication is commutative) and topic 9 (multiplication is associative). A third has been well used, and made explicit for teachers but not for pupils, in topic 6 (multiplication is distributive over addition). There are two more which perhaps I should mention for completeness, but you do not need to think about them unless you want to. These are, that addition also is both commutative and associative.

These properties make it possible to use known results to construct new knowledge, and thus to exercise the creative function of intelligence. This seems to me a good reason for continuing to teach long multiplication to those children who can grasp the principles on which it is based; and perhaps the only good reason.

The contributory concepts and abilities have been carefully prepared in earlier topics, and it is now simply a matter of putting them together.

Activity 1 Long multiplication

For any number of children. Its purpose is to show them how methods and results which they already know can be combined to multiply any 2 numbers.

Materials
- Pencil and paper for each child.
- Any source of numbers to be multiplied, such as dice, number cards, text book.

A suggested teaching approach

1. Explain that having learnt 55 multiplication results – called products for short – they can now multiply any two numbers they want, without having to memorise any new product tables. Discuss this in contrast to other learning situations. (Having learnt the names of 55 people does not enable us to know the right name for every other person we will ever meet.)

2. Recall how they worked out new products from those they already knew.
   E.g.,
   $$4 * 7 = 4 * 5 + 4 * 2$$
   $$= 20 + 8$$
   $$= 28$$

3. Show a suitable introductory example, such as 87 * 43, and invite suggestions.
4. What do they already know how to work out? Accept and list all suggestions which might be useful.
5. Depending on your own judgement of the ability of the children, you may wish to leave them time for their own investigations, or you may decide that a direct exposition is appropriate at this stage.
6. There are a number of ways of setting out the work. Here are two which show clearly the principles involved.

(a)   This is written last

$$87 * 43 = 87 * 40 + 87 * 3 = 3471$$

$$
\begin{array}{ccc}
87 & 87 & 3480 \\
* \ 40 & * \ 3 & + \ 261 \\
\hline
3480 & 261 & 3741
\end{array}
$$

(b)
$$87 * 40 = 3480$$
$$+ \ 87 * \ 3 = \ \ 261$$
$$87 * 43 = 3741$$

7. I would regard the transition to the conventional, condensed, layout as optional. It saves little time, and does not show so clearly the mathematical principles used.
8. Give the children further practice in these until the method is well established.
9. You could explain that calculators are a quick and convenient way of doing calculations like these; but it is good to be independent of calculators, and also to understand the mathematics behind the result.

Activity 2   Treasure chest

A game for two crews, each of up to 3 children. Its purpose is to give practice in using long multiplication to make the best decisions.

Materials   • Game board, see figure 8.
   • Sets of treasure cards, 4 to a set.*
   • Pencil and paper for each child.
   * One of these is illustrated. Six more sets of suitable numbers are given below. If you prefer, you may vary the objects according to your own imagination. These figures have been calculated to give close results, for which estimation is not sufficient. This makes it necessary to use long multiplication.

	Amber	Jasper beads	Garnets	Jet
First set	43 & 75,	59 & 56,	93 & 35,	39 & 64
	Amethysts	Topaz	Gold	Rubies
Second set	82 & 67,	86 & 64,	47 & 117,	24 & 230
	Silver goblets	Emeralds	Garnets	Dubloons
Third set	24 & 166,	33 & 139,	56 & 79,	31 & 145

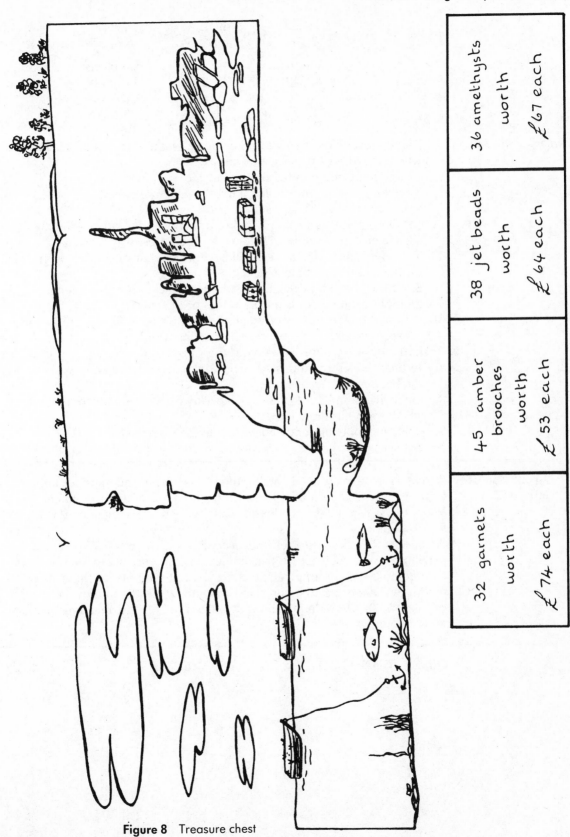

Figure 8 Treasure chest

32 garnets worth £74 each

45 amber brooches worth £53 each

38 jet beads worth £64 each

36 amethysts worth £67 each

	Amber	Amethysts	Pearls	Diamonds
Fourth set	96 & 78,	56 & 134,	36 & 208,	26 & 278

	Diamonds	Jet	Sapphires	Garnets
Fifth set	26 & 249,	225 & 29,	44 & 148,	94 & 69

	Jasper	Diamonds	Pearls	Amber
Sixth set	175 & 54,	28 & 338,	37 & 256,	263 & 36

Rules of the game

1. The two crews of treasure seekers have swum under water to the cave, where they find 4 small sealed chests.
2. The contents are painted on the outside.
3. To avoid conflict, they reach the following agreement.
   (i) Each crew will take back 2 chests.
   (ii) One crew will have first and fourth choice, the other will have second and third choice. (Why is this the fairest way?)
4. They determine which crew will have which pair of choices by guessing in which hand a pebble is held.
5. Since they have no calculator with them, they have to use long multiplication to work out the values of the chests.
6. It should be left to them to realise that it is better for the crew which guesses correctly in step 4 to delay saying whether they will choose first until after they have worked out the values of the chests.
7. In turn, as described in step 3, they take their chests and swim back to the boat.
8. On arriving on board, they may check with a calculator to find out which team has done best.
9. The game may be repeated with other sets of chests.

Discussion of activities

Activity 1 involves using a combination of concepts and methods already learnt to extend their ability to multiply into a much larger domain. When this method has been learnt, activity 2 provides a game in which to consolidate it.

There is something further to be said about calculators. What these manipulate with such speed, convenience, and accuracy are not numbers but numerals – not mathematical concepts, but symbols for these. It is their users who attach meanings to the symbols. So the more we use calculators, the more important it is to keep sight of the meaning of what we are doing.

OBSERVE AND LISTEN   **REFLECT**   **DISCUSS**

[Num 6] DIVISION
Sharing equally, Grouping, Factorising

Num 6.3   DIVISION AS A MATHEMATICAL OPERATION

Concept   The connection between grouping and sharing.

Ability   To explain this connection. (This is most easily done with the help of physical materials.)

Discussion of concept

Physically, grouping and sharing look quite different.

Start with 15.

Make groups of 3.

Resulting number of groups is 5

Start with 15.

Share between 3.

Number in each share is 5.

It is only at the level of thought that we can see that these are, in a certain way, alike. When children have grasped the connection between grouping and sharing, they have the higher order concept of division.

Activity 1   Different questions, same answer. Why?

A problem for children to work at in small groups. (I suggest twos or threes.) The purpose is for them to discover for themselves the connection between grouping and sharing.

Materials
- Two-question board, see figure 9
- Start cards 10 to 25.
- Action cards 2 to 5.

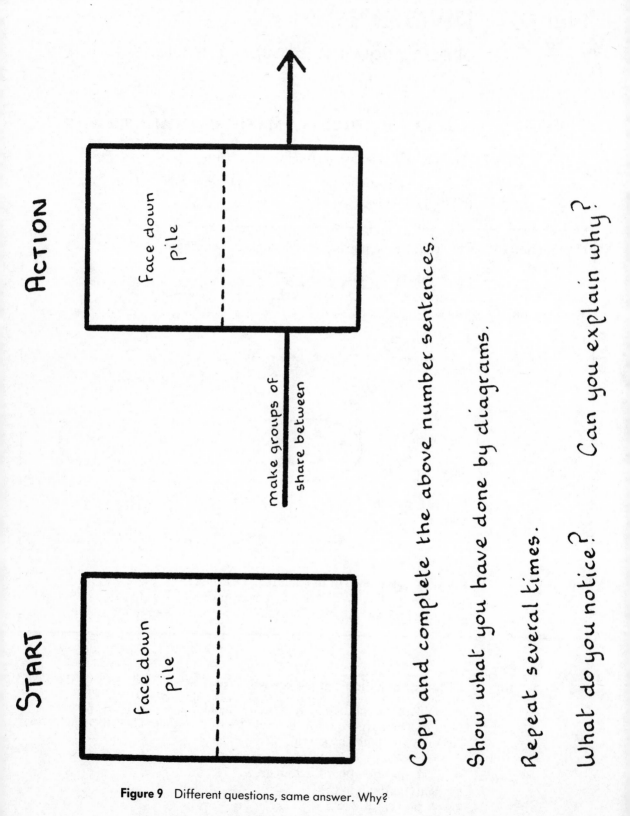

ACTION

Face down pile

make groups of

share between

START

Face down pile

Copy and complete the above number sentences.

Show what you have done by diagrams.

Repeat several times.

What do you notice?   Can you explain why?

Figure 9   Different questions, same answer. Why?

- 50 (or more) small objects.
- Pencil and paper for each child.

Introducing the problem

1. The start and action cards are shuffled and put face down in the upper spaces on the two question board.
2. The top card of each pile is turned and put face up in the lower space.
3. By reading above and below the line, there are now two unfinished number sentences. E.g.

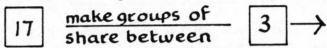

4. One (or more) in each group copy down the upper sentence, and one (or more) the lower sentence. They then complete whichever sentence they have written, using physical objects if they like. E.g.

$$17 \xrightarrow{\text{make groups of 3}} 5 \text{ groups rem } 2$$

$$17 \xrightarrow{\text{share between 3}} 5 \text{ each rem } 2$$

N.B. They should write these neatly, and keep them for later use in Activity 2.

5. They draw diagrams to show what they have done. These diagrams could be used in step 4, instead of physical objects. E.g.

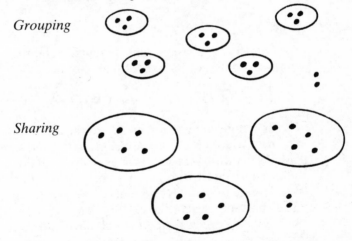

Grouping

Sharing

6. They compare the two results.
7. Steps 2, 3, 4 are repeated. Step 5 need not be repeated every time: its purpose is to emphasise that these are two different questions.
8. Ask, 'Will the two results always be the same? If so, why?'
9. Leave them to discuss this, and to arrive at a clear explanation. (One suggestion will be found in the discussion of activities.)
10. Return and hear their explanation, discussing it if necessary.

Activity 2   Combining the number sentences

An activity for a small group. Its purpose is to teach the notation for the mathematical operation of subtraction.

Materials • The number sentences which they have written in activity 1.
• Pencil and paper for each child.

What they do 1. Have them compare the first number sentence of each kind. E.g.

$$17 \quad \underline{\text{make groups of 3}} \quad 5 \text{ groups rem 2}$$

$$17 \quad \underline{\text{share between 3}} \quad 5 \text{ each rem 2}$$

2. Tell them that these two meanings may be combined in one number sentence. In this case, it would be

$$17 \div 3 \quad = 5 \text{ rem 2}$$

This is read as
'17, divide by 3, result 5 remainder 2.'
or as
'17 divided by 3 equals 5 remainder 2.'
3. They then repeat steps 1 and 2 for the other number sentences.

Activity 3 Unpacking the parcel (division)

A continuation of activity 2, for a small group. Its purpose is to remind children of the two possible meanings of a number sentence for division.

Materials • Pencil and paper for each child.

What they do 1. They all write a division number sentence on their own paper. The first number should not be greater than 20.

$$11 \div 4 \quad = 2 \text{ rem 3}$$

2. The first child shows his sentence to the others.
3. The next two on his left give the grouping and sharing meanings. In this case, 'Start with 11, make groups of 4, result 2 groups remainder 3' followed by 'Start with 11, share between 4, 2 in each share (or, each gets 2), remainder 3'. Note that '. . . groups', or '. . . in each share', are important parts of the expanded meaning.
4. Steps 2 and 3 are repeated until all have had their sentences 'unpacked'.

Activity 4 Mr Taylor's Game

This game for 2 players was invented by Mr Stephen Taylor, of Dorridge Junior School, and I am grateful to him for permission to include it here. Its purpose is to bring together addition, subtraction, multiplication, division, in a simple game.

Materials • Number cards: 1 set 0 to 25, 3 sets 0 to 9.
• Game board.
• Counters of a different colour for each player.

148

5	20	19	25	1
21	7	14	6	16
3	23	11	18	24
9	17	8	13	2
12	4	10	22	15

Figure 10 Mr Taylor's Game.

© Stephen Taylor. 1981

Rules of the game
1. The object is to get 3 counters together in a line. They must be in the same row, column, or diagonal.
2. The number cards are shuffled and put face down.
3. The first player turns over two cards. He may choose to add, subtract, multiply, or divide the numbers shown. Division must, however, be exact.
4. He puts one of his counters on the corresponding square.
5. The other player does likewise.
6. Play continues until one player has 3 in a row.
7. Another round may now be played. The loser begins.

Discussion of activities

Activity 1 poses a problem, for children to solve by the activity of their own intelligence. When they have seen the connection between grouping and sharing, they have the higher order mathematical concept of division.

The easiest path to seeing the correspondence is, I think, a physical one. If we have 15 objects to share between 3 persons, a natural way to do this is to begin by giving one object to each person. This takes 3 objects, a single 'round', which we may *think of* as a group of 3. The next round may be thought of as another group of 3, and so on. Each round gives one object to each share, so the number of rounds is the number in each share.

This verbal description by itself is harder to follow than a physical demonstration accompanied by explanation. This I see as yet another demonstration of the advantage of combining modes 1 and 2.

Activity 2 provides a notation for these two aspects of division. Note that the first number is the operand, that on which the operation is done. The operation is the division sign together with the second number, e.g. $\div 3$.

Activity 3 is another example of 'Unpacking the parcel'. There is much less in this one than in the subtraction parcel, but is still a useful reminder of the two physical meanings combined in a single mathematical notation.

After all this, they deserve a game. Mr Taylor's game fits in nicely at this stage.

OBSERVE AND LISTEN　　　　**REFLECT**　　　**DISCUSS**

Num 6.4　ORGANISING INTO RECTANGLES

Concept　A rectangular number.

Ability　To recognise and construct rectangular numbers.

Discussion of concept

A rectangular number is one which can be represented as the number of dots in a rectangular array. Here are some examples.

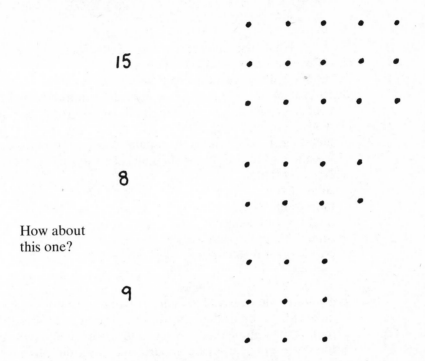

15

8

How about this one?

9

The term 'rectangle' is currently used with two meanings: any shape which has a right angle at every corner, which includes both squares and oblongs; and oblongs only. For myself, I agree with the teacher who said during a discussion of this point, 'It makes no more sense to me to talk about squares and rectangles, than about girls and children'. So I hope that we may agree on the first meaning, i.e. that oblongs and squares are two kinds of rectangle.

A rectangular number is of course the same as a composite number, but in this aspect it provides a very good link between multiplication and division, and an introduction to factorising.

Activity 1 Constructing rectangular numbers

An activity for a small group, working in pairs. Its purpose is to build the concept of rectangular numbers.

Materials For each pair:
- 25 small counters with dots at their centres.
- Pencil and paper.

What they do 1. The activity is introduced along the following lines. Explain, 'We think of these counters as dots which we can move around.'

2. Put out a rectangular array such as this one.

3. Ask, 'What shape have we made?' (A rectangle).
4. 'How many counters?' (In this case, 12.)
5. 'So we call 12 a rectangular number.'
6. Repeat, with other examples, until the children have grasped the concept. Note that the rectangles must be solid arrays like the one illustrated.
7. Next, let the children work in pairs. Give 25 counters to each pair, and ask them to find all the rectangular numbers up to 25.
8. If any of them think that a pattern like this might be a rectangle, remind them that the counters represent dots, and ask: 'Would you say this makes a rectangle?'
9. The question nearly always arises whether or not squares are to be included. I suggest that you wait until someone raises this point, and then answer along the lines given in 'Discussion of concept'.
10. Finally, let the children compare and check their lists with each other's.

Activity 2   The rectangular numbers game

A game for two. It consolidates the concept of a rectangular number in a predictive situation. Children also discover prime numbers, though usually they do not yet know this name for them.

Materials
- 25 counters.
- Pencil and paper for scoring.

Rules of the game
1. Each player in turn gives the other a number of counters.
2. If the receiving player can make a rectangle with these, she scores a point. If not, the other scores a point.
3. If when the receiving player has made a rectangle (and scored a point), the giving player can make a different rectangle with the same counters, she too scores a point. (E.g. 12, 16, 18).
4. The same number may not be used twice. To keep track of this, the numbers 1 to 25 are written at the bottom of the score sheet and crossed out as used.
5. The winner is the player who scores most points.

Discussion of activities	In activity 1, the children first form the concept of a rectangular number from physical examples (mode 1 building), and then construct further examples for themselves (mode 3 building, mode 1 testing).
	Activity 2 uses the new concept in a predictive situation (mode 1 testing).

OBSERVE AND LISTEN   REFLECT   DISCUSS

Num 6.5   FACTORISING: COMPOSITE NUMBERS AND PRIME NUMBERS

Concepts   (i)   Factorising.
(ii)   Composite numbers and prime numbers.

Abilities   (i)   To factorise a given composite number.
(ii)   To distinguish between composite and prime numbers.

Discussion of concepts

A composite number is one which can be written as the product of two (or more) numbers, other than itself and 1. E.g.,

$$15 = 3 \times 5$$
$$22 = 11 \times 2$$

Often this may be done in more than one way. E.g.,

$$24 = 2 \times 12 \qquad 24 = 3 \times 8 \qquad 24 = 4 \times 6$$

To write a number as the product of other numbers is called factorising, and these other numbers are called factors of the original number. For example 3 and 8 are factors of 24. The process may often be continued, e.g.,

$$140 = 14 \times 10$$
$$= 2 \times 7 \times 2 \times 5$$

which may be rearranged as

$$140 = 2 \times 2 \times 5 \times 7$$

In this topic we shall only deal with 2 factors, since we are here seeing it largely as a preliminary to the use of multiplication facts for dividing larger numbers.

1 is a factor of every number. A number which has no factors other than 1 and itself is called prime. So the terms 'rectangular number' and 'composite number' are interchangeable; and numbers which are not rectangular numbers are prime.

Activity 1   Factors bingo

A game for up to 6 players. Its purpose is to introduce the concept of factorisation at a level where the calculations are still easy. It only requires knowledge of the multiplication tables up to 6 × 6.

Materials
- 6 factors bingo cards.*
- Die 1–6 and shaker.
- OHP pen for each player.
- Damp rag.

* See example in step 5 below. These should be covered with plastic film, so that they can be cleaned and re-used.

Rules of the game
1. Begin by explaining the meaning of 'factor'.
2. Each player has a Factors Bingo card and an OHP pen.
3. Players in turn, throw the die, and call out the number which comes up. This number is available for use by everyone.
4. They fill their cards by writing the given number in any space where it is a factor of the number on the left. This may only be done once for each throw.
5. A partly completed card might look like this, assuming that the numbers 2, 6, 4, 5, 3 have been thrown so far. (This player was not able to use 5.)

4	=	2 ×	
6	=	×	
24	=	6 ×	4
18	=	3 ×	
12	=	×	

6. The winner is the first to fill his card.
7. This game is not quite as simple as it might first appear. If a player writes (say) 2 as one of the factors of 24, he is left with 12 as the other factor, and will not be able to fill his card. A similar problem arises with 1.

Activity 2   Factors rummy

A game for up to 6 players. Its purpose is to develop mental agility in factorising.

Materials
- Product pack: one card each of the numbers 10, 12, 14, 15, 16, 18, 20, 21, 24, 28, 30, 36.*
- Factors pack: 6 cards each of the numbers, 2, 3, 4, 5, 6, 7, 8, 9.*

* Double-headed. These 2 packs should be of different colours.

Rules of the game
1. The product pack is put face down on the table. The dealer deals 5 cards from the factors pack to each player, and puts the rest of the factors pack face down on the table.
2. He then turns over the top card of each pack, and puts it face up beside the pile.
3. The object is to get rid of one's cards by putting down pairs of cards which, when multiplied together, make the product shown on the face-up product card.

4. Players begin by looking at their cards, and putting down any pairs they can.
5. The first player then picks up a factor card from either the face up or the face down pile, whichever he prefers. If he now has a pair, he puts it down. Finally he discards one of his cards onto the face up pile.
6. In turn the other players pick up, put down a pair if they can, discard.
7. At the end of each round, the dealer turns over the top product card from the face down pile, and puts it face up beside (not on top of) the product card already showing. In this way, the number of possible products increases for every new round.
8. After step 7, players put down any pairs now made possible, before the next round is played.
9. Steps 5 to 8 are repeated, until a player puts down all his cards.
10. Play then stops, and each player scores the total of the cards still in his hand. The player who went 'out' scores zero.
11. In this game, it is possible for 2 players to go 'out' simultaneously when a new product card is turned. This does not matter: they both score zero.
12. The scores are recorded, and another round may then be played.
13. The winner is the player with the lowest total score.

Activity 3   Alias prime

A game for up to 6 players. Its purpose is to introduce children to the difference between composite and prime numbers, and give them practice in distinguishing between these 2 kinds of number.

Materials   • 3 counters for each player.

Rules of the game
1. Begin by explaining the meanings of 'composite number' and 'prime'. These concepts have been well prepared in activities 1 and 2, and in topic 4.
2. Explain that 'alias' means 'another name for', often used to hide someone's identity. In this game, all prime numbers use the alias 'Prime' instead of their usual name.
3. Start by having the players say in turn 'Eight', 'Nine', 'Ten', . . . round the table.
4. The game now begins. They say the numbers round the table as before, but when it is a player's turn to say any prime number, they must not say its usual name, but say 'Prime' instead.
5. The next player must remember the number which wasn't spoken, and say the next one. Thus the game would begin (assuming no mistake) 'Eight', 'Nine', 'Ten', 'Prime', 'Twelve', 'Prime', 'Fourteen', 'Fifteen', 'Sixteen', 'Prime', 'Eighteen' and so on.
6. Any player who makes a mistake loses a life – i.e. one of his counters. Failing to say 'Prime', or saying the wrong composite number, are both mistakes.
7. When a player has lost all his lives he is out of the game, and acts as an umpire.
8. The winner is the last player to be left in the game.

Note. When the players are experienced, they may begin counting at 'One'. This gives rather a lot of primes for beginners!

Activity 4 The sieve of Eratosthenes

An activity for children to play individually, or in small groups. Its purpose is to teach them a classical piece of mathematics for identifying primes.

Materials
- Number squares 1-100 (see figure 11).*
- Pencil for each child.
* One each, or shared.

What they do
1. In the previous game, when players are good enough to reach largish numbers, there is sometimes doubt whether a number is prime or not. Explain that this is a method which gets rid of all the composite numbers and leaves only primes.

1	2	3	4	5	6	7	8	9	10
11	12	13	14	15	16	17	18	19	20
21	22	23	24	25	26	27	28	29	30
31	32	33	34	35	36	37	38	39	40
41	42	43	44	45	46	47	48	49	50
51	52	53	54	55	56	57	58	59	60
61	62	63	64	65	66	67	68	69	70
71	72	73	74	75	76	77	78	79	80
81	82	83	84	85	86	87	88	89	90
91	92	93	94	95	96	97	98	99	100

Figure 11   The sieve of Eratosthenes.

2. Starting with 2 (the smallest prime other than 1), they cross out every multiple of 2 *except 2 itself*.
3. The next prime is 3, so they cross out every multiple of 3 except 3 itself.
4. Likewise for each successive prime.
5. The numbers remaining when the process is complete are all primes.
6. After a while, the children will notice that no new numbers are being crossed out. With numbers up to 100, the process is complete when all the multiples of 7 have been crossed out.
7. The intriguing question is, 'Why? When we come to cross out the multiples of 11, 13, etc, why do we find that these have already been done?' While steps 1 to 6 are straightforward, this requires careful thought.
8. A simpler question is, 'Why do we only cross out multiples of primes?'
9. This method is quite general, and may be extended beyond 100 if desired.

Discussion of activities	In this topic we are mainly concerned with introducing the concept of factorisation as a preparation for its use in division, so that children will later be able to use their knowledge of the multiplication tables for dividing. This saves learning a whole new body of facts. For this reason the numbers involved are kept small. Activities 3 and 4 develop an off-shoot of factorisation, namely prime numbers. We do not develop the study of primes any further than this, but they have long intrigued mathematicians and children should at least know what they are. Using their knowledge of multiplication results to arrive at division results is, of course, a strong example of mode 3 schema building. Doing things backwards is usually harder than forwards, and it certainly is in this case. So division, both conceptually and as a skill, is prepared and developed carefully over a number of topics.

OBSERVE AND LISTEN   **REFLECT**   **DISCUSS**

Num 6.6   RELATION BETWEEN MULTIPLICATION AND DIVISION

Concept   The relation between multiplication and division.

Ability   To express the same relationship in a variety of different ways: as multiplying, grouping, sharing, dividing.

Discussion of concept

The new concept to be formed in this topic is an awareness of how all of the following are connected.

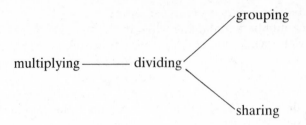

This is also a convenient place to introduce vertical notation for division, in preparation for dividing larger numbers in the next topic.

Activity 1 Parcels within parcels

A game for up to 6 children. Its purpose is to make explicit the relationships between multiplication and the various aspects of division.

Materials
- 6 or more parcel cards.
- Pencil and paper for each child.
- Bowl of counters.

Rules of the game *Stage (a)*

1. The parcel cards are shuffled and put face down.
2. The first player turns over the top parcel card.
3. She then starts to 'unpack the parcel' by first writing a number sentence which she shows to the others, and then reading it aloud in as many ways as she can. (See example below.)
4. If the others agree, they say 'Agree'. The first player takes a counter for each agreed statement.
5. If they disagree, the first player has to justify her statement by reference to the parcel card. E.g. for 3(5) = 15, she would point out that there are 3 rows of 5, making 15.
6. Steps 3, 4, 5 are repeated by the other players in turn until the parcel has been fully unpacked.
7. The next player turns over the top card, and steps 1-6 are repeated.
8. The winner is the player with the most counters at the end.

Example
Parcel card turned over

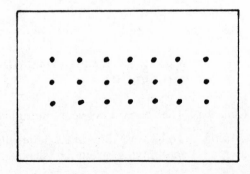

Contents
A. Writes: 3(7) = 21
    Reads: '3 sets of 7 make a set of 21' or '3 sevens are/make/equal 21'
    (One point)
B. Likewise for 7(3). (One point)
C. Writes: 3 * 7 = 21.
    Reads: '3 star 7 equals 21.'
    '3 sevens are 21.'
    '7 threes are 21.'
    (Three points)
D. Writes: 21 ÷ 3 = 7
    Reads: '21 divided by 3 equals 7'
    '21, make groups of 3, result 7 groups.'
    '21, share between 3, result 7 in each share.'
    (Three points)
E. Writes: $21 \xrightarrow{\text{make groups of 3}} 7$
    Reads: '21, make groups of 3, result 7 groups.'
    (One point)
F. Writes: $21 \xrightarrow{\text{share between 3}} 7$
    Reads: '21, share between 3, result 7 each.'
    (One point)
G., H., I. Likewise for 21 ÷ 7 = 3.
As may be seen from this example, it is quite a sophisticated game. C, D and G are clearly the ones to choose first. But there are still points to be collected when these have been used.
Stage (b)
1. When they have a good grasp of the foregoing, introduce the following notation. Explain that this is another way of writing a division sentence, which is needed for larger numbers.

$$5 \overline{)15}^{\ 3}$$

This is read as:

'How many 5s in 15? Answer, 3.'
2. This should *not* be read as 'five into fifteen . . .', as one sometimes hears. We are certainly not dividing 5 into 15 shares.
3. Continue as in stage 1, including this notation.

Discussion of activities

Stage (a) is conceptually quite complex. This is a necessary consequence of the great variety of information which can be extracted from one 'parcel'. All these ways of thinking are needed for different purposes; and it is much more efficient, and economical of memory, to learn them all as different ways of thinking about the same number-relationship. This relationship is represented much more clearly by the rectangular array than it can be by any notation, each of which shows only a particular aspect. All these aspects are concepts already learnt. What the children are now doing is becoming more aware of their inter-relationships.

Stage (b) is simpler, since it only involves learning a new notation for what they already know.

Note that in both these activities, the main links which are being strengthened are between notations and their various meanings, not between one notation and another. Their various meanings are all implicit in the rectangular arrays – the parcel cards.

OBSERVE AND LISTEN　　　　　　**REFLECT**　　　　**DISCUSS**

Num 6.7   USING MULTIPLICATION RESULTS FOR DIVISION

Concept　The use of multiplication results in reverse, to obtain division results.

Ability　To arrive at a division result mentally by recalling an appropriate multiplication result.

Discussion of concept

The close relationship between the two statements

　　'3 fives are 15' and
'How many fives in 15? Answer 3.'

has already been learnt, using small numbers and visual representations. In this topic the concept is expanded to include all products up to and including 10×10, and made independent of visual representations.

Activity 1　**A new use for the multiplication square**

An activity for children to do in pairs. Its purpose is to develop the ability described above.

Materials　● Multiplication square for each child.*
　　　　　● 1 to 9 die.
　　　　　● Pencil and paper for each child.
　　　　　* They should still have the squares they made for themselves in Num 5.6/3. A photo-master is also provided in Vol. 2a.

What they do　1.　Player A has his multiplication square face up. Player B has his square face down.
　　　　2.　Player A throws the die. Suppose it shows 7. He therefore takes the row starting with 7, and writes　　**7**

　　　　3.　He then chooses any number in this row, say 35. He writes

$$7 \overline{)35}$$

and passes the paper to his partner.

4. His partner first reads this aloud, as 'How many sevens in 35?'
5. Next, if he can, he recalls from his multiplication tables that 5 sevens are 35. He says this aloud, and completes the written division.

$$\frac{5}{7)\overline{35}}$$

6. If he cannot do this, he turns over his multiplication table, finds the row starting 7, and then locates 35 in this row. He uses this to say aloud, '5 sevens are 35', and then continues as in step 6.
7. In either case, play A checks B's result and says 'Agree'.
8. The players then interchange roles, and steps 2 to 6 are repeated.
9. Players should be encouraged to give each other practice with all the products in a row, and not just the harder ones. For this reason, no scoring system is included in this activity, which might cause players to give each other only the more difficult examples.

Activity 2 Quotients and remainders

An activity for up to 4 children. Its purpose is to give practice in division, and to introduce the terms 'quotient' and 'remainder' using easy numbers.

Materials
- Q and R board, see figure 12.
- Start cards 9 to 30.
- Die 1-6.
- For each child, 5 counters of 1 colour.
- Pencil and paper for each child (optional).

Rules of the game
1. The start cards are shuffled and put face down.
2. The first player throws the die, and then turns over the top start card. This gives a number to divide by, and a starting number; e.g. 3 and 23.

$$\frac{7}{3)\overline{23}} \text{ rem } 2$$

3. He says, 'Quotient 7, remainder 2,' so that the others can check.
4. He may then place one of his counters on a 7 and one on a 2, the aim being to get 3 counters in a row. This row may be across, down, or diagonal. He may also choose to put down only one counter, or no counter.
5. The next player repeats steps 2 to 4, and so on in turn until either a player has won by getting 3 in a row, or this has become impossible.
6. A player who throws 1 may have another turn. If the quotient is a number not on the board, only the remainder is used.
7. A new game may then be played.
8. (Optional) Pencil and paper may be used for written calculation.
Note This board has been designed to give a quick result. For a longer game, play continues until each player has put down all his counters. For the last counter, he chooses either the quotient or the remainder. The winner is then the player with the longest row.

0	6	2	5	1	7	0
3	1	8	2	4	3	1
9	8	4	6	5	4	10
3	1	5	0	10	2	4
9	7	2	5	1	3	10
4	3	5	4	3	5	2
0	9	7	2	6	8	0

Figure 12 Q and R board.

Activity 3 Village Post Office

A game for 2 to 6 children. Its purpose is to use the relationship between division and multiplication in situations where division involves a remainder.

Materials
- Multiplication square.
- Notice.*
- Stamp cards, 3 to 10.
- Parcel cards.**
- Pencil and paper for each child.

* See illustration in step 3 below.
** As many as you like. I suggest that children begin with an easy pack, with numbers up to 30p; and progress to a harder pack, up to 70p. Suitable numbers are:

Easy   14, 17, 19, 23, 25, 26, 28, 29, 30.
Hard   31, 33, 35, 36, 37, 40, 41, 43, 46, 53, 55, 57, 62, 65, 67, 69.

With the harder set of parcel cards, only stamp cards 7-10 should be used.

Rules of the game   *For 2 children*
1. One acts as postmistress, the other as customer.
2. The postmistress shuffles the stamp cards, the customer shuffles the parcel cards, and these are then put face down in separate piles.
3. The postmistress opens the shop by turning over the top stamp card and putting it in the space in the notice. It now reads (e.g.),

4. The customer then takes the top parcel card and turns it over. Suppose it reads 26p. He calculates $26 \div 6 = 4 + 2$ and should therefore ask for 4 sixpenny and 2 penny stamps. Note that the postmistress likes customers to ask for the least number of stamps which gives the required total. (She doesn't take kindly to requests for 26 penny stamps.)
5. The postmaster checks: $4(6) + 2 = 26$.
6. If correct, he says 'Correct' and accepts the parcel. If the results do not agree, the multiplication square may be used to discover where their mistake lies.
7. The next parcel card is then taken by the customer, and steps 4 to 6 are repeated.
For up to 6 children
In addition to the postmistress, there are now 1 or 2 assistant postmistresses. The remaining children are customers, and are served by whichever postmistress is free. Otherwise the game is played as above.

Discussion of activities   In the earlier topics, learning has been directed towards the establishment of the concept of division in its two aspects, grouping and sharing; and with relating it to multiplication. In the present topic, the purpose is to develop fluency in calculation.

The basis of this is the use of already-known multiplication facts for division (activity 1). The notation which children will need for dividing larger numbers is also used here. Activity 2 gives further practice at these in the form of a game, still using fairly small numbers. Activity 3 is important for linking these calculation skills back to the concepts involved.

The terms 'quotient' and 'remainder' are useful ones for later work. I leave it for you to decide whether to include 'divisor' and 'dividend' also.

OBSERVE AND LISTEN   **REFLECT**   **DISCUSS**

Num 6.8   DIVIDING LARGER NUMBERS

Concept   The concept of division, as already learnt.

Ability   To divide a 2-, 3-, or 4-digit number by a single digit number, first without re-grouping and then with re-grouping.

Discussion of concept   The concept of division has already been learnt. What we are here concerned with is extending the ability to larger numbers. The method for doing this uses non-canonical form, which has already been used in addition, subtraction, and multiplication.

Activity 1   **'I'm thinking in hundreds . . .'**

An activity for children in groups of 3. Its purpose is to teach them the first steps in the ability described above.

Materials   For each group:
- H T U division board, laminated.*
- OHP pen and wiper.
- Examples card.**

* See illustration in step 2 below. Alternatively, duplicated expendable sheets may be used.

** These are the examples:

$$684 \div 2 \quad 936 \div 2 \quad 848 \div 4 \quad 408 \div 2 \quad 630 \div 3$$
$$880 \div 4 \quad 690 \div 3 \quad 906 \div 3 \quad 208 \div 2 \quad 550 \div 5$$

What they do   1. The children need to sit facing the same way.
2. The first of the examples is copied in the left hand space of the HTU division board by the child sitting in the middle, using the notation shown.

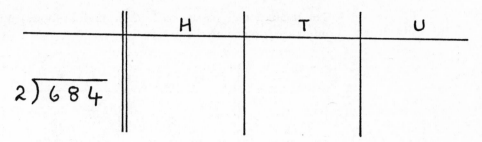

She reads this aloud: 'How many 2's in 684?', and passes the board and OHP pen to the child on his left.

3. The left hand child says, 'I'm thinking in hundreds', and writes the hundreds figure in the hundreds column.

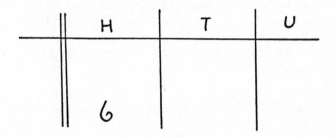

4. Next she writes, reading aloud as she does so: 'How many 2's in 6 hundreds? Answer, 3 hundred'. (NB 3 hundred, not 3.)

5. Steps 3 and 4 are repeated for the tens figure by the middle child. She begins by saying, 'I'm thinking in tens'.

6. Steps 3 and 4 are repeated for the units figure by the right hand child. She begins, 'I'm thinking in units'.

7. The lower part of the board should now look like this.

8. The board is then passed back to the middle child, who completes the number sentence on the left.

	H	T	U
$3\,4\,2$ $2\overline{)6\,8\,4}$	3 $2\overline{)6}$	4 $2\overline{)8}$	2 $2\overline{)4}$

She reads it aloud. 'How many two's in six hundred and eighty four? Answer, three hundred and forty-two.'

9. The board is wiped clean, and steps 2 to 8 are repeated with the next example on the card.
10. The order in which the children sit should be varied.

Activity 2   'I'll take over your remainder'

A continuation of activity 1, for children in groups of 3. Its purpose is to teach them how to deal with remainders in each column.

Materials   For each group:
- H T U division board, laminated.*
- OHP pen and wiper.*
- Examples card.**
* The same as for activity 1.
** Here are 10 examples. Others may be taken from a suitable textbook. You may wish to grade the difficulty more slowly.

$$743 \div 2 \quad 851 \div 3 \quad 783 \div 4 \quad 680 \div 5 \quad 705 \div 6$$
$$241 \div 7 \quad 354 \div 8 \quad 559 \div 9 \quad 303 \div 4 \quad 600 \div 7$$

What they do   1. The first example is copied in the left hand space of the HTU division board by the child sitting in the middle, and read aloud, as in activity 1. The board is then passed to the child on the left.

	H	T	U
$3\overline{)743}$			

2. The left-hand child writes the hundreds figure in the hundreds column.

H	T	U
7		

3. Next she writes, reading aloud as she does so: 'How many 3's in 7 hundreds? Answer, 2 hundreds, remainder 1 hundred.'

H	T	U
$3\overline{)7}$ 2 rem1		

4. The question is now, what to do with the remainder?
5. The middle child writes the tens figure in the tens column.

H	T	U
$3\overline{)7}$ 2 rem1	4	

6. Next, she says, 'I'll take over your remainder. 1 hundred is 10 tens, so that makes 14 tens.' The remainder in the hundreds column is crossed out.

H	T	U
$3\overline{)7}$ 2	14	

7. He writes, and reads aloud: 'How many 3's in 14 tens? Answer, 4 tens remainder 2 tens.'

H	T	U
$\overset{2}{3\overline{)\,7}}$	$\overset{4\ r\ 2}{3\overline{)14}}$	

8. The right-hand child deals similarly with the units. She takes over the remainder of 2 tens, which are 20 units, making 23 units altogether.

H	T	U
$\overset{2}{3\overline{)\,7}}$	$\overset{4}{3\overline{)14}}$	$\overset{7\ r\ 2}{3\overline{)23}}$

9. The board is then passed back to the middle child, who completes the number sentence on the left.

$$\overset{2\ 4\ 7\ r\ 2}{3\overline{)\,7\ 4\ 3}}$$

H	T	U
$\overset{2\ r\ 1}{3\overline{)\,7}}$	$\overset{4\ r\ 2}{3\overline{)14}}$	$\overset{7\ r\ 2}{3\overline{)23}}$

She reads it aloud. 'How many threes in seven hundred and forty three? Answer, two hundred and forty seven, remainder 2.'

10. The board is wiped clean, and steps 1 to 9 are repeated with the next example. The order in which the children sit should be varied.

11. When children have had plenty of experience of the above, transition to the condensed notation is straightforward. To begin with, the same calculation should be re-written in the condensed notation to show the correspondence. In the above example, this would be:

$$\overset{2\ 4\ 7\ \ r\ 2}{3\overline{)\,7\ ^1\!4\ ^2\!3}}$$

This condensed notation is a good one, provided that its meaning is well understood. Now that calculators are widely available, I attach little importance to children's acquiring a high degree of skill in this kind of computation; but it is good to understand the principle.

Activity 3   Q and R ladders

This game is suitable for 4 or 6 children, playing in teams of 2. Its purpose is first, to expand the abilities developed in activities 2 and 3 to larger numbers; and second, to develop fluency in these calculations.

Materials
- Game board.*
- Markers: a pair of one colour for each team of 2.
- Start cards 50 to 100.
- Die 5 to 10.**
- Pencil and paper for each pair, or single player.

*See photomaster in Vol. 2a. It consists of two ladders, one for quotients and one for remainders.

** Make your own from 1 cm cubes.

Rules of the game
1. The start cards are shuffled and put face down.
2. Each team puts one of its markers on the zero rung in each ladder. These represent climbers.
3. The first pair begins as follows. One player turns over the top start card, and the other throws the die.
4. They then cooperate in dividing the number on the start card by the number on the die, using the method learnt in activity 2. This gives them a quotient and a remainder.
5. These 2 numbers show how many rungs their 2 pieces may climb, each up its respective ladder.
6. The other teams in turn repeat steps 3 to 5.
7. The winning team is that which gets both of its 2 climbers to the top of the ladder, or beyond. The exact number is not required in this game.

Note This game usually takes 6, 7, or 8 rounds; occasionally, fewer. It has been designed so that the likelihood of being first at the top is approximately equal for climbers on the 2 ladders. There is also about a 1 in 5 chance of both getting there at the same time.

Activity 4   Cargo Airships

A game for up to 4 players. Its purpose is to give them plenty of practice in division of numbers up to 1000, by numbers from 3 to 9.

Materials
- Cards representing airports, one for each player.*
- 7 cards representing airships.*
- Cards representing loads.**
- Calculators.
- Pencil and paper for each player.
- A paper clip for each airship.

* See figure 13, and in Vol. 2a.

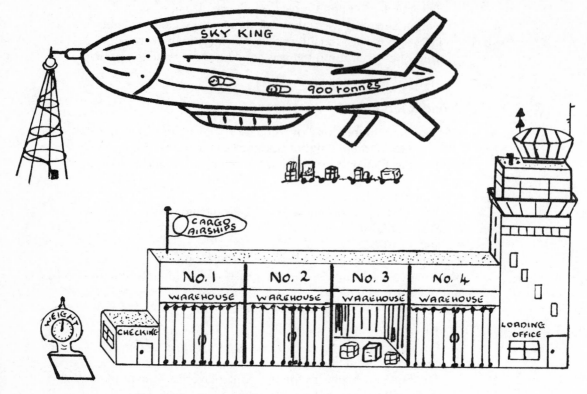

Figure 13 Cargo airships.

** A suitable set of numbers is 325, 108, 473, 235, 90, 156, 209, 392, 267, 340, 440, 60, 83, 116, 180, in each case followed by 'tonnes'.

Rules of the game

1. This game is like 'One Tonne Van Drivers', but harder since it involves dividing.
2. Each cargo airship can carry from 600 to 1000 tonnes, according to size. They also vary from 3 to 9 in their number of compartments, and the loads must be equally shared between the compartments to keep the airship level. This is the task of every loading officer.
3. All the players except one act as loading officers at distant airports. The remaining player is the checking officer in the home airport. She has a calculator.
4. Each loading officer has a card representing her airport, and an airship. The airships are assigned randomly.
5. To begin the game, the load cards are shuffled and put face down in the middle of the table.
6. The loads arrive by road at the distant airport. To represent this in the game, the first loading officer takes the top load card.
7. This must be shared equally between whatever number of compartments the aircraft has. So the loading officer calculates the correct part-loads, equal for each compartment. These will be carefully weighed out on the weighbridge before loading. E.g., if she has a 6 compartment airship, and a 473 tonne load arrives, she would instruct her loaders to make part-loads of 78 tonnes each, leaving a remainder of 5 tonnes. She writes this on a loading slip, as shown in step 10.

8. Since the remainders are small compared with the part loads, the cargo officer on the airship uses her own discretion where to put these.

9. Steps 6 and 7 are repeated in turn by the other loading officers, and this continues until one of them receives a load which would make her airship over-loaded. She must then send that airship off to the home port, together with a loading slip which might look like this.

10.
Airship *Sky Queen*

Max. load 900 tonnes, 6 compartments.

Load	*6 part-loads, each*	*remainder*
473	78	5
108	18	0
235	39	1
Totals 816	135	6

11. The other loading officers send home their airships when these can take no more.

12. When all the airships are back at the home airport, players change roles and become checking officers. They check by calculator all the calculations, including part-loads and remainders. There is good opportunity for discussion about how best to do this. The unused capacity is also calculated, in the above example 84 tonnes $(900 - 86)$.

13. Miscalculations are penalised by adding 100 tonnes to the unused capacity for each error in a part load, and 5 tonnes for each error in a remainder.

14. The best loading officer is the one with the least unused capacity.

Discussion of activities

Activities 1 and 2 are for extending children's calculating skills to larger dividends, still with single figure divisors. These would conventionally be done by children working singly, using pencil and paper and very likely the conventional notation.

The thinking behind the present approach, in which three children work together using a shared calculation board, is as follows. By making it a social activity, it becomes more interesting and introduces discussion. Each child sees and checks the accuracy of the calculations of the others. In activity 1, by having 3 children each say aloud, 'I'm thinking in . . .', they emphasise the changes in thinking between columns. This is important preparation for passing down the remainders in activity 2. Both the headed columns, notation, and saying aloud what they are doing, are being used to retain awareness of what is happening at each stage, so that when this method is eventually replaced by the conventional (and highly condensed) notation, children will, we hope, have established their understanding of the thinking processes which it represents.

I have introduced the method with HTU from the start, rather than TU, because it is no harder and gives two examples of passing on the remainder each time rather than one. But if you prefer to begin with TU, by all means do so.

The method of calculating used in this topic is a hybrid. It is much easier to think of

$$2\overline{)6}^{\,3}$$

as 'How many 2s in 6? Answer 3' than as 'Start with 6, share between 2, 3 in each share'; so it is presented the first way. (The reason for not using physical materials here is that very large quantities would be needed. With a divisor (say) 8, there could be a remainder of 7 hundred-cubes to be exchanged for 70 ten-rods.) And as already noted, '2 into 6 goes 3 times' does not describe what is being done – it is inaccurate and confusing.

My justification for this hybrid is that once we have established grouping and sharing as mathematically equivalent (topic 3), they become interchangeable for purposes of calculation. (We think in the same way when we know that 3 tens and 30 units are equivalent, and therefore interchangeable for the purposes of calculation.) So when we are concerned with the mathematical operation of division, we are justified in using whichever of the two varieties best serves our thinking.

Activities 3 and 4 are games which give plenty of practice in these new methods. Activity 3 (Q and R ladders) involves only division of tens and units; activity 4, division of hundreds, tens and units.

OBSERVE AND LISTEN   **REFLECT**   **DISCUSS**

Num 6.9   DIVISION BY CALCULATOR

Concept   The calculator as a tool by which we can divide whatever the numbers, easily and quickly.

Abilities   (i)   To use a calculator correctly.
(ii)   To interpret the results.
(iii)   To deal appropriately with any decimal fractions which appear in the results.

Discussion of concept

The widespread availability of inexpensive calculators has a number of advantages for school mathematics. By reducing the amount of time which has to be spent on calculating, time is released which can be spent more usefully in other ways. They also allow the use of numbers which arise naturally: there is no longer any need to use artificially simplified numbers which 'work out nicely'.

In general, I think that children should continue to learn the skills of addition, subtraction, multiplication, division. This will be obvious from the amount of space given to these in the networks. But I cannot see any good reason why children should continue to learn long division. No new mathematical understanding results, and compared with the time and effort involved the benefits are negligible.

What I do see as important is that calculators should be used with understanding, and this is the aim of this topic.

Decimal fractions are dealt with in the Fractions network, which is where they belong. Rounding also comes there, with the help of the number line. Both of these topics should be done before the present one.

Activity 1 **Number targets: division by calculator**

A game for up to 6 children, though a smaller number is better. Its purpose is to develop further the relationships between dividend, divisor, quotient, with more difficult numbers. The use of a calculator frees the mind from the distraction of laborious calculations, and allows full attention to be given to these relationships. This is also a convenient time to introduce the terms 'dividend' and 'divisor', if this has not been done already.

Materials
- Calculator.
- Three 0-9 dice.
- Paper and pencil.

Rules of the game
1. The 3 dice are thrown to give a 3-digit number. This is written on the paper as the dividend.
2. 2 dice are then thrown to give a 2-digit number. This is written as the target. E.g.,

Dividend	Target
747	64

3. The aim is to find a number which, when used as divisor, gives the target number as quotient when the calculator result is rounded to the nearest whole number. Each player in turn writes his attempt, and passes paper, pencil, and calculator to the next player. Example:

Dividend	Target
747	64

$747 \div 12 = 62.25$
(Good for a first trial)
$747 \div 13 = 57.461539$
(This player changed the divisor in the wrong direction)
$747 \div 11 = 67.909091$
(This player learnt from the other's mistake)
$747 \div 11.5 = 64.956522$
(Nearly there, but this rounds to 65)
$747 \div 11.6 = 64.396552$
(He wins this round)

4. Another round may now be played, repeating steps 1 to 3. The winner of the last round starts, since the first attempt is the most difficult.

Discussion of activity

Activity 1 uses a calculator to test predictions. It is quite a difficult activity, requiring children to take into account both the direction in which the divisor needs to be changed from the last trial, and also what is a likely amount. This seems to me a much better direction in which to develop their understanding than learning the laborious, time-consuming, and no longer necessary procedure of long division.

OBSERVE AND LISTEN   **REFLECT**   **DISCUSS**

FRACTIONS

Double operations
Numbers which represent these
Fractions as quotients

Num 7.1 MAKING EQUAL PARTS

Concepts (i)   The whole of an object.
(ii) Part of an object.
(iii) Equal parts and their names.

Ability To make, name, and recognise wholes, halves, third-parts, fourth-parts, fifth-parts, etc., of a variety of objects.

Discussion of concepts

Many children have difficulty with fractions, and I think there are several causes which continue to bring this about.
(i) Fractions *are* difficult. Work with fractions is begun too early, and taken too far for children of primary school age.
(ii) The same notation is used with three distinct meanings. For example, $\frac{2}{3}$ can mean a fraction, or a fractional number, or a quotient.
(iii) The authors of many text books for children appear to confuse these three meanings, and they pass on their confusion to the children. It is rather like confusing the different physical embodiments of $7 - 3$: take-away, comparison, complement. But in this case the confusion is at a more abstract level. The distinction is not an easy one, and a full discussion of this I would consider as at least O level mathematics, perhaps A level.

In the present network I have tried to present only the truth, but for the reasons above not the whole truth. We begin as usual by introducing the concept in several different physical embodiments. The terms 'third-part', 'fourth-part', etc, are used to distinguish fractions from the ordinal numbers third, fourth, etc; and also as reminders that we are talking about parts *of something*. This is implicit in the word 'part', but to start with we need to say so explicitly. Note that in this topic we are not yet talking about fractions, but about wholes and parts. This is just the first stage of the concept.

Activity 1 Making equal parts

An activity for up to 6 children. Its purpose is to make a start with the concept of a fraction, using two different physical embodiments.

Materials • SAR boards, Fractions 1, Fractions 2, and Fractions 3.*
• Plasticine.

- Blunt knives.
- Cutting boards.

* See figure 14. A full-size version, together with boards 2 and 3, will be found in Vol. 2a. For board 2, it is helpful also to have a cardboard template the size and shape of a 'fruity bar', which children can cut round.

START	ACTION	RESULT	NAME
a plasticine sausage.	Leave this one as it is.	(Put it here.)	The <u>whole</u> of a sausage.
a plasticine sausage.	Make **2** equal parts.	(Put them here.)	These are <u>halves</u> of a sausage.
a plasticine sausage.	Make **3** equal parts.	(Put them here.)	These are <u>third-parts</u> of a sausage.
a plasticine sausage.	Make **4** equal parts.	(Put them here.)	These are <u>fourth-parts</u> of a sausage. Also called quarters
a plasticine sausage.	Make **5** equal parts	(Put them here)	These are <u>fifth-parts</u> of a sausage

Figure 14   SAR board 1. Making equal parts

What they do   *(Apportioned between the children)*

1. Six equal-sized round Plasticine 'sausages' are made, by rolling 6 equal amounts of Plasticine and trimming the ends to fit the sausage shapes on the left of board 1. One sausage is put into each outline.
2. The children do the actions described on the board. The lines of division may be marked lightly before cutting. In this way, trials can be made and corrected by smoothing out the marks.

3. After cutting, the separated parts are put in the RESULT column next to their descriptions.
4. Steps 1 and 3 are repeated using Fractions Board 2 and fresh plasticine. Board 1 should if possible remain on view. With board 2, a variety of division lines are easily found. E.g. fourth-parts:

At this stage accept any correct results. These possibilities will be explored further in the next activity.

5. Steps 1 to 3 are now repeated using Fractions Board 3. If possible, fresh plasticine should be used, the other two boards remaining on view. The lines of division should be radial, as shown below.

 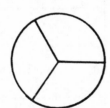  

Activity 2   Same kind, different shapes

An activity for up to 6 children. Its purpose is to develop the idea that parts of the same kind may not look alike. In activity 1, this arose from the use of different objects. Here we see that this can be so even with the same object.

Materials   ●   * S-A-R boards: halves, fourth-parts, third-parts, see figure 15.
Plasticine.
Blunt knives.
Cutting boards.

The first of these is illustrated overleaf. The others are in Vol. 2a.

START	ACTION	RESULT	NAME
a fruity bar			

Make **2** equal parts. — (Put them here) — These are <u>halves</u> of a fruity bar.

Make **2** equal parts in different ways. — (Put them here.) — These are also <u>halves</u> of a fruity bar.

Make **2** equal parts in a different way — (Put them here) — These are also <u>halves</u> of a fruity bar

There are three simple ways. Later you may be able to find others.

Figure 15 SAR board 1. Same kind, different shapes. *Halves*

What they do 1. Begin with the halves board. This is used in the same way as the SAR board for activity 1. The 3 straightforward ways are:

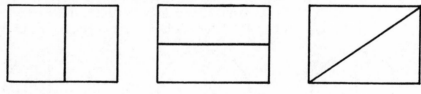

2. Next, they use the third-parts board. This offers only 2 straightforward ways.

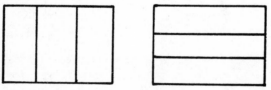

3. Next, they use the fourth-parts board. There are 6 ways of doing this which are fairly easy to find.

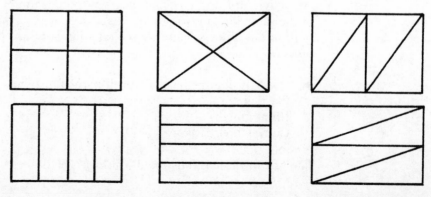

4. Finally, they may like to return to the halves board, and try to find more ways. Here are 2 more, which can be varied indefinitely.

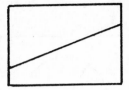 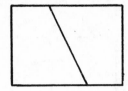

Activity 3   Parts and bits

A teacher-led discussion for up to 6 children. Its purpose is to emphasise that when we talk about third-parts, fourth-parts, etc., we mean equal parts. To make this clear, we use the word 'bits' when these are unequal.

Materials
- Plasticine.
- Blunt knives.
- Cutting boards.

Suggested sequence for discussion

1. Make 2 Plasticine 'sausages' of equal size. Cut one into 3 equal parts, the other into 3 bits. Ask whether both of these have been cut into third-parts.
2. If necessary, explain the difference, as described above.
3. Have the children make some more sausages, all of the same size, and cut some into halves, fourth-parts, fifth-parts, and some into 2, 4, 5 bits.
4. These are put centrally together with the parts and bits made in step 1.
5. The children then ask each other for parts or bits. E.g. 'Sally, please give me a fourth-part of a sausage'; or 'Mark, please give me a bit of a sausage.'
6. The others say whether they agree.
7. Steps 5 and 6 are repeated as necessary.

Activity 4   Sorting parts

An activity for up to 5 children. Its purpose is to consolidate the concepts formed in activities 1 and 2, moving on to a pictorial representation.

Materials
- Parts pack of cards.*
- 5 name cards.**
- 5 set loops.

* Some of these are illustrated in figure 16. The complete pack is in Vol. 2a.
** These are marked WHOLES, HALVES, THIRD-PARTS, FOURTH-PARTS, FIFTH-PARTS.

What they do

1. Begin by looking at some of the cards together. Explain that these represent the objects which they made from Plasticine, in the last activity – sausages, fruity bars, biscuits; and some new ones. They also represent the parts into which the objects have been cut, e.g. third-parts, fourth-parts, halves, fifth-parts. Some have not been cut: these are wholes.

179

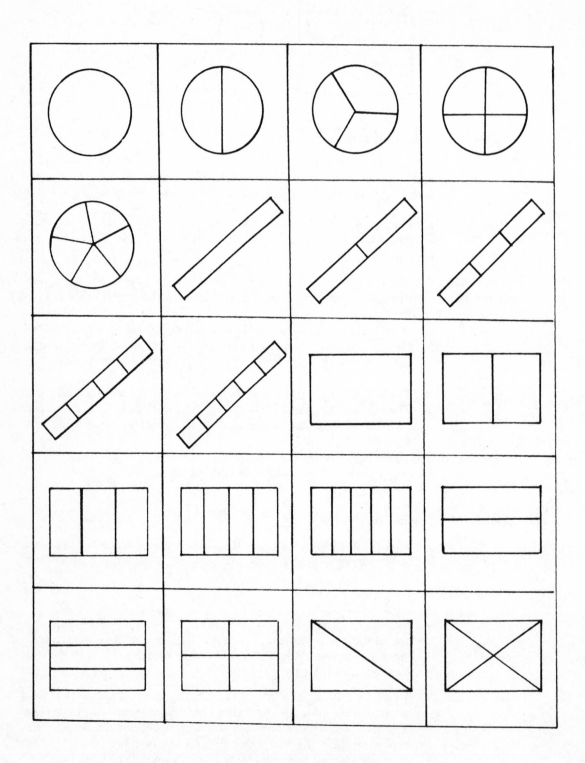

Figure 16 Cards for *Sorting parts* and *Match and Mix: parts*.

2. The parts pack is then shuffled and spread out face upwards on the table.
3. The name cards are put face down and each child takes one.
4. Each child puts in front of her a set loop with the name card she has taken inside, face up.
5. They all then collect cards of one kind, according to the name card they have taken.
6. They check each other's sets, and discuss, if necessary.
7. If they are fewer than 6 children, they may then work together to sort the remaining cards.
8. Steps 2 to 7 may be repeated, children collecting a different set from before.

Activity 5 Match and mix: parts

A game for 2 to 5 players. Its purpose is further to consolidate the concepts formed in activity 1.

Materials
- Parts pack of cards.*
- A card as illustrated below.
* The same as for activity 4.

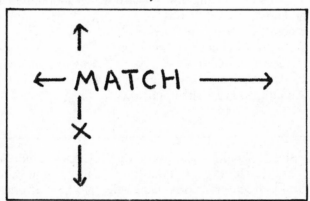

Rules of the game
1. The cards are spread out face downwards in the middle of the table.
2. The MATCH and MIX card is put wherever convenient.
3. Each player takes 5 cards (if 2 players only, they take 7 cards each). Alternatively the cards may be dealt in the usual way.
4. They collect their cards in a pile face downwards.
5. Players in turn look at the top cards in their piles, and put cards down next to cards already there (after the first) according to the following three rules.
(i) Cards must match or be different, according as they are put next to each other in the 'match' or 'mix' directions.
(ii) Not more than 3 cards may be put together in either direction.
(iii) There may not be two 3's next to each other.
('Match' or 'mix' refers to the kind of part.)
Examples (using A, B, C . . . for different kinds of part)
A typical arrangement.

```
                    C

                  A  A  A

                B  B  B

                    D  D  D

                    B

                    A
```

None of these is allowed.

```
A        B B B B        C C C      A A        A

A                       D D D      B B        B

A                                  C C        A

A
```

A card which cannot be played is replaced at the bottom of the pile.
6. Scoring is as follows.
   1 point for completing a row or column of three.
   2 points for putting down a card which simultaneously matches one way and mixes the other way.
   2 points for being the first 'out'.
   1 point for being the second 'out'.
   (So it is possible to score up to 6 points in a single turn.)
7. Play continues until all players have put down all their cards.
8. Another round is then played.

Discussion of activities

Activities 1, 2 and 3 make use of mode 1 schema building (physical experience). This is every bit as important when introducing older children to fractions as physical sorting is when introducing young children to the concept of a set. In the present case, it is the physical action of cutting up into equal parts from which we want the children to abstract the mathematical operation of division. In this case, the operand is a whole object, so it is important to have something which can easily be cut up. Plasticine is ideal for this, since children can first make the right shapes and then cut them up.

Activities 4 and 5 move on to pictorial representation of these physical actions. This is where most textbooks begin. What is not understood is that the diagrams condense no less than six ideas, as will be seen in Num 7.3. These diagrams are likely to be helpful if and only if the children already have the right foundation schema to which these can be assimilated. Otherwise, here is the first place where children can get confused.

So in this topic, we begin with physical actions on objects: making equal parts. We then introduce diagrams representing these and no more. We are not yet into fractions; just objects, and parts of objects.

The key ideas are that the parts must all be equal in size (or we call them 'bits'); and that the kind of parts we are talking about depends only on how many the object is cut up into, not on their shape, nor on what the object is. These ideas are encountered first with physical objects, then with diagrams.

OBSERVE AND LISTEN　　　　**REFLECT**　　　　**DISCUSS**

Num 7.2　TAKE A NUMBER OF LIKE PARTS

Concept　That of a number of like parts.

Abilities　(i)　To put together any required number of any required kind of part.
　　　　(ii)　To recognise and name any such combination.

Discussion of concept　This is the next step towards the concept of a fraction. It is much more straightforward than that of topic 1, which entailed (i) separating a single object into part-objects (ii) of a given number (iii) all of the same amount. Here we only have to put together a given number of these parts.

Activity 1　**Feeding the animals**

An activity for up to 6 children working in 2 teams. Its purpose is to introduce the concept described above.

Materials　● 3 sets of animals.*
● Menu for each set, on separate cards.*
● Cards for each menu showing standard sizes of eel, meat slab, biscuit. (One between 2 children.)**
● 5 food trays.
● Plasticine.
● Blunt knives.
● Cutting boards.
● 5 set loops.
* As listed below. The animals may be models, or pictures on cards. Quite a lot of these are needed: sorry, but if they help children to like fractions it's worth it!
** A template for the meat slab is useful. See Num 7.1 under 'Materials'.

SET 1

Animals   2 bears, 3 walruses, 5 seals, 6 penguins, 8 otters.

> *Menu*
>
> These all eat fish.
>
> Today, the menu is eels (beheaded and tailed).
> Each bear gets the whole of an eel.
> Each walrus gets half of an eel.
> Each seal gets a third-part of an eel.
> Each penguin gets a fourth-part of an eel.
> Each otter gets a fifth-part of an eel.

SET 2

Animals   2 lions, 2 cheetahs, 4 wolves, 4 hyenas, 6 wild cats.

> *Menu*
>
> These all eat raw meat, supplied in large slabs.
>
> Each lion gets the whole of a slab.
> Each cheetah gets half of a slab.
> Each wolf gets a third-part of a slab.
> Each hyena gets a fourth-part of a slab.
> Each wild cat gets a fifth-part of a slab.

SET 3

Animals   3 rats, 3 voles, 5 shrews, 5 house mice, 7 harvest mice.

> *Menu*
>
> These all eat biscuits.
>
> Each rat gets the whole of a biscuit.
> Each vole gets half of a biscuit.
> Each shrew gets a third-part of a biscuit.
> Each house mouse gets a fourth-part of a biscuit.
> Each harvest mouse gets a fifth-part of a biscuit.

What they do   1.   One team acts as animal keepers, the other works in the zoo kitchen. The latter need to be more numerous, since there is more work for them to do.

2.   A set of animals is chosen. Suppose that this is set 1. The kitchen staff look at the menu and set to work, preparing eels, as in Num 7.1/1. The animal keepers put the animals in their enclosures (segregated, not assorted). They may choose how many of each.

3. The animal keepers, one at a time, come to the kitchen and ask for food for each kind of animal in turn. The kitchen staff cut the eels as required. E.g.

Animal keeper	*Zoo kitchen staff*
'Food for 3 walruses, please.'	'Here it is: 3 halves of an eel.'
'Food for 4 otters, please.'	'4 fifth-parts. Tell them not to leave any scraps.'
'Food for 5 seals, please.'	'Here it is: 5 third-parts of an eel.'
'Food for 2 bears, please.'	'Here you are: 2 whole eels.'
'Food for 3 penguins, please.'	'3 fourth-parts. Lucky penguins.'

4. Each time, the animals' keeper checks that the amounts are correct, and then gives its ration to each animal. The keepers also check each other.
5. When feeding time is over, the food is returned to the kitchen for re-processing. Steps 1 to 4 are then repeated with different animals, keepers, and kitchen staff.
6. Note that the eels, after their head and tails are removed, resemble the sausages of Num 7.1/1; and the slabs of meat are oblongs. Note also that the eels, slabs, biscuits should be of standard sizes.

Activity 2 Trainee keepers, qualified keepers

An activity for up to 6 children. Its purpose is to consolidate their recognition of the combination, number of parts and kind of parts.

Materials As for activity 1, without the animals and set loops.

What they do *Stage (a) Trainee keepers*
1. The children are acting as trainee keepers. In this part of their course, they are learning to ensure that they can recognise the right food for all their animals.
2. Initially they work with one menu at a time. A standard card (eel, meat slab, or biscuit) is put at the top of the menu.
3. Each of them then makes up a food tray for a given number of animals of a particular kind.
4. In turn, one of the food trays is put in the middle and the others say what kind of animal it is for, and how many. E.g.

a standard eel

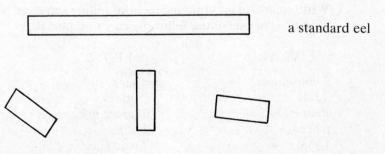

This is for 3 penguins.

5. It is difficult to judge the difference in size between, e.g. fourth-parts and fifth-parts. So the unused parts should be left on the cutting board, with any remaining plasticine cleared away. Thus in the example above, the remaining fourth-part should be left on the cutting board.

6. As they become more expert, they work with 2, then 3 menus.

Stage (b)   Qualified keepers

1. When one of them thinks he is ready to take his test, the others prepare 5 trays including at least 1 from each menu.

2. If the one taking his test can identify all of these correctly, he qualifies. (A pass mark of 100 per cent may seem severe, but every animal has to be correctly fed.)

Activity 3   Head keepers

An activity for up to six children. Its purpose is for children to write the two operations which together go to make a fraction in their own words, as preparation for the standard notation which they will learn in the next topic.

Materials   For each child:
- The 3 menus already used on one sheet of paper.
- Lists of animals to be fed (see below.)
- Pencil and paper for each child.

What they do   1. A head keeper has to be able to write clear instructions for feeding any of the animals.

2. Those who wish to be considered for this job are each given one list of animals to be fed. Specimen lists are given below.

3. They write, in their own words, instructions for preparing a food tray for each cage of animals on their list.

4. When they have finished, all but one of the children act as examiners. The remaining one reads out the questions, and his answers. The others decide whether these are both clear and accurate.

5. If all the answers meet these requirements, the candidate is eligible for head keeper when there is a vacancy.

Write clear and accurate instructions telling someone how to prepare a food tray for one of the following cages of animals.

LIST A	LIST B	LIST C
3 house mice	2 seals	1 vole
2 rats	2 otters	3 harvest mice
2 cheetahs	3 house mice	4 wolves
6 hyenas	4 voles	2 hyenas
1 seal	7 wild cats	3 bears
4 penguins	3 lions	5 walruses

LIST D	LIST E	LIST F
3 wildcats	3 bears	3 cheetahs
4 lions	1 penguin	2 hyenas
1 shrew	2 wolves	5 walruses
5 voles	8 wild cats	2 otters
1 bear	3 voles	5 rats
2 penguins	5 shrews	4 shrews

Discussion of activities

In this topic we bring in the second contributor to the concept of fraction, returning for this to the same physical embodiments as in Num 7.1/1. As in the previous activity, these physical embodiments are of two kinds. The Plasticine is of the first kind: a physical operand, in different shapes representing different imaginary operands. The actions of making a given number of equal parts, and taking a given number of these, are of the second kind. It is the second kind which leads to the mathematical concept of a fraction, independently of what the operand is.

However, a fraction has to have *some* operand. So in step 3 of activity 1, I have kept in the words '. . . of a biscuit' (etc.) to help us all to remember this. (You can skip the rest of this paragraph if you like.) This leads to a slight problem of syntax. Should 'biscuit' be singular or plural? After thought, I have settled for singular. 'Third-part of a biscuit' leads to '2 third-parts of a biscuit', and even to '5 third-parts of a biscuit'. In the last case, they won't all come from the biscuit – but each part will come from *a* biscuit, not several.

In activity 1, the fractional parts were the end-point of the activity, leading to the concept. In activity 2, they are the starting point. Children have to use their newly formed concepts to recognise what number of what kind of parts they are looking at. Their decisions are confirmed or otherwise by the rest of the group (mode 2 testing).

Activity 3 requires them to think about and describe the physical actions of making equal parts, and then taking a given number of these, instead of actually doing these actions. This takes them a step further towards fractions as mental operations.

OBSERVE AND LISTEN   **REFLECT**   **DISCUSS**

Num 7.3   FRACTIONS AS A DOUBLE OPERATION: NOTATION

Concepts

(i) A fraction as a mathematical operation which corresponds to two actions: making a given number of equal parts, and putting together a given number of these.

(ii) A notation which represents this double operation.

Abilities   (i)   To match this operation (as represented by its notation) with a
                    physical embodiment.
             (ii) To match this operation (as represented by its notation) with a
                    diagram for the same fraction.

Discussion of concepts

As soon as we are dealing with mathematical operations, which are purely mental, we require a notation by which to communicate, manipulate, and record these. So the introduction of a notation, and the transition to the concept of a fraction as a combined operation, come together.

The traditional notation is a good one,

$$\frac{1}{2}$$ how many parts
        of a given kind   (numerator)

        what kind of
        parts   (denominator)

What kind of parts is determined by how many equal parts are made from the operand, so a number is sufficient to specify what kind of part. This is implied by the way we read it, 'two thirds'; or as I think we should continue to say at this stage, 'two third-parts'.

As has been said already, 'part' implies part *of* something. It implies an operand. There are now two further points to be made.

(i) In the present treatment of fractions, the numerator is not the operand, and 2/3 does not mean the same as 2 ÷ 3. (The latter meaning is also correct, but to introduce it at this stage complicates the concept further, and I am trying to simplify.)

(ii) The whole is not the operand either. The operand is what this whole is whole *of*.

The traditional way of representing fractions by diagrams is also good, but very condensed.

This diagram
for ⅔

simultaneously represents no less than 6 ideas:

the object we
start with
(the operand);

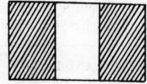

the number of
cuts we make,
and where we
make them
(cuts as actions);

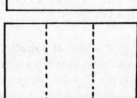

the cuts we have
made (cuts as
results), and the
parts which result;

and the number
of parts which
we are taking.

So is it small wonder that children have problems when their learning of fractions *begins* with these diagrams.

In topic 1, these diagrams were introduced after children had met with these ideas separately, in physical form. Here we shall renew the connection, and link it with the notation.

Activity 1   Expanding the diagram

An activity for up to 6 children, working singly or in twos or threes. Its purpose is to relate the conventional fraction diagrams to the 6 concepts which they combine.

Materials
- SARAR board (see figure 17).
- Pack of fraction diagram cards (see figure 18).*
- Reminder card.**
- Plasticine.
- Knives.

* This figure shows two specimen cards. A full pack is provided in Vol. 2a. You can invent more, if further practice is needed.
** As illustrated below.

> REMINDER CARD
> FOR
> EXPANDING THE DIAGRAM
>
> The diagram shows:
> the object we start with
> *first action*   the cuts we make
> *first result*   the parts we make
> *second action*   the parts we take
> *combined result*   a fraction of an object

What they do
1. The SARAR board is put where all can see it. To begin with, all except the diagram at the top is covered.
2. Explain that this diagram shows the result of two actions combined. This combination is called a fraction.

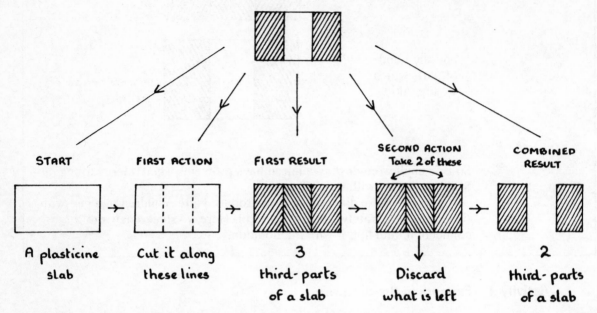

Figure 17 Expanding the diagram

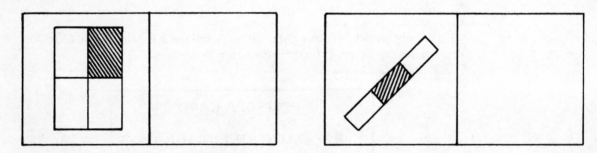

Figure 18 Specimen fraction diagram cards

3. Uncover the rest of the board, and help them to work through the 5 steps shown. Help them to see how each step is embedded in the combined diagram. Leave this on view with the final result in Plasticine still in position.

4. Choose a suitable fraction diagram card. Help them to work through the steps which it represents, using the reminder card as a guide. The Plasticine objects are put in the blank half of the card. Repeat this step if necessary.

5. When they are ready to continue, each pair or trio takes a fraction card from the set. They may choose cards they think they can do. Note that the long thin oblong may be modelled as a sausage, and the torus as a ring doughnut. The children may use either description.
6. For each card, they work through the steps which this represents, agreeing each step with each other.
7. When finished, they agree what the result is called. (E.g. 2 fifth-parts of a ring doughnut.)
8. Steps 5, 6, 7 are repeated until they are confident that they can interpret every part of the meaning of a fraction diagram.

Activity 2   'Please may I have?' (Diagrams and notation)

A game for 5 or 6 players. Its purpose is to link the diagrams with the conventional notation.

Materials
- Set of fraction diagram cards.*
- Set of fraction notation cards.**

* As used in activity 1.
** As illustrated in step 2 below.

Rules of the game
1. All the cards are dealt to the players, each pack separately. If there are 5 players, each will thus get 3 cards of each sort. If there are 6 players, each will receive 2 cards of one sort and 3 of the other.
2. The purpose is to get rid of one's cards by making pairs. Each pair must consist of a notation card and a diagram card. E.g.

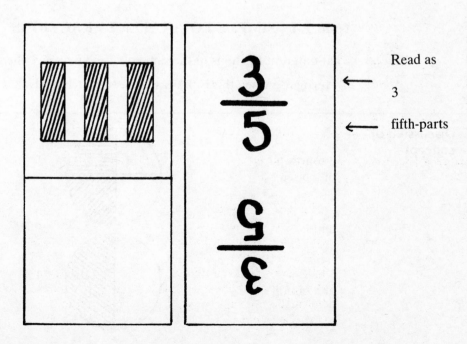

Read as

← 3

← fifth-parts

3. After the deal, the players first put down any pairs which they already hold.
4. They then try to make more pairs by asking each other, taking turns. E.g. 'Please, Susan, may I have a diagram for two third-parts?' Or, '. . . a notation for two third-parts?'
5. The winner is the player who has most pairs when all have played out their hands.

Discussion of activities

Because so many children (and adults) have difficulty with fractions, I think that it is important to continue with physical embodiments of both the actions and the operands in order to give plenty of mode 1 learning to establish a good foundation. This is particularly important when, as in this case, diagrams are used which themselves are highly condensed. So in activity 1 we return to physical actions on physical operands.

The notation, which represents the same concept as a fraction diagram, must therefore inevitably be more condensed even than the diagram. So the children need – and I hope by now will have had – plenty of experience of the separate operations, before they learn the conventional notation.

In activity 2, the words 'of . . .' have been dropped for two reasons. The same operator can act on a variety of operands; and we have therefore begun to treat fractions independently of any particular embodiment.

OBSERVE AND LISTEN   **REFLECT**   **DISCUSS**

Num 7.4   SIMPLE EQUIVALENT FRACTIONS

Concept   That different fractions of the same operand may give the same amount.

Ability   To recognise when this is the case, i.e. to match equivalent fractions.

Discussion of concept

2 fourth-parts
of a biscuit

and

1 half
of a biscuit

are not identical, but we get the same amount to eat (assuming no crumbs). So we say that 2/4 and 1/2 are equivalent fractions, meaning that if applied to the same operand they result in the same amount: though these may not look exactly alike.

The idea of equivalence is an important one throughout mathematics. (For a fuller discussion, see chapter 9 of *The Psychology of Learning Mathematics*). It is important in this network because it makes the bridge between fractions as double operations, and fractions as representing numbers.

It is the idea which is important, and in this topic I have therefore kept to simple examples.

Activity 1   'Will this do instead?'

An activity for up to 6 children. Its purpose is to introduce the concept of equivalent fractions. It also introduces eighth-parts.

Materials
- Plasticine.
- 8 small cards, all the same size. (6 cm by 4 cm is suitable.)
- Knife.
- Board to cut on.
- A small rolling pin is also useful.

What they do
1. One of the children acts as the owner of a sweetshop. He sells very good fruity bars.
2. Before the shop opens, he makes a number of these, each the size of one of the cards. The cards are used as supports.
   (Initially you may find it better to do this yourself. It helps to prevent sticking if the cutting board and rolling pin are wetted).
3. Fruity bars are expensive, and pennies are scarce. So the shopkeeper, a kind old man, cuts them up so that children can buy them in parts. Two he cuts into halves, two into fourth-parts, and two into eighth-parts. (This leaves two spare cards.)
4. He is also eccentric, and tries never to give exactly what he is asked for.
5. When the shop opens, a customer comes in and asks for (e.g.) half of a fruity bar. The shopkeeper takes 2 fourth-parts, or 4 eighth-parts, and puts these on a spare card. He offers these to the customer, saying 'Will these do instead?'
6. The customer says (in this case) '2 fourth parts – that will do nicely, thank you'. (Or 4 eighth-parts, as the case may be.)
7. Another customer enters the shop, and steps 5 and 6 are repeated.
8. The stock is replenished when necessary.
9. Sometimes the old man makes a mistake. (If this does not arise naturally, he does so 'accidentally on purpose'.) In this case the customer politely explains.
10. The game may be extended by the inclusion of other goodies, of various shapes.

Activity 2   Sorting equivalent fractions

An activity for up to 6 children. Its purpose is to expand the concept of equivalent fractions to diagrams and notation.

Materials   • Equivalent fractions pack 1 (see specimens below).
• 3 set loops.

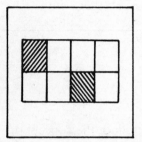 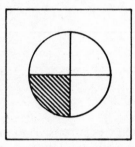 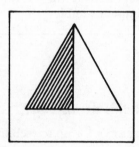 

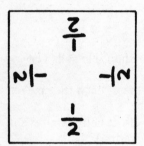 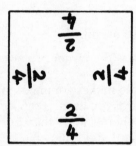 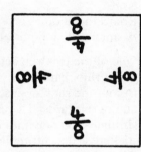 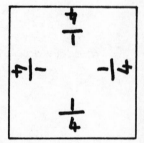

What they do   1.   The fraction pack is shuffled and spread out face upwards on the table.
2.   Children work in ones or twos, according to how many there are. Each child (or pair) takes a set loop.
3.   To begin with, the notation card for a whole, 1 half, and 1 fourth-part are found. One is put in each set loop.
4.   They then collect all fractions which are equivalent to this, whether diagrams or notation.
5.   They check each others' sets, and discuss if necessary.
6.   As a continuation activity, each equivalence set may be sorted into subsets. E.g. within the set of fractions equivalent to one half, one subset would be all the diagrams representing the fraction 2 fourth-parts, together with its notation.

Activity 3   Match and mix: equivalent fractions

An activity for 2 to 5 players. Its purpose is to give further practice in recognising equivalent fractions.

Materials
- Equivalent fractions pack 1.*
- Match and mix card.**

* The same as for activity 2.
** Like that for Num 7.1/5.

Rules of the game This is played in the same way as Match and Mix: parts (Num 7.1/5). Here, 'match', or 'mix' refers to equivalence of fractions, as represented by diagrams and notation.

Discussion of activities

In activity 1, the physical embodiments provide a good mode 1 refresher of earlier work, and foundation for the concept of equivalent fractions. And the imagined situation embodies one of the meanings of equivalent (equi-valent: equal in value). Equivalent fractions of a fruity bar contain the same amount to eat, and are worth the same amount of money.

You will notice the omission of third-parts. While these fit well into the schema as so far developed, I see no object in children's learning about sixth-parts just to provide something two of which are equivalent to third-parts. And looking forward to the equivalent decimal fractions, I have little enthusiasm for teaching children recurring decimals just in order to keep going with third-parts. Eighth-parts, on the other hand, form part of the sequence formed by successive halving and are still with us in everyday life. Both the rulers on my desk as I write still have inches along one edge, and these are sub-divided into halves, quarters, eighth-parts, and sixteenth-parts.

In activity 2, they extend the new concept to the more abstract representations of fractions provided by diagrams and notation. They have already learnt the connections between these, in Num 7.3/2. Activity 3 consolidates these in a game which they have already learnt to play, with simpler materials.

I would not encourage teaching the cancelling rule, which is a convenient technique but does not relate clearly to the concepts. Children will themselves notice the inverse, that equivalent fractions may be obtained by doubling numerators and denominator. This corresponds to cutting every part in two.

OBSERVE AND LISTEN   **REFLECT**   **DISCUSS**

Num 7.5   DECIMAL FRACTIONS AND EQUIVALENTS

Concepts
(i)   Decimal fractions.
(ii) Equivalence between decimal fractions and fractions of other denominations.

Abilities
(i)   To find decimal fractions of a variety of operands.
(ii) To match decimal fractions with other equivalent fractions.

<table>
<tr><td>

Discussion of concepts

</td><td>

The common usage of the term 'decimals' confuses (i) a particular kind of fraction, and (ii) place-value notation. Unless we separate these two ideas, we would have to say that 0.5 is a decimal, while 5/10 is not. So I hope that you will accept my proposal, that we use the term 'decimal' to mean what it says, i.e. related to 10 (as in 'decimal coinage'); and 'decimal fraction' to mean a fraction whose denominator is a power of 10 (10, 100, 1000 . . .), whichever way it is written. If this is agreed, then the term 'common fraction' (or 'vulgar fraction') is no longer a useful one.

Decimal fractions have the great advantage that they can be represented in two notations: bar notation (the one used in this network up to now), and place-value notation. The latter offers considerable simplification when it comes to calculations – not least, that we can use a calculator!

In this topic we shall confine ourselves to the introduction of decimal fractions, and their equivalences with fractions of other denominators. Their representation in place-value notation is a separate topic in itself.

</td></tr>
</table>

Activity 1   Making jewellery to order

An activity for up to 6 children. Its purpose is to introduce decimal fractions in verbal form.

Materials
- A metre measure, divided in decimetres and centimetres.
- Jewellery catalogue (see figure 19).
- Purchasing guide (see figure 20).

What they do
1. (Introductory discussion) They already know that 100 cm is the same length as 1 m; so they should find it easy to answer the question 'What is a hundredth-part of a metre?' Next, they learn that the other length on the metre measure is called a decimetre, because there are ten of these in a metre. So a tenth-part of a metre is called . . . ?
2. Two children take the roles of jeweller and jewellers' supply merchant. The others in turn act as customers.
3. The jeweller works at home, making jewellery to order. She has a catalogue to show to the customers, and a purchasing guide for her own use.
4. The first customer calls, looks at the catalogue, and chooses what she would like, e.g., a coiled brooch.
5. The jeweller looks at her purchasing guide, and sees that a metre of silver wire will make five of these. She only wants enough for one.
6. So she goes to the supplier and asks for one fifth-part of a metre of silver wire.
7. The supplier looks at her metre measure, and says 'I'll measure you 2 decimetres; that is, 2 tenth-parts of a metre'.
8. The purchaser says 'I agree'; or if he has any doubts, the matter is discussed with the help of the metre measure.
9. The jeweller returns home, another customer calls, and steps 4 to 8 are repeated.

Plaited bracelet.

Filigree pendant.

Coiled brooch.

Pair of ear-rings

Figure 19   Jewellery catalogue.

I metre of silver wire makes

Plaited bracelet	2
Filigree pendant	4
Coiled brooch	5
Pair of ear-rings	10

Figure 20   Purchasing guide.

10. When all the remaining children have acted as customers, two more children take the roles of jeweller and supplier, and steps 4 to 8 are repeated.

11. Note that since a filigree pendant takes a fourth-part of a metre, the jeweller in this case says 'I'll measure you 25 centimetres; that is, 25 hundredth-parts of a metre'. For variety, centimetres may be used on other occasions. E.g. for a coiled brooch, the jeweller could also say 'I'll measure you 20 centimetres; that is, 20 hundredth parts of a metre'.

Activity 2 Equivalent fraction diagrams (decimal)

A teacher-led discussion for up to 6 children. Its purposes are (i) to make explicit the concepts of a decimal fraction, introduced in activity 1 (ii) to extend their use of fraction diagrams to those for decimal fractions (iii) to use these diagrams for recognising equivalences between decimal and non-decimal fractions, and also between decimal fractions of different denominations.

Materials
- For each child, a pair of equivalent fraction diagrams (decimal), as illustrated below. These may be on the same card.
- Something to point with.

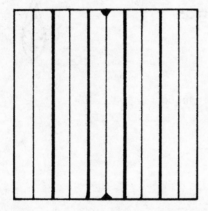 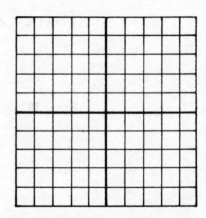

Suggested sequence for the discussion

1. Give each child a pair of equivalence diagrams. It doesn't matter which way up they look at these. Begin by asking them to look at the one shown above on the left.

2. What kind of parts are represented by the narrowest oblongs? (Tenth-parts.) By the oblongs between the thicker lines? (Fifth-parts.) And by the oblongs marked off by the arrowed line? (Halves.)

3. What equivalences can we deduce? (1 fifth-part is equivalent to 2 tenth-parts. 2 fifth-parts are equal to 4 tenth-parts, etc. and 5 tenth-parts are equivalent to one half.)

4. Next, ask them to look at the other diagram. Discuss this in a similar way. (We can deduce that 1 fourth-part is equivalent to 25 hundredth-parts, etc. And that 1 half is equivalent to 50 hundredth-parts.)

5. Next, tell them to put the two diagrams side by side. What can they say by comparing these? (1 tenth-part is equivalent to 10 hundredth-parts.

1 fifth-part is equivalent to 20 hundredth-parts. Also, 3 tenth-parts are equivalent to 30 hundredth-parts, etc. And 2 fifth-parts are equivalent to 40 hundredth-parts etc.)

6. Finally, tell them that there is a special name for the kind of fractions they have been talking about: decimal fractions. These include tenth-parts, hundredth-parts. Can they think of another decimal fraction? (What part of a metre is a millimetre? What part of a kilometre is a metre?)

Activity 3   Pair, and explain

A game for up to 6 children. Its purpose is to relate the equivalence they have learnt in activity 2 to the notation which is common to all kinds of fraction (common fraction notation).

Materials   • Fractions, pack 2 (see specimens below).
• For each child, a pair of equivalent fraction diagrams (decimal).*
* The same as in activity 2.

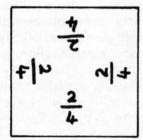
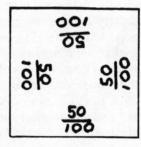
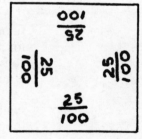

Rules of the game   1. The fractions pack is shuffled and put face down on the table. The top card is turned face up and put separately.
2. In turn, each player takes the top card from the pile and puts it face up on the table. The face-up cards are spread out so that all can be seen at the same time.
3. The object is to form pairs of equivalent fractions. These will gradually show us more cards are turned face-up. Pairs may be made from identical fractions since these too are equivalent.
4. The player who has just turned a card has first chance to make a pair. He takes these, puts them side by side in front of him, and explains the equivalence in terms of the equivalence diagram/s. If the others agree, he keeps the pair. If not, there is discussion.
5. If a pair is overlooked, the player whose next turn it is may claim it *before* turning over a card. He then turns over a card as in step 4. If another pair results, he may take this also.
6. When there are no more cards to turn over the winner is the player who has most pairs.

Note   The explanation in step 4 is a very important part of this activity. It must be in terms of the diagrams; not in terms of the cancelling rule, which is a convenient short-cut but makes no contribution to understanding.

Activity 4   Match and mix: equivalent decimal fractions

A game for 2 to 5 players. Its purpose is to give further practice in recognising decimal equivalent fractions.

Materials
- Fractions pack 2.*
- Match and mix card.**

* The same as used for activity 2.

** The same as used for Num 7.1/5 and Num 7.4/3.

Rules of the game   This is played in the same way as Match and Mix: equivalent fractions (Num 7.4/3), using fractions pack 2.

Discussion of activities   In this topic we are still using bar notation, for both decimal and non-decimal fractions. (See 'Discussion of concepts'.)

In activity 1, the metre and its sub-divisions into tenth-parts, hundredth-parts, thousandth-parts, provides a familiar and useful physical embodiment of the new concepts to be learnt. I have introduced the decimetre here for two reasons. First, because we need it as a representation of the fraction a tenth-part; and second, because it is a useful unit which in my view deserves to be more widely used than it is.

In activity 2, the new concept is made more explicit by discussion (mode 2), and related to equivalence diagrams like those already used for non-decimal fractions. No new material is introduced in activity 3. It consolidates the new concepts by mode 2 testing. As we all know, there is nothing so good as trying to explain something to others, to make one get it clear in one's own mind. Activities 3 and 4 work entirely with symbols, and so complete the process by which a concept is detached from any particular physical embodiment.

OBSERVE AND LISTEN   **REFLECT**   **DISCUSS**

Num 7.6   DECIMAL FRACTIONS IN PLACE-VALUE NOTATION

Concept   Extension of place-value notation to represent decimal fractions.

Abilities   (i)   To represent, and recognise, decimal fractions in place-value notation.

(ii)   To recognise the same fraction written in place-value and in bar notation.

Discussion of concept

We are very dependent on notations of many kinds not only for communicating and recording our ideas, but as a help to the thinking process itself. Some notations do their job much better than others. Place-value notation is a very good one, so the combination of decimal fractions and place-value notation is a very useful one. With the advent of calculators and computers, I see no reason for children to learn to calculate in bar notation until such time as they are about to learn algebraic fractions.

Note that we are here talking about *equal* fractions. These

$\frac{4}{100}$ and .04

are two notations for the same fraction.

Note   Children should already have done topics NuSp 1.9 (Interpolation between points on a number line) and NuSp 1.10 (extrapolation of place-value notation) before beginning the activities which follow.

Activity 1   **Reading headed columns in two ways**

An activity for up to 3 children. (They all need to see the activity board the same way up.) Its purpose is to refresh their knowledge of place-value notation for decimal fractions, and give additional practice in pairing the two notations for decimal fractions.

Materials
- Activity board.*
- Number cards.**

* See illustration in step 4 below. The full version is in Vol. 2a. Two should be provided, so that up to 6 children can play at a time.
** 1 to 9, 3 cm square, 2 of each.

What they do   1.   To introduce the activity, show the children the familiar headed columns.

H | T | U

Starting at the units, each column we go to the left means that the numbers are 10 times bigger. So what would it mean if we had some more columns on the right of the units column? Like this.

H | T | U | |

What are 10 times smaller than units? Tenth-parts. And what are 10 times smaller than these? Hundredth-parts. To emphasise the boundary between wholes and parts, we will use a dotted line. So we now have headed columns like these, using t-p and h-p for tenth-parts and hundredth-parts. (Note the use of lower case letters for parts of a unit, as in the metric system of abbreviations.)

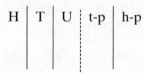

We can have as many columns as we like, extending to the left and right of the dotted line. For the present activity 3 columns are enough. (See illustration in step 4.)

2. The activity board is then put on the table where all the children can see it right way up. The number cards are shuffled and put in a pile (or heap) face down.

3. In turn, the children take number cards from the pile and put them face up where indicated by squares on the activity board. They take one, two, or three cards as needed to fill a line.

4. They then read the resulting fraction in two ways, as in the examples below. (It does not matter which is said first, and it is a good idea to vary this.)

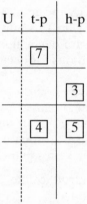

First child: '7 tenth-parts. Zero point 7 zero.'
Second child: '3 hundredth-parts. Zero point zero 3.'
Third child: '4 tenth-parts and 5 hundredth-parts. Zero point 4,5.'
('Four, five' not 'forty-five'.)
(Next time round, they could speak these the other way about.)

5. At this stage a zero is spoken for every empty column. This is never incorrect. Sometimes it is essential as a place-holder, sometimes it is not needed. This is a separate question which is dealt with in the next activity.

6. When all the lines are filled, the board is cleared and steps 3 and 4 repeated.

Activity 2   Same number, or different?

An activity for up to 3 children. Its purpose is for them to learn when a zero is essential as a place-holder, and when it is optional.

Materials
- Activity board.*
- Number cards.*
- Pencil and paper for each child.

* The same as for activity 1.

What they do
1. The activity board and number cards are put out as for activity 1.
2. The first child puts number cards on the board as in activity 1.
3. He then reads these in two ways, with and without zeros for the empty columns.
4. The other two write exactly what is said, both ways. They then decide whether each of these is the same number as the one on the board, or different.
5. Steps 2, 3, 4 are repeated, the next child putting down the cards and reading them.
6. Examples:

U	t-p	h-p
	6	
		2

(Top line)	Spoken:	'Zero point 6 zero.	Point 6.'
	Written:	0.60	.6
		same number	same number
(Second line)	Spoken:	'Zero point zero 2.	Point 2.'
	Written:	0.02	.2
		same number	different number

7. This continues until the board is filled.
8. Steps 2 to 7 may be repeated.
9. They may then try to put into words what determines the outcome – i.e. when zeros are necessary for place-value notation to represent correctly the fraction given by the headed columns, and when they are optional. This is not very easy, so I suggest it as suitable only for the brighter children.
10. A concise formulation is: 'Leading and trailing zeros are optional. Sandwiched zeros are necessary as place-holders.' ('Sandwiched' means between two digits, or a digit and the decimal point.) This is a convenient rule, but children should be able to give reasons as well. Nor should they be given this to memorise. If they can produce a correct formulation of their own all the better.

Notes

(i) In the context of measurement, .6 and .60 do have different meanings. The first means that we are measuring to the nearest decimetre; the second, to the nearest centimetre, the result being .60 as against .61 or .62.
(ii) Many people prefer to write and speak (e.g.) 0.4 rather than .4 on the grounds that this helps to prevent the decimal point from being overlooked. I see this as a purely personal preference. Mathematically, both stand for the same number, and this is what the present activity is about.

Activity 3 Claiming and naming

A game for 5 or 6 players. Its purpose is to give practice in recognising the same decimal fraction written in two notations, bar and place-value.

Materials   • Fractions, packs PV and B.*
* See specimens shown in figure 21. (A complete set of each is shown in Vol. 2a).

Pack PV is in place-value notation.

Pack B is in bar notation.

A limited range of digits is used to reduce the cues from these.

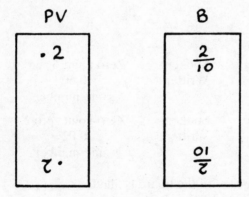

Figure 21 Fractions packs PV and B (specimens).

Rules of the game   1. Pack PV is shuffled and dealt to the players. Pack B is shuffled and put face down on the table.
2. Players look at their hands.
3. Each player in turn picks up the top card from the pack on the table and puts it face up.
4. Whichever player has in his hand the card for the same fraction says 'I claim that', and takes it.
5. He puts the 2 cards together in front of him, and names both aloud. E.g. '4 hundredth-parts. Point zero 4.' The others check.

6. The game continues as in steps 3, 4, 5. The first to put down all his cards is the winner, but the others play out their hands.
7. Next time the game is played, the packs are used the other way about. That is, B is dealt to the players and PV is put on the table.

Discussion of activities	We are now working at a purely abstract stage, without the support of physical materials or diagrams. So the earlier work, devoted to establishing the concepts firmly with the help of the above, is of great importance in preparation for this. If children have difficulty at this or later stages, then they need more time working at the more concrete levels.
	This topic is concerned with notations rather than concepts (which emphasises further the need for the concepts to have already been well established). Headed column notation continues to provide a way of showing what the numbers stand for which is clearer and more explicit than place-value notation, but which can be translated easily to and from place value notation. Bar notation provides a link with the earlier work on fractions of all denominators.
	And the expansion of place-value notation to represent fractions implies also the expansion of the concept of number to include fractional numbers, which is another meaning for the word 'fractions'. This implication will be made explicit in the next topic.

OBSERVE AND LISTEN   **REFLECT**   **DISCUSS**

Num 7.7   FRACTIONS AS NUMBERS. ADDITION OF DECIMAL FRACTIONS IN PLACE-VALUE NOTATION

Concept   Fractions as a new kind of number.

Ability   To add decimal fractions, using place-value notation.

Discussion of concept	Fractions are often treated as numbers right from the start. This almost guarantees confusion for the children, since they are seldom told that we are *expanding* our concept of number to include a *new kind of number*. Place-value notation makes this transition smoother, but does not remove the need to explain what is going on, so that children have a chance to adjust their thinking.
	Moreover, there are two distinct concepts involved, each with much interiority. The first is that of fractions – a new category of mathematical ideas. The second is that of other possible number systems. (Until now,

205

children have only met one number system.) So one of the concerns of this topic is to introduce children to thinking of fractions as numbers. This we do in activity 1. Here we show that fractions, in place-value notation, may be added in the same way as whole numbers; and that the results make sense. So in this respect they 'behave' like the numbers with which we are already familiar.

Whether we are justified in adding fractions in the same way as the familiar counting numbers is another question, and a more difficult one.

The problem is not unlike that of a naturalist who discovers a new species. First, he has to become aware of its existence. Then he has to decide how to categorise it, in the same way as one has to decide whether a bat is a bird or a rodent. And the most important characteristic for classifying may not be the most obvious, which in this case is flight.

To qualify for acceptance as a number system requires that these new (mental) objects 'behave' like the numbers we are already familiar with. The characteristics required by mathematicians are, again, not the most obvious. They have already been described in Num 5.10; namely, that addition is commutative and associative, likewise for multiplication, and multiplication is distributive over addition.

All this is, of course, far beyond our present needs, and I mention it for your information rather than for your detailed consideration. Also, so that you will understand why I do not treat it as a separate topic for the children. For the brighter children, however, I think it is worth touching lightly on this question, in the context of addition only. This is done in activity 2.

Activity 1   Target, 1

A game for up to 3 players (since they need to see the cards the same way up). Its purpose is to introduce the idea of adding decimal fractions, using place-value notation.

Materials
- Tenth-part cards.*
- Hundredth-part cards.*
- Pencil and paper for each player.

*See illustration in step 2 below.

Introduction   1. 'Now that we are writing decimal fractions like this they look rather like the ordinary numbers we're used to. Suppose we decide to treat them like numbers, how would we add them?' E.g.

$$\cdot 4\,7$$

$$\begin{array}{r} \cdot 4\,7 \\ + \;\cdot 3\,2 \\ \hline \end{array}$$

2. Follow this with other
    examples, including those
    which involve 'carrying';
    first only to the right of
    the decimal point, e.g.

$$\begin{array}{r} \cdot 2\ 6 \\ +\ \cdot 3\ 9 \\ \hline \end{array}$$

3. Then across the decimal point, e.g.

$$\begin{array}{r} \cdot 7\ 4 \\ +\ \cdot 5\ 2 \\ \hline \end{array}$$

Rules of the game   *Easier version*

1. The two packs of cards are shuffled and put separately, face down.
2. Each player in turn takes the top card from each pack. She may use
    one of these, or both combined, the smaller card on top; or she may
    decide to use neither if she wishes.

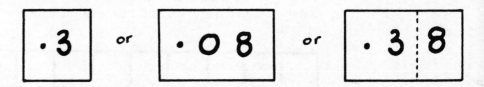

3. Each player writes this number, and adds it to the previous number or
    total to give a cumulative total.
4. The used cards are replaced at the bottom of the pile.
5. The player who reaches 1 unit exactly is the winner.
6. Overshooting is not allowed. If the numbers turned would take the
    total past 1 however they are used, then they are not used.

Harder version

This is played as above, except for step 5. In this version, all the cards
which have been turned over remain face up, and are spread out so that all
are visible. The player whose turn it is may use any one, or two, of these.
So at each turn, there are two more cards to choose from.

Activity 2   'How do we know that our method is still correct?'

A teacher-led discussion, for the more able pupils only. Its purpose is first
to put the above question, and then to answer it so far as addition is
concerned.

Materials
● 2 decimal unit squares (see figure overleaf).
● Base 10 material.
● Pencil and paper for each child.

*Suggested
sequence for the
discussion*

1. Begin by putting the question, along the following lines. 'When we
    started writing decimal fractions in place-value notation instead of bar
    notation, they looked much the same as ordinary whole numbers
    except for the decimal point. But of course they are not the same.'

2. Emphasise the difference by asking them to read each of the following in two ways.

3 7   'Thirty-seven.
          Three tens, seven units.'

(Now insert a decimal point.)

• 3 7   'Point three seven.
            Three tenth-parts, seven hundredth-parts.'

Note   Never tolerate 'point thirty seven', which guarantees self-confusion.

3. 'So when we've been adding decimal fractions like ordinary whole numbers, we have assumed that the way of adding which is correct for ordinary whole numbers is still correct for fractions. How do we know that our method *is* still correct, now that the figures mean something different?'

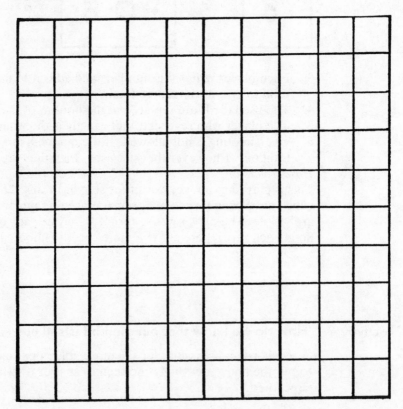

Decimal unit square.

4. Show a decimal unit square. 'If each of the little squares stands for a unit, what does the big square stand for?' (A hundred.) But if we change the meaning so that the *big* square stands for a unit, what does each little square now stand for?' (A hundredth-part.)

5. Put a rod from the base 10 materials in a column of the unit square. 'And what does this now stand for?' (A tenth-part.)
6. So how can we represent (e.g.) .34 on this unit square? (3 rods, 4 cubes.)
7. The continuation to addition is now straightforward. The 2 numbers to be added are first represented separately on the 2 unit squares. The rods and cubes are then put together on one square, and the result interpreted. Begin with examples which do not require carrying; then, carrying from hundredth-parts to tenth-parts; then, from tenth-parts to units (whole numbers). You can continue, according to your own judgement, by combining both kinds of carrying.
8. Again, use your own judgement about how many examples the children need to use in order to establish the deeper meaning of children's use of the symbols for adding fractions.

Discussion of activities	In this topic, we use our extrapolation of place-value notation to extrapolate the idea of number, from the familiar whole numbers to a new kind called fractional numbers. The word 'fraction' has now acquired a second meaning. This meaning is assumed in topic 1, where the familiar methods for adding are applied to numbers of this new kind. This is concept building (mode 3). Provided that this makes sense to them intuitively, I think that for many children it may be best to leave it at that. However, there will be some who can see the point of the question put in topic 2. For these, the same base 10 materials which helped to provide good conceptual foundations for the early number work in place-value notation are useful in helping them to strengthen their conceptual foundations for the new number work. This topic makes a start with mode 3 testing, that these new concepts are consistent with our mathematical knowledge.

OBSERVE AND LISTEN   REFLECT   DISCUSS

Num 7.8 FRACTIONS AS QUOTIENTS

Concepts
(i) A fraction as a result of sharing.
(ii) A fraction as a quotient.

Abilities
(i) To share equally a number of objects greater than 1 when the result includes fractions of objects.
(ii) To predict the results of (i) as it would be shown in place-value notation by a calculator.
(iii) To use calculators to save time and labour, but thoughtfully.

| **Discussion of concepts** | One of the ways in which many textbooks create unnecessary difficulties for children is to confuse fractions as quotients with the other aspects of fractions which have already been discussed. This is like confusing the comparison and take-away aspects of subtraction; but worse, because fractions are harder even when correctly explained. |

If we read $\frac{2}{5}$ as 'two-fifth' parts, short for 'two fifth-parts', the corresponding physical actions are: start with an object, make five equal parts, take two of these parts, result two fifth-parts.

Now however we are going to think of $\frac{2}{5}$ in a different way, as the result of division. The corresponding physical actions are: take two objects, share equally between five, each share is how much?

At a physical level these are quite different, just as physically 3 sets of 5 objects and 5 sets of 3 objects are quite different, and mathematically 3(5) and 5(3) are different; although the results are the same.

So we should be more surprised than we are that the division $2 \div 5$ gives $\frac{2}{5}$ as result. And to teach that $\frac{2}{5}$ is just another way of writing $2 \div 5$ is to beg the whole question. $2 \div 5$ is a mathematical operation, a division. $\frac{2}{5}$ is the result of this operation, a quotient. The distinction becomes even sharper if we write this quotient as 0.4. To put this another way: would we say that 45 was just another way of writing 5×9?

Finally, I suggest that we should be more surprised than most people seem to be that a quotient is a number at all. It is, in fact, a new kind of number: a fractional number. A full discussion of this expansion of our schema for numbers, and what makes it legitimate and useful, is beyond the scope of what we are doing here; nor is it necessary. But I hope that the sequence in which the ideas have been offered, and the activities, will at least help to build a clearer understanding of the various aspects of fractions than children have usually been able to acquire.

Activity 1   Fractions for sharing

An activity for a small group of children. Its purpose is to introduce them to the connection between fractions and the sharing aspect of division.

Materials
- Plasticine.
- Knives. ⎫
- Cutting boards. ⎬ Preferably one per two children.
- Cards 6 cm by 4 cm. ⎭
- SAR board: fractions for sharing (see figure 22).*
- Number cards 2 to 5.**
- OHP marker.
- Wiper.

* The full-sized one should be covered with film.

** To fit the spaces on the board.

START

Take this number of fruity bars.

ACTION

Share them equally between this number of children.

1. Complete the number sentences below recording what was done and the result.

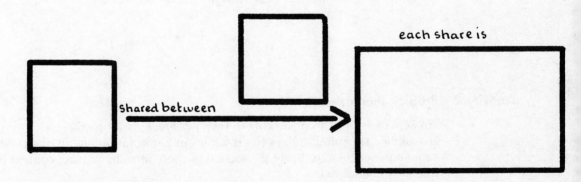

each share is

shared between

2. Write a shorter number sentence with the same meaning.

Figure 22 Fractions for sharing

What they do
1. About 5 Plasticine 'fruity bars' are made, using templates to give a uniform size.
2. To begin with, put a 2 in the left-hand space, a 3 in the right-hand space of the SAR board. Ask the children to do as it says. The first time they may need a little help.
3. One way to do this is to put 2 fruity bars, one on top of the other, and cut these into 3 equal parts. When taken apart, each share is 2 third-parts of a fruity bar. This may introduce practical difficulties, e.g. the layers of Plasticine may stick together if too warm; but conceptually it is probably the clearest.
4. So they should write a number sentence something like this:

'2 fruity bars, shared between 3, result $\frac{2}{3}$ of a fruity bar each.'

5. Let them experiment with other numbers in the START and ACTION spaces. To begin with, the smaller number should be in the START space.
6. When they fully understand the foregoing in physical terms, continue to step 7. This corresponds to the second instruction on the SAR board.
7. Remind them that sharing is one kind of division. So they can shorten their number sentences to (e.g.)

$$2 \div 5 = \frac{2}{5}$$

8. This is read as '2 divided by 5 equals (or "is equal to") 2 fifth-parts.' Emphasise that we are not saying that $\frac{2}{5}$ is another way of writing $2 \div 5$.
   The left-hand side says what is *done*. It stands for making equal shares. The right-hand side says *how much* each person gets. It is called a quotient. (The word means 'how much', or 'how many'.)

Activity 2   Predict, then press

An activity for children working in twos or threes. Its purpose is to consolidate the relation between fractions in bar notation and in place-value notation; and to bring the second of these into the present context of fractions as quotients.

Materials   For each group:
- Activity board (see figure 23).
- Start cards (numbered from 2 to 10).*
- Action cards numbered 2, 4, 5, 8, 10.*
- Calculator.
- Pencil and paper.
* To fit the squares on the activity board.

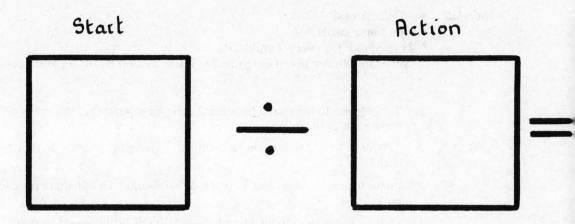

Start   Action

Copy the above.

Write the quotient in fraction bar notation.

Then write it as it would be shown by a calculator

Test your prediction.

Figure 23   Predict, then press.

What they do   1.   A card is put into each of the Start and Action squares. These may be randomly chosen (top of a shuffled pile); or children may be allowed to choose if they wish to experiment systematically.

2.   Each child then writes the quotient first in bar notation, and then in decimal notation. E.g.,

$$7 \div 5 = 1 \text{ and } \frac{2}{5}$$

$$= 1.4$$

(Thinking: 7 shared between 5 gives 1 each, and 2 over. These 2 shared between 5 give $\frac{2}{5}$ each, as in activity 1).

3.   Their prediction is then tested by using the calculator to give the quotient.

4.   The 8 card should be taken out of the Action pack until the children are proficient with the easier divisors.

Activity 3   'Are calculators clever?'

A teacher led discussion for up to 6 children. Its purpose is to encourage them to be critical about the results obtained by calculator.

Materials • Calculators.*
• Example cards.**
* At least one for every 2 children.
** Six examples are given in figure 24. These should be on separate cards.

1. 7 people are to be shared between 2 cars, for a journey. How many will there be in each car?

2. 3 children have 2 parents between them. How many parents do they have each?

3. I have 9 carrots, to give to 4 horses. What would be a fair share for each horse?

4. I have 7 pot plants, to give to 4 friends for their birthdays. How many should I give to each?

5. A householder gives 3 children who do some gardening £1.80 to be shared equally between them. How much should they have each?

6. A packet contains 8 fish fingers. How should these be shared equally between a family of 3?

Figure 24 Are calculators clever?

What they do 1. Begin with this example.
'7 people are to be shared between 2 cars, for a journey. How many will there be in each car?'

2. Ask them to use their calculators to work out the answer, just to see what happens.
$7 \div 2 = 3.5$
What do they think about this?

3. Ask if they can think of a number story for which this number sentence would make sense. Here is one. '7 biscuits are to be shared between 2 climbers. How many should they have each?' It makes even better sense if instead of 3 whole biscuits and 5 tenth-parts each, they get 3 and 1 half! Did any one remember that 5 tenth-parts is equivalent to 1 half?

4. Repeat steps 1 and 2 with other number stories. Of the 6 given here, 3 make sense and 3 do not. For those that do not step 3 should be repeated. For those that do, they should invent a number story which does not make sense. (Number 6 may need discussion, and possibly even the introduction of plasticine fish fingers!)

Activity 4 **Number targets by calculator**

A game for children to play in twos or threes, sharing a calculator. Its purpose is to increase children's knowledge of the relationships between quotients and decimal fractions.

Materials For each group of 2 or 3:
• A calculator,
• Set of calculator target cards.*

- Pencil and paper for each child.

* See examples in steps 2 below. A full set is provided in Vol. 2a.

Rules of the game   *Stage (a)   Fractions only*

1. The fraction cards are shuffled, and put face down. (The unit cards are not used in stage 1.)

2. In turns, each player turns over the top card from the pile. E.g.,

3. He is then allowed 3 'shots' with the calculator. Each shot consists of 4 entries: (number) (÷) (number) (=). 1 point is scored for each shot which hits the target. In this case, some successful shots would be

$$4 \div 10 \qquad 8 \div 20 \qquad 2 \div 5$$

4. 3 hits could also be scored by

$$4 \div 10 \qquad 40 \div 100 \qquad 400 \div 1000$$

For beginners there is nothing against this – they learn something from it. But more experienced players may agree to allow only one shot with a power of 10 as divisor.

5. It is a good idea for one player to make his shots verbally, and another to enter these on the calculator and show the result.

6. After an agreed number of turns, the winner is the player who has scored most hits.

Stage (b)   Mixed numbers

1. Both packs of cards are now used. These are shuffled and put face down in two piles.

2. In turns, each player turns over the top card from each pile, and puts these side by side to give a mixed number. There are 72 possible combinations; e.g.,

When the units pile is finished, it is shuffled and used again.

3, 4, 5   These are the same as steps 3, 4, 5 in Stage 1.

Discussion of activities

In activity 1, we go back to mode 1 to relate the new meaning of fractions, namely quotients, to a typical physical situation. This helps to show that although the two aspects of division give the same result, this is not something to be taken as obvious from the beginning. This new meaning is additional to the other earlier meanings, not a replacement.

Calculators are the best way for doing all but the simplest divisions. It is however important that they be used with understanding, of two kinds. One kind is relating the answers obtained by calculator to their existing number schema; the other kind is relating these answers critically to situations such as those described in the number stories. These are the purpose of activities 2 and 3 respectively.

Activity 4 is a game for exercising and consolidating their understanding.

OBSERVE AND LISTEN   **REFLECT**   **DISCUSS**

[Space 1] **SHAPE**
Shapes in the environment and in mathematics

Space 1.4   PARALLEL LINES, PERPENDICULAR LINES

Concepts (i)   'Is parallel to'
         (ii) 'Is perpendicular to'
             as relationships between two lines.

Abilities (i)   To recognise examples of parallel or perpendicular lines.
         (ii) To construct examples of parallel or perpendicular lines.

Discussion of concepts

Just as we have relationships between two numbers (e.g. 'is greater than', 'is equal to'), so also we have relationships between two lines such as those in the present topic. If line a is parallel to line b, then line b is parallel to line a, so we may also say that these lines are parallel (meaning, parallel to each other). This is true also of the relationship 'is perpendicular to'. This reversibility does not hold for all relationships. E.g. it is true for 'is equal to', but not for 'is greater than'. Here, however, our main concern is with the particular relationships named in this topic, not with the ways in which relationships themselves may be classified.

Activity 1   **'My rods are parallel / perpendicular.'**

An activity for up to 6 children. Its purpose is to help children learn these two relationships.

Materials • A pack of 20* cards. On 10 of these is written 'parallel' with an example, and on the other 10 is written 'perpendicular' with an example.
       • For each child, 2 rods of different lengths. A square section is useful to prevent rolling.
    * Any even number of cards will do, provided that there are enough to give a good variety of examples. In the examples, it is important that the pairs of lines should be of different lengths, and oblique relative to the edges of the paper. (See illustrations in the Discussion of activities.) Parallel and perpendicular are relationships between lines, independently of how these lines are positioned on the paper.

What they do Stage (a), with cards
1. The cards are shuffled, and put face down.
2. Each child in turn takes a card and puts it in front of him face up.
3. The children then put their rods on top of the lines in the illustration.

4. In turn, they show their cards to the others and say, 'My rods are parallel', or 'My rods are perpendicular', as the case may be.
5. Each child then takes another card, which he puts face up on top of the card he has already. Steps 3 and 4 are then repeated.

Stage (b), without cards

1. Each child in turn puts his rods either parallel or perpendicular, and says 'My rods are parallel/perpendicular' (as the case may be).
2   The others say 'Agree' or 'Disagree'.
3. A child may deliberately give a false description if he chooses. The others should then all disagree.

Activity 2   'All put your rods parallel / perpendicular to the big rod'

An activity for up to 6 children. Its purpose is to consolidate the concepts parallel and perpendicular.

Materials
- Ruler or big rod
- Small rod for each child. (It is good if the small rods are of assorted length.)

What they do
1. The teacher puts down the big rod and says 'All put your rods parallel to the big rod.'
2. The children do so.
3. Steps 1 and 2 are repeated several times. Encourage variety in the placing of the children's rods.
4. Then, after step 2, the teacher removes the big rod and asks the children what they notice about their own rods. It should be brought out in discussion that the children's rods are all parallel *to each other*.
5. Steps 1, 2, 3, 4 are repeated with the instruction '. . . perpendicular to the big rod.'

Activity 3   Colouring pictures

An activity for 2 to 6 children.

Materials
- A picture for each child, made up of lines which are all in parallel or perpendicular pairs. The pictures should be in feint lines, e.g. from a spirit duplicator. (See illustration below.)
- A pack of parallel / perpendicular cards, as used in activities 1, 2, 3.

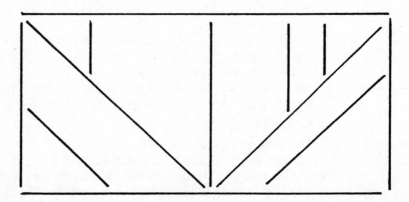

What they do
1. The pack is shuffled and put face down.
2. The first child turns over the top card.
3. He is then allowed to colour two lines in his picture, which must be either parallel or perpendicular according to the card.
4. The other children in turn do steps 2 and 3.
5. Putting pencils on top of the lines helps to show up which lines are parallel or perpendicular.
6. Continue until all the pictures have been coloured.

Discussion of activities

Activity 1 is for building the concepts parallel, perpendicular from a variety of examples. Again I emphasise the importance of choosing examples which do not link these concepts either with length of line, or position on paper. If this mistake is not avoided, children will be able to recognise examples like these:

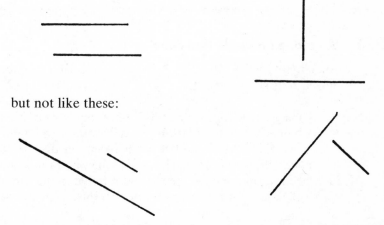

but not like these:

Activity 1 is also for linking the concepts with the appropriate vocabulary. 'Perpendicular' is quite a hard word, so you may decide to practise children in saying it. Initially they are not expected to read these words from the cards. They learn them orally, linked with the visual examples of parallel and perpendicular lines. In this way they will gradually learn to recognise the written words. Stage (b) of this activity uses the newly formed concepts to generate examples, with peer-group checking. Activity 3 is similar, but develops a situation in which more than two rods are involved. Of these, a given pair may be either parallel or perpendicular.

Activity 4 is the payoff. We now have a picture with many lines. Correct recognition of relationships between these lines allows children to colour their lines. You will recognise the development of the earlier activity Space 1.3/1 to make use of these more advanced mathematical ideas. Why more advanced? Because being straight or curved is a property of a single line; being parallel or perpendicular is a property of a pair of lines – a relational concept.

OBSERVE AND LISTEN   **REFLECT**   **DISCUSS**

Space 1.5   COMPARISON OF ANGLES

Concept   The shape and size aspects of angle.

Ability   To decide which of two angles is the larger/smaller.

Discussion of concept

When two straight lines meet, they form a shape which we call an angle. The everyday and mathematical meanings are in this case much the same. An angle can also represent a difference between two directions. Here we concentrate on angles as shapes, which may be considered either by themselves, as in this topic, or as contributing to descriptions of other shapes, as in topic 10.

Objects may be ordered in various ways; e.g. persons by age, names alphabetically, lines by their lengths, sets by their number. Angles may be ordered by their size, which is independent of the length of their arms.

Activity 1   **'All make an angle like mine'**

An activity for 2 to 6 children. Its purpose is to introduce the concept of an angle, in its shape aspect.

Materials   • An angle disc for every child, preferably each of a different colour.
• A hinged angle made from two milk straws and a pipe cleaner.
Note   An angle disc is made from two circular discs of thin cardboard, one white and one coloured. Each is cut along one radius, and the two are then interlaced so that one can be rotated relative to the other. In this way a coloured angle is formed which can be adjusted to any desired size.

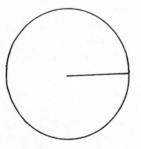 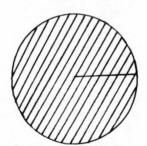 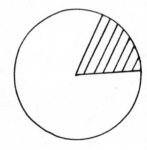

What they do   Stage (a) using angle discs only
1. On receiving their angle discs, children are allowed a little time to explore and manipulate.
2. Explain that the coloured shape shows an angle.
3. Child A sets her disc to any angle she likes, puts it in the middle of the table, and says 'All make an angle like mine.'
4. The other children make angles of the same size, and put them near that of child A.
5. Child A then compares them with her own, and pointing to each in turn says 'Agree' or 'Disagree'. (The match need only be approximate, and visual comparison is all that is required at this stage.)

6. Another child becomes child A, and steps 3 to 5 are repeated.
Stage (b) using the hinged angle
The steps are the same as in activity 1, except that child A uses the hinged angle. This allows physical comparison if there is disagreement.

Activity 2 'Which angle is bigger?'

An activity for 2 to 6 children. Its purpose is to introduce comparison by size of angles.

Materials
- Two angle discs, of different colours. For stage (a) these should be of the same size, for stage (b) of different sizes.
- Acetate sheet.
- OHP pen.
- Damp rag.

What they do   Stage (a) uses discs of the same size.
Stage (b) uses discs of different sizes.
Otherwise, the stages are alike.
1. Child A and child B each makes an angle. These are put in the middle of the table.
2. Child C then says (e.g.) 'The red angle is bigger than the green angle.' (Or if she likes, 'The green angle is smaller than the red angle.')
3. In the event that the angles look alike, C would say, 'These angles are about the same size'.
4. The other children say in turn 'Agree', or 'Disagree'.
5. If there is disagreement, a check may be made by putting the acetate sheet on top of one angle and tracing this angle, using the overhead projector pen.
6. Other children take over the roles of A, B, C, and steps 1 to 4 are repeated.

Activity 3 Largest angle takes all

A game for 3 to 5 children, based on activity 2. Its purpose is to consolidate the concept of comparison by size of angle.

Materials
- A pack of cards on which are drawn angles, 6 of each of the following sizes: 30, 60, 90, 120, 150 degrees. The arms of the angles should vary considerably in length among angles of the same size: see 'Discussion of activities'.
- Paper and pencil for scoring.
- Acetate, OHP pen, damp rag.*
* As for activity 2.

Rules of play
1. The pack is shuffled. Five cards are then dealt to each player.
2. Players put their cards in a pile face down.
3. Starting with the player to the left of the dealer, each player puts down one card in front of her, face up.
4. The player who puts down the largest angle takes all the others. She

puts this set of cards in a pile in front of her. Comparison may be visual, or by the acetate method as in activity 2.

5. If two angles are equal in size, each player takes one angle for her pile.
6. The winner of a round is the first to put down for the next round. The others follow in turn, clockwise.
7. When all the cards have been played, the players scores are recorded according to the number of cards they have taken.
8. Another game may then be played, and the scores added to those of the previous game.
9. This game may also be played as 'Smallest angle takes all'.

Activity 4   Angles in the environment

Materials   • An angle disc for each child, as in activity 1.

What they do   1. Each child looks around the room and finds an angle. (Suitable sources are angles made by hanging strings, angles between books on shelves, corners of tables, hands of a clock. Many environmental angles are right angles. This does not matter: it prepares the way for the next topic.)
2. Each child adjusts her angle to the same size as whatever she has chosen.
3. In turn, each child holds up her angle and says (e.g.) 'I've made my angle the same size as the angle of that string' (pointing).
4. The others in turn say whether they agree.

Discussion of activities   Activity 1 is for forming the concept of an angle, by making and copying a variety of angles of different sizes and colours. A different example of the same concept is introduced in stage 2, in the form of a hinged angle made from milk straws and a pipe cleaner.

Once the concept of an angle has been established, children are in a position to compare angles of different sizes. Note that the size of an angle has nothing to do with the length of its arms. Of the two angles below, the left is the larger. This is the point of the second stage of activity 2, and of activity 3.

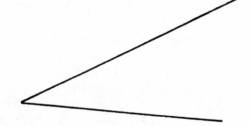

Activity 4 relates the concept of angle to environmental examples. Here there is more irrelevant detail to be ignored, so it comes last, after the concept has been established by simpler examples.

OBSERVE AND LISTEN   **REFLECT**   **DISCUSS**

Space 1.6   CIRCLES

Concepts   (i)   Circles as shapes.
　　　　　 (ii)   Diameter, radius, circumference of a circle.

Abilities   (i)   To recognise circles.
　　　　　 (ii)   To name the above parts of a circle.

Discussion of concepts	In this topic we focus on the shape aspect of circles. The various interesting relations between circles and other shapes, such as triangles, polygons, will be dealt with in a later topic, Space 1.12/2. So this is a simple, introductory treatment only, except for activity 4.

Activity 1   Circles in the environment

A teacher-led discussion for up to 6 children. Its purpose is to teach the concept of a circle as the shape common to a variety of objects in the environment.

Materials   ● A cut-out circle for each child. The circles should be of varying colours and size, the smallest being at least 10 cm in diameter.

Suggested sequence for the discussion

1. Give each child a circle.
2. Ask if they know the name of this shape. Probably they will: if not, tell them.
3. Ask them to try and find objects in the environment which have this shape. Some (e.g. a traditional-style clock) will be seen flat-on, others, though in fact circular (e.g. top of a waste bin) will be seen foreshortened. These may need to be moved before it is clear to some children that the shape is like that of their cut-out model circle.

Activity 2   Parts of a circle

A teacher-led discussion for up to 6 children. This is a continuation of activity 1. Its purpose is to add further detail to the concept of a circle.

Materials   ● The same as for activity 1, with an additional circle for yourself.

Suggested sequence for the discussion

1. Fold your circle in half, and open it out again.

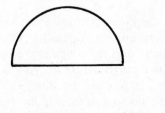 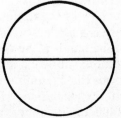

2. Tell the children to do likewise.
3. Tell them the name for the new line (diameter). Label your diameter, and let them copy yours. You may like to have a line ruled along the diameter to make it show up more.
4. Fold along another diameter, preferably not perpendicular to the first, and open out again. Put a dot where the creases cross.

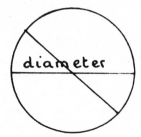

5. Ask the children to suggest names for this point. 'Middle' is a good name. The mathematical term is 'centre'.
6. Give them the names for the other parts, and let them label these as before. Only the radius (i.e. half diameter) should be pencilled in.

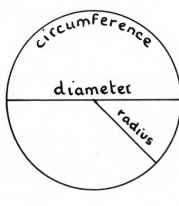

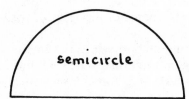

Activity 3 Circles and their parts in the environment

A teacher-led discussion for up to 6 children. This is a continuation of activity 2. Its purpose is to consolidate the newly developed aspects of the concept of a circle.

Materials ● The labelled circles from activity 2.

Suggested sequence for the discussion
1. Ask the children to find circular objects in the environment where they can also find some of the other parts which they now have labelled in their own circles.
2. A clock of the traditional kind provides a good example. The whole face is a circle; the rim round the edge is its circumference; the spindle of the hands is the centre; and the long hand is most of a radius.
3. A more subtle example is provided by the rim of a waste bin. This forms the circumference of a circle, but the rest of the circle (its interior) is missing. The bottom of the bin has both.
4. Radii and diameters are harder to find. They may be added to available

objects (e.g. the waste bin again) by stretching strings across. One will provide a diameter. A second string crossing the first will give four radii.

Activity 4   Patterns with circles

An exploratory activity for up to 6 children. Its purposes are to develop skill in drawing, and to provide a ground from which further properties of a circle may be found.

Materials   For each child:
- safety compasses
- paper
- pencil.

What they do   1. Introduce the children to the use of the safety compasses, and allow them time to practise drawing circles of various sizes. In some of these they should draw and label the centre, a radius, and a diameter, to revise and consolidate activity 2.
2. Each then experiments with making patterns from circles. Some interesting ones can be produced: a few examples are shown in figure 25 overleaf. It may be good for them near the beginning to copy these, since there are various things to be found out this way. Straight lines may be added if desired.
3. One at a time, the diagrams are looked at together and discussed. The purpose is to find properties of the circle which are brought into view by the design. For example, in design A each circle is half the diameter of the big circle. In B, the large circle is divided into two equal parts. (Why?). This pattern may be extended, as in C. Returning after topic 12, there are more properties to be found. E.g. in D, the lines joining the centres form an equilateral triangle, and pass through the points where the circles touch. With one more equal touching circle, we get a rhombus. (Why?)

Discussion of activities

We begin with cut-out circles, rather than objects in the environment, in order to provide physical examples with the minimum of other qualities which have to be ignored. The technical term is 'low-noise examples'. When the concept of a circle has been formed, it is consolidated by looking for and recognising examples where there are more distractors – where more abstracting has to be done. This process is repeated in activities 2 and 3 for those parts of a circle which we want the children to learn at this stage. These 3 activities should follow each other fairly closely.

Activity 4 is more advanced, and requires the physical skills involved in drawing; so it is good for developing these. Children enjoy making patterns with circles, and there are many important properties which can be found by studying these patterns. At this stage our task is to help children find them and put them into words: geometric proof is something for much later.

OBSERVE AND LISTEN   **REFLECT**   **DISCUSS**

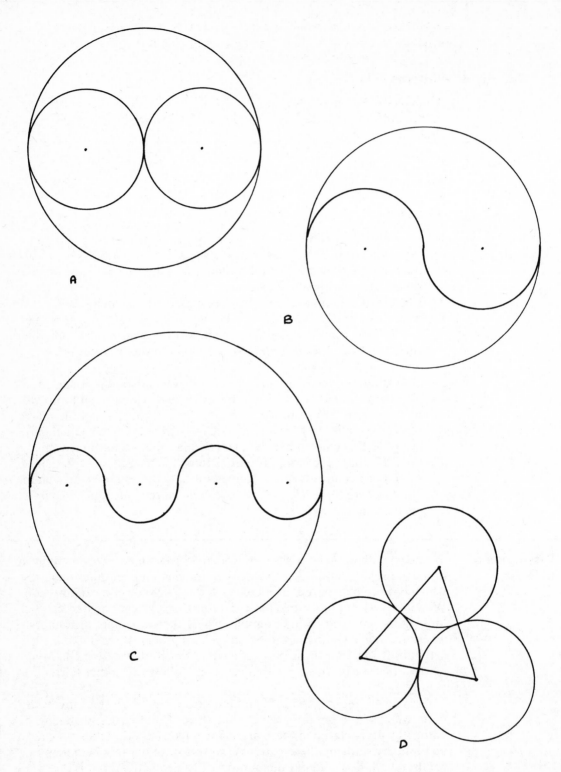

Figure 25 Patterns with circles.

Space 1.7   CLASSIFICATION OF ANGLES

Concepts   (i)   Acute angle, obtuse angle, right angle.
(ii)   (Later) Straight angle, reflex angle.

Abilities   (i)   To classify angles into these categories.
(ii)   To produce examples of these categories.

Discussion of concepts

These are simple concepts, once children can compare angles by size. An acute (sharp) angle is one which is less than a right angle, an obtuse (blunt) angle is one which is greater than a right angle. Among obtuse angles, we do not usually include angles greater than a straight angle, which is two right angles put together. These are called reflex angles.

Activity 1   Right angles, acute angles, obtuse angles

A sorting activity for 1 to 3 children. Its purpose is to help children form the concepts of acute angle, obtuse angle, right angle.

Materials
- A piece of paper for each child. (The size is not critical.)
- Coloured crayon or felt tip pen.
- An assortment of cut-out angles, in the form of sectors of a circle. (See illustration below.) There should be roughly equal numbers of acute, obtuse, and right angles.
- The circles should be of assorted sizes; assorted colours too if you like.
- 3 set loops.
- 3 small cards labelled 'Acute angles', 'Obtuse angles', 'Right angles' respectively.

What they do   1.   Each child makes herself a right angle by folding her paper twice.

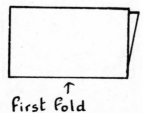

first fold

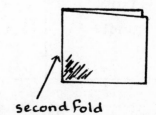

second fold

2. The right angle (at the double fold) is then marked with coloured crayon or felt tip.
3. The cut out angles are mixed together in the middle of the table.
4. The 3 set loops are put out, with a card labelling each: respectively acute angles, obtuse angles, right angles.
5. The children work together to sort these into 3 sets: acute, obtuse, right angle. They do this by comparing each with their right angles.
6. A good way is for each child in turn to put an angle into a set loop, saying as she does so (e.g.) 'Obtuse angle'.

Activity 2   Angle dominoes

A game for 2 to 4 players. Its purpose is to consolidate the concepts formed in activity 1.

Materials • A set of 24 angle dominoes. These are of two kinds, see figure 26. A full set is provided in Vol 2a. Note that the right angles are not marked as such, so that the players have to decide for themselves, either by looking or by comparing with their own right angles.

Rules of play 1. The rules are the same as for ordinary dominoes. There are however various ways of playing. A way we find goes well is described in steps 2 to 5.
2. 5 dominoes are dealt to each player. The rest are put face down in the middle.
3. A player who cannot go takes a domino from the middle. This counts as her turn.
4. When all are taken from the middle, a player who cannot go knocks once. If she cannot go a second time she knocks twice; if a third time, she knocks thrice and is out of the game.
5. The winner is the first to use all her dominoes; or the one left with fewest, if none can go.
6. In the present game, the match must be between an angle and a word,

Figure 26   Angle dominoes.

or between two angles of the same kind (acute, obtuse, right). Two
words may not be matched, since this does not depend on
understanding their meaning.

Activity 3   'Mine is the different kind'

A game for exactly 3 players.

Materials
- 30 cards, on 10 of which are drawn 10 acute angles, on 10 right angles,
  and on 10 obtuse angles. The arms of the angles should vary
  considerably in length.
- They also keep their right angles from activity 1, to check.

Rules of play
1. The cards are shuffled, and all are then dealt to the players.
2. The players hold their packs face down.
3. Starting with the player to the left of the dealer, each in turn puts down
   his top card face down in front of her.
4. If all are alike or all are different, the players continue in turn to put
   down another card on top of their earlier one(s), until there are two
   alike and one different. Here 'alike' refers to the 3 categories acute,
   obtuse, right angle.
5. The player whose pile shows the odd one out says 'Mine is the different
   kind', or 'mine is the odd one out', and explains why. E.g. 'Yours are
   acute, and mine is obtuse'. She then takes all 3 piles, which she puts
   face down at the bottom of her own pile.
6. This player then puts down a card, and steps 3, 4, 5 are repeated.
7. If a player has no more cards in his hand to put down, her pile stays as
   it is until step 5 applies.
8. Play continues until one player has lost all her cards. The winner is
   then the one with most cards.
9. If this takes too long, the winner is the player who finishes with most
   cards.

Activity 4   'Can't cross, will fit, must cross'

An activity for up to 4 children.

Materials
- An assortment of cut-out angles.*
- 12 instruction cards. On 4 of these is written 'Each of you take an acute
  angle'; on 4, 'Each of you take a right angle'; and on four, 'Each of you
  take an obtuse angle'.
- One angle card as illustrated in step 2.
* The same as for activity 1.

What they do   *Stage (a)*
1. The cut-out angles are mixed together and spread out in the middle of
   the table.
2. The angle card is put on the table with the side 1 showing.

> Put two angles together
> with their points on the
> dot, on the same side
> of the line if you can.
>
> ──────────●──────────
>
> side 1

3. The instruction cards are shuffled and put face down.
4. The top instruction card is turned over, and the children do as it says.
5. They then follow the instruction on side 1 of the angle card.
6. Steps 4 and 5 are repeated until all the instruction cards are used.

Stage (b)

1. Steps 1 to 6 are the same as in stage 1, except that side 2 of the angle card is used. Examples of correct predictions are shown below:

> Predict whether two
> angles of the kind you
> have can't cross, will
> fit, or must cross.   Then
> test on this.
>
> ──────────●──────────
>
> side 2

'Can't cross'
(2 acute angles)

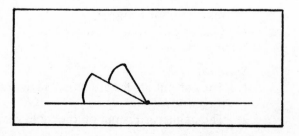

'Will fit'
(2 right angles)

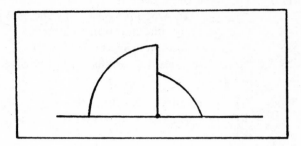

'Must cross'
(2 obtuse angles)

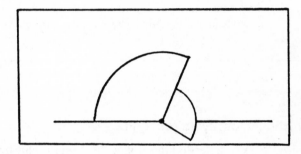

7. The intention is that children discover the basis for prediction, as shown above in the three parentheses.
8. When they have done so, they may be invited to put this into words.
9. They may also be asked if they can think out why this is so. This, however, is difficult for children of this age.

Discussion of activities	Activity 1 is for concept building from physical examples (mode 1). Activity 2 is for consolidating the link between words and concepts, using a variety of examples. Testing in this case is by agreement and if necessary discussion (mode 2). Activity 3 consolidates these concepts and their associated words in another game, involving finding two of a kind and one of a different kind. Activity 4 investigates some further consequences of the properties, and sets children on the path of making mathematical generalisations.

OBSERVE AND LISTEN   **REFLECT**   **DISCUSS**

Space 1.8   CLASSIFICATION OF POLYGONS

Concepts   (i)   That of a polygon.
(ii)   Ways in which polygons may be classified:
    (a)   regular and non-regular
    (b)   number of sides.
Note   Varieties of triangles and quadrilaterals are dealt with in later topics.

Abilities   (i)   To classify polygons in the ways described above.
(ii)   To name them, and state their characteristic properties.

Discussion of concepts

In this topic we make a start with thinking about various kinds of shapes which can be made from straight lines. These are called polygons. We look for ways of classifying them, and start by using regular / irregular, and number of sides. In subsequent topics, further classifications within the set of triangles and the set of quadrilaterals will be introduced.

Activity 1   Classifying polygons

A teacher-led discussion for up to 6 children. Its purpose is to help children to differentiate the various kinds of polygon.

Materials   • Polygons, pack 1. This consists of 30 square cards on which are 15 regular polygons and 15 non-regular polygons. The regular polygons consist of 3 equilateral triangles, 3 squares, 3 pentagons (5 sides), 3 hexagons (6 sides), 3 octagons. The 15 non-regular polygons are as above, except that no two sides or angles are of equal size. (So the triangle is scalene, and the squares are replaced by non-regular quadrilaterals.) The sizes of the polygons are varied: but there is not a clear large / small distinction. A complete set is provided in Vol. 2a.

Suggested sequence for discussion
1. Lay out an assortment of the polygon cards, about half the pack.
2. Ask for suggestions how these might be sorted. The two ways we have in mind are (a) number of sides (b) regular and irregular. These we hope are the most noticeable.
3. If other ways of sorting are proposed', give them a fair hearing and let children try to sort their way. Size is quite a reasonable one, but we have tried not to embody this in the materials.
4. Eventually the children will arrive at (a) and (b). Usually (a) is noticed first.
5. Put down the rest of the pack, and let each child collect the set of all shapes which have a particular number of sides.
6. When they have done this, let each describe in his own words the set he has collected. E.g. 'I have collected the set of shapes with 5 sides.'
7. Then tell them the mathematical names for these, and let them all describe their sets again.

8. Ask them to look at their sets, and see if they can sort them further. Usually they will now see the regular / irregular distinction.
9. When they have sorted into these sub-sets and described in their own terms, introduce them to the generally used words. E.g. 'The set of regular hexagons, and the set of non-regular hexagons.'
10. Mix all the pieces, and repeat steps 5 to 9 with children collecting different sets.

Activity 2 Polygon dominoes

A game for 2 to 4 players. Its purpose is to consolidate the concepts formed in activity 1, and link them with their names.

Materials • A set of dominoes as provided in Vol. 2a.

What they do This game is played according to the usual rules of the game of dominoes, except that a match of word with word is not allowed. (See Space 1.7/2, 'Angle dominoes', for these rules.) The following are some further suggestions which may be incorporated if and as desired.
1. It is good for each player to have a mixture of word dominoes and figure dominoes. To achieve this, first sort the cards into words and pictures. Then deal these two packs in succession.
3. If they want to score, the first to go 'out' scores 5, the next 4, etc. Players who do not go 'out' score zero.
3. When learning, it is good to help each other. Later, 'No help' may be agreed. Players can then often help themselves by looking at existing matches of words with polygons.

Activity 3 Match and mix: polygons

A game for 2 to 5 players. Its purpose is further to consolidate the concepts formed in activity 1.

Materials • Polygons, pack 2. This is a double pack of the regular polygons as in activity 1, so there will be 30 cards, now including 6 of each kind of regular polygon. It might be helpful to have this pack of a different colour from pack 1.
• A card as illustrated below.

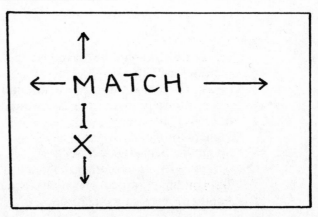

Rules of the game

1. The cards are spread out face downwards in the middle of the table.
2. The Match and Mix card is put wherever convenient.
3. Each player takes 5 cards (if 2 players only, they take 7 cards each). Alternatively the cards may be dealt in the usual way.
4. They collect their cards in a pile face downwards.
5. Players in turn look at the top card in their piles, and put cards down next to cards already there (after the first) according to the following three rules.
   (i) Cards must match or be different, according as they are put next to each other in the 'match' or 'mix' directions.
   (ii) Not more than 3 cards may be put together in either direction.
   (iii) There may not be two 3's next to each other.
   ('Match' or 'mix' refers to the kind of polygon).
   Examples (using A, B, C . . . for different kinds of polygon)
   A typical arrangement:

None of these is allowed:

```
A        B B B B        C C C        A A        A
A                       D D D        B B        B
A                                    C C        A
A
```

A card which cannot be played is replaced at the bottom of the pile.
6. Scoring is as follows.
   1 point for completing a row or column of three.
   2 points for putting down a card which simultaneously matches one way and mixes the other way.
   2 points for being the first 'out'.
   1 point for being the second 'out'.
   (So it is possible to score up to 6 points in a single turn.)
7. Play continues until all players have put down all their cards.
8. Another round is then played.

Discussion of activities	Sorting and classifying are among the most fundamental ways in which intelligence functions, and activities based on these have been in use from the very beginning. Activity 1 is a sorting activity, leading to two of the most noticeable ways in which polygons can be classified. Once these categories have been learnt, they are consolidated by the games in activities 2 and 3.
	The cards used for sorting and classifying polygons have 2 advantages over the printed page. First, they show the figures in a variety of positions, since (being square) they may be any way up. This helps to establish that a figure is the same whatever its position, and accustoms children to recognising figures in all positions. Second, by allowing physical sorting, it leads children to form the categories for themselves rather than the usual method of presenting them with the finished article.
	Once again we use a combination of modes 1 (physical experience) and 2 (discussion, communication of vocabulary by teacher) for schema building, followed by using the newly formed concepts in the co-operative situation provided by a game.

OBSERVE AND LISTEN   **REFLECT**   **DISCUSS**

Space 1.9   SYMMETRIC PROPERTIES

Concept   Symmetry about a line.

Ability   To recognise figures which have line symmetry, and locate the axis (or axes) of symmetry.

Discussion of concept	Congruence is a relation between 2 figures. Symmetry is a relationship of a figure with itself. Here we consider only line symmetry. Being a visual property, it is easier to recognise from examples than words. In the figures below, the broken line is the axis of symmetry. It is a line which divides the figure into 2 halves such that one half is congruent with the other, but would need turning over before the 2 halves could be made to coincide.
	If a figure has one or more axes of symmetry, we describe it as symmetrical about these axes. The X below has 2 axes of symmetry; the pentagon has 5. In each case only one has been shown.

235

These figures are symmetrical:

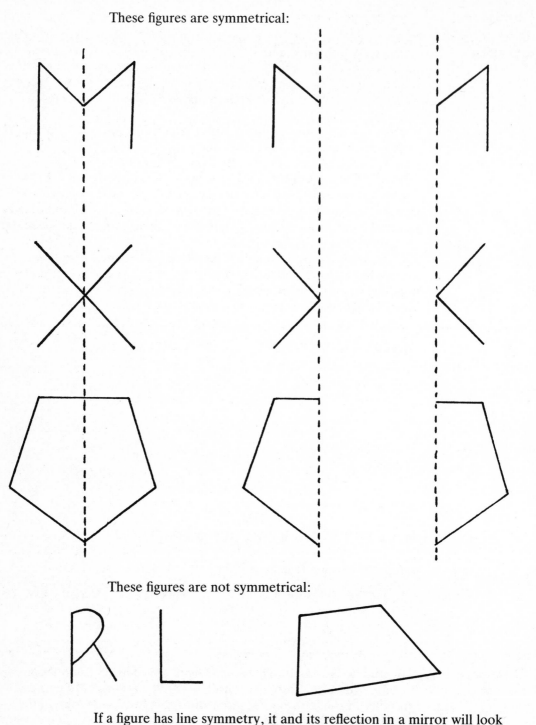

These figures are not symmetrical:

If a figure has line symmetry, it and its reflection in a mirror will look alike. Also if you fold the paper along an axis of symmetry and hold this axis against a mirror, you can see the complete figure again. For this reason an axis of symmetry is sometimes called a mirror line. Note that there is another kind of symmetry, called rotational symmetry, which is not introduced here.

Activity 1   Testing for line symmetry

An activity for children working in pairs. Its purpose is to make explicit their intuitive perception of line symmetry.

Materials
- A small pack of symmetry cards. The pack used for the next activity may be shared among several pairs.
- A piece of transparent acetate sheet, as used for overhead projectors. One full-size sheet may conveniently be cut into 4 for this purpose.
- Each sheet has on it a straight line in waterproof OHP marker.
- For each pair, a water-washable OHP marker and a damp rag.

What they do
1. The pack is put face down on the table.
2. The top card is turned over and examined. If the children agree that it is not symmetrical, they start a pile of non-symmetrical figures and go on to the next card.
3. If they both think that it is symmetrical, they test as follows.
4. One of them puts the acetate on top of the card with the line where she thinks the axis of symmetry is.
5. She then traces half the figure on to the acetate.
6. The other tests for symmetry by turning the acetate over and checking for congruence between the two halves. (N.B., it must be turned over not rotated.)
7. If symmetry is confirmed, the card is put with a pile of symmetrical figures.
8. Steps 2 to 7 are repeated until all the cards are sorted.

Activity 2   Collecting symmetries

A game for 5 or 6 players. Its purpose is to consolidate the concept of symmetry, and to practise children in finding all the axes of symmetry when a figure has more than one.

Materials
- A pack of symmetry cards, as provided in Vol. 2a. This consists of 45 cards, of which 30 have figures which are symmetrical and 15 not. These figures should include letters of the alphabet, regular and irregular polygons having 3, 4, 5, 6, 8 sides, and patterns having 0 to 6 lines of symmetry.

Rules of the game
1. The object is to collect as many axes of symmetry as possible.
2. The pack is shuffled and put face down. The top 3 cards are then turned and laid face up.
3. The first player picks up whichever card she likes, from those which are face up.
4. She then turns over the top card from the face-down pile, and puts it face up to fill the gap ready for the next player.
5. Steps 3 and 4 are repeated until each player has 5 cards.
6. If at any time all 3 face-up cards are non-symmetrical, the player whose turn it is says 'No symmetry.' She is then entitled to put aside all 3, and lay out 3 new cards for herself to choose from.
7. The players in turn claim their scores, claiming for each card the number of axes of symmetry which it has. If challenged, she must prove

her claim to the satisfaction of the others. If necessary the method of activity 1 should be used.

8. Another round may then be played.

Discussion of activities	Activity 1 establishes the concept of symmetry by physically showing the congruence of the 2 halves of the figure.
	Activity 2 consolidates it, and emphasises the extended concept of multiple symmetry, in a game which depends on this as a shared schema.

OBSERVE AND LISTEN   **REFLECT**   **DISCUSS**

Space 1.10   TRIANGLES: CLASSIFICATION, CONGRUENCE, SIMILARITY

Concepts
(i) Ways in which triangles may be further classified: equilateral, isosceles, scalene, right angles.
(ii) Congruence of triangles.
(iii) Similarity of triangles.

Abilities
(i) To classify triangles in the ways described above.
(ii) To recognise whether two triangles are congruent or not.
(iii) To recognise whether two triangles are similar, and say in what ways they are the same and in what ways different.

Discussion of concepts	(i) An equilateral triangle has all its sides equal in length, and all its angles equal in size. An isosceles triangle has two (but not three) equal sides and two equal angles. A scalene triangle has no two sides equal, and no two angles equal. A right-angled triangle has one right angle. Further categories are possible, e.g. obtuse angled; but the above are sufficient for the present. The categories of right-angled and isosceles overlap, and so do right angled and scalene.
	(ii) Two triangles are congruent if one fits exactly on top of the other, turning it over if necessary.
	(iii) Two triangles are similar if they are the same shape but not necessarily the same size. (So congruent triangles are also similar, but would usually be called 'congruent'.)

Activity 1   Classifying triangles

A teacher-led discussion for up to 6 children. Its purpose is to help children form group (i) of the concepts above.

Materials
• Triangle pack 1. A complete set is provided in Vol. 2a. This is like the polygons pack used for activity 1 in the previous topic, but consists only

of triangles. These are of 5 varieties, 6 assorted examples of each. The varieties are:

Equilateral.
Isosceles, not right-angled.
Right angled, scalene.

Isosceles right-angled.
Scalene, not right-angled.

- Set loops.

Suggested sequence for discussion This follows the same lines as Space 1.8/1, classification of polygons. There is a difference, in that the categories right-angled and isosceles overlap. After children have discovered this for themselves, it may be shown using set loops. Start with the loops not overlapping and let children discover the need to overlap them. The same applies to right-angled and scalene.

At this stage, informal descriptions are satisfactory. Children may then be told the mathematical names in preparation for activity 2.

Activity 2   Triangle dominoes

A game for 2 to 4 players. Its purpose is to help children attach the mathematical names to the concepts formed in activity 1, while also consolidating the concepts.

Materials • A set of dominoes as provided in Vol. 2a.

What they do This game is played as in Space 1.7/2 and Space 1.8/2. Reminder: each match must be between a word and an angle.

Activity 3   Match and mix: triangles

A game for 2 to 5 players. Its purpose is to combine and practise further the concepts formed in activities 1 and 2.

Materials • Triangles pack 1. This is the same as used in activity 1.
• Match and Mix card as in Space 1.8/3.

Rules of the game The game is played in the same way as space 1.8/3, Match and mix: polygons. An interesting development is provided by the overlapping categories. These may be used for either matching or mixing, provided that the player states his reason, E.g.,

'Match:
both isosceles.'

'Mix:
one right angled
the other not.'

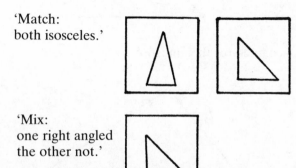

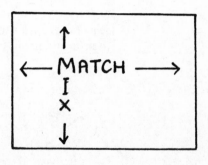

Activity 4   Congruent and similar triangles

A teacher-led discussion for up to 6 children. Its purpose is to introduce these concepts, with some of their further properties.

Materials • Triangles pack 2, as provided in Vol. 2a. This consists of 24 cut-out triangles in 12 pairs. Of these, 6 are pairs of congruent triangles, and 6 are pairs of similar triangles. Most of these are scalene, but 2 pairs in each set are of the 'special' kinds (equilateral, isosceles, right angled). Sizes are assorted. In 2 of the similar pairs, the larger have sides twice as long as the smaller; in 2 similar pairs, three times as long; and in 2 similar pairs, one-and-a-half times as long.

Suggested sequence for the discussion

1. Put all the triangles in the middle of the table and ask children to find pairs of triangles which are alike. Depending on the number of children, each will get 2 or 3 pairs.
2. Ask them in turn to describe in their own words the ways in which the triangles in each pair are alike. E.g. (for congruent triangles) 'They are exactly the same.' 'They fit exactly.' (For similar triangles) 'They are the same shape but different sizes.'
3. Tell them the mathematical names for these relationships, and let them in turn describe their pairs again. (E.g. 'I have a pair of congruent triangles and a pair of similar triangles.')
4. Ask them what else they can find out about their pairs of similar triangles. Among the more important properties are:

(i) If you put the smaller on top of the larger like this, with two sides coinciding, the third sides are parallel:

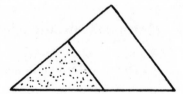

(ii) This can be done in 3 ways. Here are the other 2:

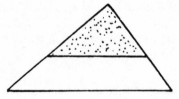 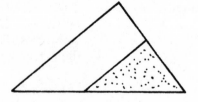

(iii) This is easier to follow in pictures than in words. E.g. (measurements in cm),

 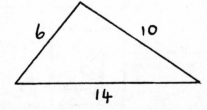

In mathematical language, the ratios of the lengths of corresponding sides are in the same proportion. This formulation lies several years into the future for the children. At the present stage, any kind of description which shows an intuitive grasp is acceptable.

Discussion of activities	These activities parallel those in the previous topic, so it may be worth re-reading the discussion at the end of Space 1.8. The advantage of the present approach over the printed page shows particularly clearly in activity 4, step 4(ii), when the smaller triangle can be physically fitted onto the larger triangle in 3 different ways.

OBSERVE AND LISTEN   **REFLECT**   **DISCUSS**

Space 1.11   CLASSIFICATION OF QUADRILATERALS

Concepts   Ways in which quadrilaterals may be classified:
- (i)   kite
- (ii)   trapezium
- (iii)   parallelogram
- (iv)   rhombus
- (v)   rectangle
- (vi)   square
- (vii)   oblong

Abilities
- (i)   To classify quadrilaterals in the ways described above.
- (ii)   To name them, and state their characteristic properties.
- (iii)   To relate these classifications.

Discussion of concepts	In Space 1.9, we classified polygons by two criteria: number of sides, and regular/irregular. Then in Space 1.10, we took one of these categories, 3-sided polygons (triangles) and made further distinctions between different kinds of triangle. Now we do the same for 4-sided polygons (quadrilaterals). These we sort by 2 criteria: (a) how many sides are equal, and which: (b) how many pairs of sides are parallel. These are not independent, e.g., if a quadrilateral has two pairs of parallel sides, then these pairs of opposite sides must also be equal. This results in interesting relationships between categories: e.g. a square is also a rhombus, a rectangle, and a parallelogram.

Squares and oblongs, as we shall use the terms, are both kinds of rectangle. One sometimes hears people talk about squares and rectangles as though these were distinct categories, but this is rather like talking about girls and children. Girls and boys are both kinds of children. Likewise, squares and oblongs both satisfy the criteria for rectangles, which is to have 4 right angles.

The categories are described and illustrated below:

Kite	2 pairs of adjacent sides equal, but not 4 equal sides.	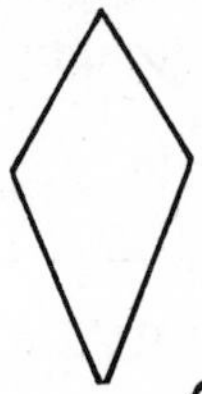
Trapezium	1 pair (only) of opposite sides parallel.	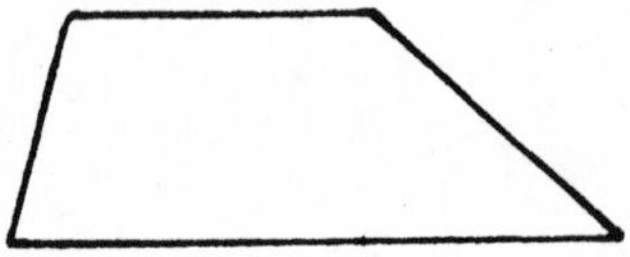
Parallelogram	2 pairs of sides parallel. (Also, 2 pairs of opposite sides equal.)	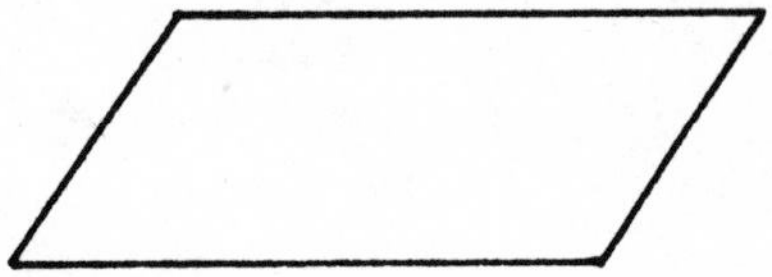
Rhombus	All 4 sides equal. (It is also a parallelogram.)	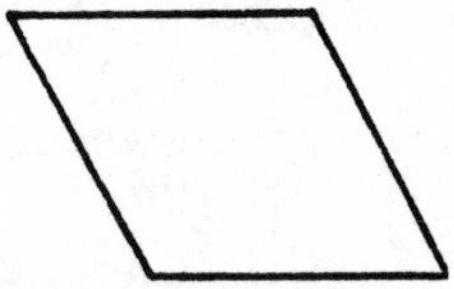
Rectangle	4 right angles. (It is also a parallelogram.)	or
Square	4 right angles. 4 equal sides. (It is also a rectangle a rhombus, and a parallelogram.)	
Oblong	A rectangle which is not a square.	

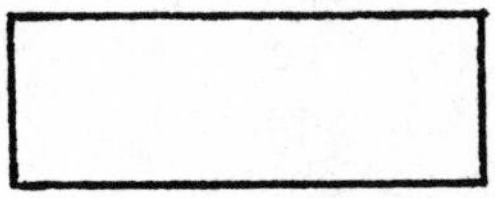

Activity 1 Classifying quadrilaterals

A teacher-led discussion for up to 6 children. Its purpose is to teach children the above categories and their names.

Materials
- Quadrilaterals pack, as provided in Vol. 2a. This consists of 36 cards, with 6 examples each of categories (i) to (iv) as listed above, 6 squares, and 6 oblongs. (So there will in fact be 12 rectangles: 6 square rectangles and 6 oblong rectangles.) The examples vary in size, shape (except squares), and orientation, e.g., the rectangles are not all drawn with their sides parallel to the sides of the card.
- Notebook or sheet of paper for each child.
- Pencils.

What they do
1. Lay out an assortment of the quadrilaterals cards, about half the pack.
2. Explain that the object is to sort these.
3. Invite the children to look for shapes which belong together. Accept any reasonable suggestions, and let each child collect all the examples of that shape.
4. Put down the rest of the pack, and let them continue until all are sorted.
5. Let each child describe in her own words what she has collected, and then tell her the mathematical term for this.
6. If any cards remain unsorted, sort these too. What happens now will depend on the categories which have been used.
7. If parallelograms and rhombi have been put together, ask if they can be sorted further.
8. If squares and oblongs have been separated, leave them so since this will be dealt with in activity 2.
9. By now the categories are likely to be fairly near the ones illustrated. If it is not quite the same, explain that there are various reasonable ways of sorting. The way you are going to show them is a useful one which is widely used, and not very different from theirs.
10. The one to aim at in the present activity is, I suggest, the one shown above with oblongs and squares, parallelograms and rhombi, all separated.
11. Tell them the mathematical names for these, if they do not know already. At this stage, oblongs may be called rectangles (which they are), or oblongs.
12. Each child describes her set using its mathematical name. E.g. 'I have collected a set of squares.'

Activity 2 Relations between quadrilaterals

A continuation of activity 1. Its purpose is to help children find the relationships between the various categories of rectangles.

Materials The same as for activity 1.

Suggested sequence for discussion
1. Tell the children to keep 2 examples of each of their categories, and collect the rest.
2. Ask for all the parallelograms.

3. Depending on what you have been given, query other examples which you have not been given. E.g. (pointing to the oblongs) 'Aren't those parallelograms too?'

4. Discuss what properties a shape must have to be a parallelogram, and get them to formulate the outcome. E.g. 'Rectangles are a kind of parallelogram.'

5. Repeat steps 2, 3, 4 until children have come to realize that squares, oblongs, rhombi are all kinds of parallelogram.

6. Repeat as in steps 2 to 6.
    (a) by asking for all the rectangles. You should get squares and oblongs.
    (b) by asking for all the rhombi (or rhombuses). You should get squares and other kinds of rhombus.
    In each case discuss the criteria, and get the children to formulate the outcome. E.g. 'Squares and oblongs are both kinds of rectangle.'

Activity 3   **'And what else is this?'**

A game for up to 6 children. Its purpose is to consolidate the shape concepts, and relations between them, learnt in activities 1 and 2.

Materials   • Quadrilaterals pack. The smaller set with only 2 examples of each kind, used in activity 2, is more convenient, but the full pack may be used.

Rules of the game   1. The cards are spread out face up in the table in such a way that it is easy to find an example of whichever kind is wanted.

2. Then player 1 picks up a card and asks player 2 (on her left) 'What is this?'

3. Player 2 might reply 'An oblong'.

4. Player 1 asks player 3 (the next player after player 2) 'And what else is this?'

5. Player 3 might reply 'A rectangle'.

6. Player 1 repeats the question to players 4, 5 . . . in turn. Replies might be 'A quadrilateral', 'A polygon with 4 sides', and eventually 'That's all'.

7. Steps 2 to 6 are then repeated with the next player acting as player 1.

Activity 4   **'I think you mean . . .'**

A game for 4 or 6 children. Its purpose is further to exercise the shape concepts and relations learnt in this topic, with emphasis on language and vocabulary.

Materials   • Quadrilaterals pack as in activity 1, without kites or trapezia. This leaves 24 cards, all parallelograms of one kind or another.
  • Card listing the pairs which may be formed: squares, oblongs, rhombi, parallelograms which are none of the foregoing.

Rules of play   1. The cards are shuffled and dealt.
  2. Each player looks at her cards.
  3. The object is to collect pairs of the same kind: squares, oblongs,

rhombi which are not squares, parallelograms which are none of the foregoing.

4. Any pairs which players already have in their hands, they put down.
5. They then try to acquire more pairs by asking in turn, starting with the player on the left of the dealer.
6. They may ask whom they like, but must not ask for the card by name. So a player wanting, say, a rhombus might say 'Please may I have a parallelogram with all its sides equal?' The one asked might reply 'I think you mean a rhombus', followed by 'Here you are' or 'Sorry'.
7. A player asking by name loses her turn.
8. When a player makes a pair, she puts it down.
9. Scoring is as follows. 2 points for first 'out', 1 point for second 'out', plus 1 point for each pair.
10. Another round may then be played.

Note Rule 6 requires that a parallelogram which is not a square, oblong, or rhombus, must not be called a parallelogram at all. It might be called 'A quadrilateral with two pairs of parallel sides, not all equal.'

Discussion of activities

Activity 1 is concerned with sorting and classifying – fundamental activities of intelligence which have been in frequent use from the beginning. Activities 2, 3, 4 are more sophisticated, however, since the present classes overlap. This gives the opportunities for reflection on the way these categories are related to each other. Activity 3 starts with an example, and asks in what ways it can be categorised. Activity 4 starts with a category, and ends with a particular member of that category (if the asker is lucky). It also emphasises the language of description and relationships.

OBSERVE AND LISTEN   **REFLECT**   **DISCUSS**

Space 1.12 INTER-RELATIONS OF PLANE SHAPES

Concept A variety of part/whole relationships between smaller and larger geometrical figures.

Abilities (i) Combining smaller figures to make larger figures.
(ii) Finding smaller figures within larger figures.

Discussion of concept

The ability to see how parts fit together to make a whole, and to find shapes within other shapes, is an important one for later geometry. Here we are concerned with being able to think of, e.g., a parallelogram as made up of two congruent triangles. It is a good example of relational thinking in geometry, analogous to the relationships between numbers which are so important in numerical mathematics.

Activity 1   Triangles and polygons

An activity for up to 6 children. Its purpose is to teach relationships, including angular relationships, between triangles and regular polygons.

Materials • Triangles/polygons set. These are made by cutting out regular polygons, and then cutting these into isosceles triangles. Two typical ones are illustrated in figure 27. All the angles should be marked, on both sides.

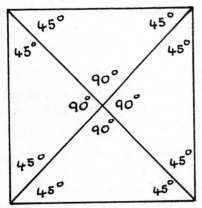
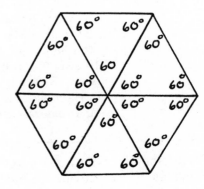

Figure 27   Triangles/polygons set.

What they do   *Stage (a)*
1. Each child takes a triangle of a different shape.
2. They collect all the triangles which are congruent with the one they have.
3. Each makes a regular polygon with their triangles. (A square may be made using 2 or 4 right angled isosceles triangles.)
4. They examine their polygons, and add together all the angles surrounding the centres.

Stage (b)
1. The first child shuts his eyes and takes a triangle.
2. He looks at it and predicts what kind of regular polygon can be made using it, and how many congruent triangles will be needed.
3. The others help him to collect all the triangles congruent with the one he has.
4. He tests his prediction.
5. If successful he explains how he knew.
6. Steps 1 to 5 are repeated by another child.

Activity 2   Circles and polygons

An activity for up to 6 children. Its purpose is to teach relationships between circles and polygons.

Materials   For each child:
• safety compasses
• pencil and paper
• scissors.

What they do

1. Each child draws a circle on paper and cuts it out.
2. He folds it along a diameter, then again, and opens it flat.

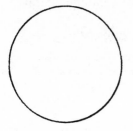 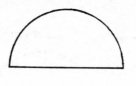 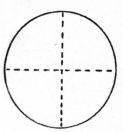

3. He draws a square.

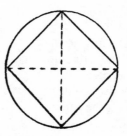

4. Each child cuts out another circle, and repeats step 2, but folds once more.
5. In this way he draws an octagon.

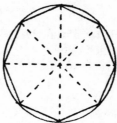

6. They mark the sizes of angles at the centre. These are arrived at by calculation, not measurement.
7. Next, a hexagon. The circle for this is not cut out.
8. A first point is marked anywhere on the circumference. Using the same length of radius as that by which the circle was drawn, they use the compasses to mark second, third . . . points round the circumference, as shown below. The distance from the sixth to the first point should be found to be the same as all the others.

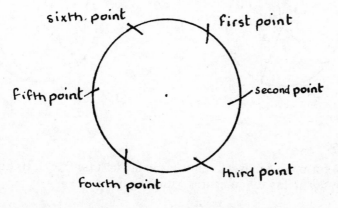 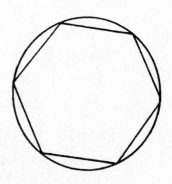

9. The points are joined to form a hexagon, as above.
10. This is a very satisfying method. Ask 'Why does it work?' Hint: join all the points to the centre. Second hint if necessary: look for equilateral triangles.
11. Next, the equilateral triangle. This uses circles in a different way.
12. Start with a circle.

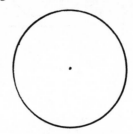

13. Take any point on the circumference as centre for another circle, using the same radius.

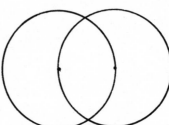

14. This gives 2 equilateral triangles, of which only one is shown here.

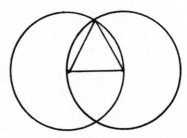

15. Ask: 'Do we need to draw the whole circles? If not, how little can we do with?'
16. A pentagon cannot be drawn by a method of the kind above. It is necessary to calculate the central angle, and use a protractor to draw angles of the required size, as below.

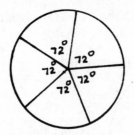

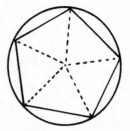

Activity 3 'I can see . . .'

A game for up to 6 players, but is probably best for 2 or 3. Its purpose is to develop the ability to see figures within figures.

Materials
- A complex figure, such as figure 28. This should be covered with transparent film.*
- OHP pens, a different colour for each player.*
- Scoring rules on a piece of thin card.
- A bowl of counters.

* Alternatively, the figure could be duplicated and expendable. In this case any kind of coloured marker will do.

Rules of play

1. The figure is circulated from player to player.
2. Each in turn 'collects' embedded figures, such as a pair of congruent triangles, a right angle, a pair of congruent angles or lines, a parallelogram.
3. He names these, and claims them by marking them with his colour. This is done on or within the shape, as is best in the particular case.
4. If the other players agree, he takes a counter from the pool.
5. The same embedded figure may be claimed in various ways, but not twice in the same way.
6. The winner is the one with most counters, when no one can think of anything new to claim and gain agreement thereto.
7. One point is scored for each of the following (by agreement, this list may be extended):
   A pair of parallel lines.
   A pair of congruent triangles.
   A pair of congruent lines.
   A pair of congruent angles.
   A parallelogram.

(List continued overleaf)

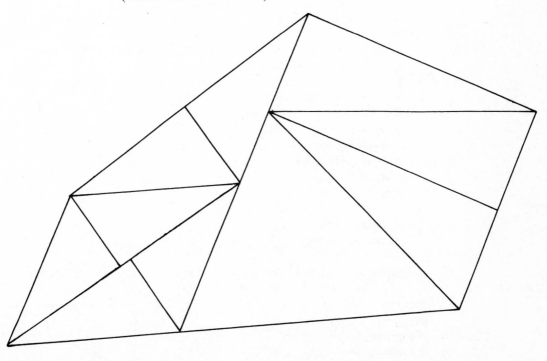

Figure 28 'I can see . . .'

An oblong.
A square.
An isosceles triangle.
An equilateral triangle.

Activity 4 Triangles and larger shapes

A game for up to 6 children, but is probably best for 2 initially. Its purpose is to develop awareness of the relationships between triangles and other shapes.

Materials
- A set of cut-out triangles, as provided in Vol. 2a. For the larger groups a double set will be needed. It is useful to make these sets of different colours.
- Scoring rules on a piece of thin card.

Preliminary Allow the children time to experiment with putting the cut-out pieces together in various ways, and finding out what larger shapes they can make.

Rules of play
1. The object is to collect triangles and make larger shapes, e.g. parallelograms.
2. The triangles are spread out in the middle of the table.
3. Each player in turn takes a triangle, with which (from the second round on) he starts building larger figures.
4. When there are no longer enough triangles for each player to take one more, one more round is played as in step 5.
5. In this final round, each player may if he wishes exchange one of his triangles for one in the pool.
6. Players then count up their scores, each in turn explaining to the others what points he claims and why.
7. The scoring rules are as follows:

composite parallelogram	1
composite rhombus	1
composite rectangle	1
composite square	1
composite right angle	1
composite straight line	1
composite kite	1
composite oblong	1

The same figure may be scored in as many ways as possible. Example:

composite oblong	1
composite rectangle	1
composite parallelogram	1
2 composite right angles	2
total	5

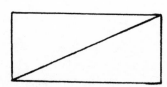

composite rhombus	1
composite parallelogram	1
total	2

composite rhombus	1
2 composite right angles	2
composite parallelogram	1
composite rectangle	1
composite square	1
total (if he says them all)	6

3 composite parallelograms	3
3 composite straight line	2
total	5

Players may re-arrange their pieces at any time up to their final declaration.

Discussion of activities	In activity 1, physically putting shapes together is used as the means for learning part-whole relationships. Activity 2 takes a step towards pencil-and-paper geometry. It is still based on physical manipulation, but calculation and inference are also used. Activity 3 diversifies from regular polygons to all kinds of larger shapes. Prediction is also involved: triangles are chosen because, by combining it with other shapes in imagination, the player expects a desired result. He has to commit himself to taking the piece before this can be tested. So in these three activities, we have another clear example of mode 1 schema building and testing.
	The preliminary to Activity 4 consists of combining the cut-out triangles physically, and observing the outcome. The activity itself involves combining the shapes first in imagination, and then testing the prediction physically. So here we have a very clear example of mode 1 schema building followed by testing.

OBSERVE AND LISTEN   **REFLECT**   **DISCUSS**

251

Space 1.13   TESSELLATIONS

Concept   That of a tessellation.

Ability   To discover whether a given shape will tessellate, or not.

Discussion of concept

A tessera is one of the pieces of marble, glass, or tile from which a mosaic pavement is made, and tessellating is combining these so as to form a mosaic. The everyday meaning of tessellation (which is centuries old) and the mathematical meaning are the same; except that mathematicians, as one might expect, do it on paper. So the transition from cardboard or plastic tessella (little tessera) to drawing, which we follow in this topic, also follows its historical sequence.

A shape can be tessellated if a number of them, all the same size, can be fitted together (rotated if necessary) to cover a surface without gaps. Here we shall concern ourselves with tessellations using one shape only.

Activity 1   Tessellating regular polygons

A group investigation for up to 6 children, working singly or in pairs. Its purpose is to teach the concept of tessellation, and introduce some of the easier examples.

Materials
- About 20 of each of the following regular polygons, cut out in cardboard and stored in separate plastic bags. Some of those in each bag have their interior angles marked, on both sides. If the polygons in a bag can be of assorted colours, so much the better.
- Equilateral triangles.
- Squares.
- Pentagons.
- Hexagons.
- Octagons.

What they do
1. Using the equilateral triangles, demonstrate what is meant by tessellation.
2. Each child or pair then takes a bag.
3. Their first task is to discover, by experiment, whether the polygons they have can be tessellated, or not.
4. Their second task is to find out why they can or cannot be tessellated. The marked angles provide a clue.
5. In turn, the children tell the rest of the group what they have found out.

Activity 2   Tessellating other shapes

A group investigation for up to 6 children, working singly or in pairs. Its purpose is to expand children's concept of tessellation to include rectangles, parallelograms, all triangles, and a variety of other shapes. It also takes children from physical tessellation to doing it on paper.

Materials   For each child:
- plain paper
- pencil and rubber
- ruler
- Instruction card for the group, as below.

TESSELLATIONS

Which of these shapes can be tessellated? Which cannot?
  Rectangles, any shape.
  Parallelograms, any shape.
  Triangles, all varieties.
What else can you find out?
Share out the task among yourselves, and produce a combined report.

What they do   1.   They follow the instructions on the card.
2.   In fact, all these shapes can be tessellated.
3.   Rectangles are fairly obvious. Their right angles fit together to form straight lines.
4.   Parallelograms also tessellate quite easily. Opposite sides, being parallel, have the same direction; so they fit if the parallelogram is slid along any side without rotation.

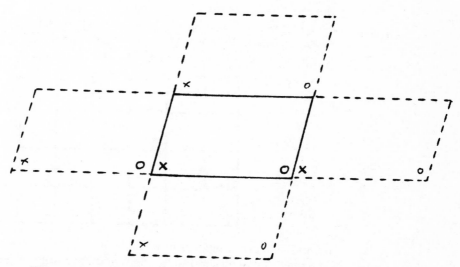

From this we can see that the angles at each end of a side combine to give a straight line.
5.   Any kind of triangle can be tessellated, since two congruent triangles make a parallelogram. To get the second in position, rotate the first half a turn about the mid point of any side.

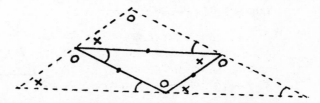

From this we can see that the 3 angles of a triangle together make a straight line.

The dotted larger triangle is similar to each of the smaller ones, since the angles of the original triangle are each reproduced once.

Activity 3   Inventing tessellations

An investigation which may be followed singly or in pairs. Its purpose is to open up the concept of tessellation and teach children two ways of generating their own.

Materials   For each child:
- plain and squared paper
- tracing paper
- pencil and rubber
- ruler

What they do   1. Demonstrate one of the methods for generating tessellations described below.
2. Then allow the children time for inventing their own.
3. Let them show and discuss their results.
4. Repeat steps 1 to 3 with the other method.
5. These tessellations may be coloured.

Method 1   Dissection of a rectangle
If a rectangle is dissected into two halves of the same shape, these will tessellate. Squared paper is useful for this. A suitable dissection line may be obtained by working inwards from the two ends, as below.

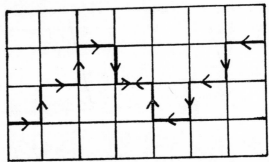

Method 2   Parasquigglegrams
I discovered this method for myself, and have not yet seen it elsewhere, though it is too simple not to have been discovered by others. The name is my own. Tracing paper is useful for reproducing the squiggles.

This is a nice use for translations.

Start with 2
intersecting squiggles.

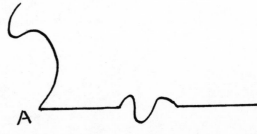

Move A without
rotation to the
other end of
one squiggle,
taking the other
squiggle with it.

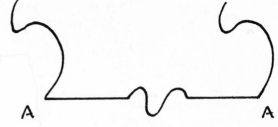

Now the
other way.

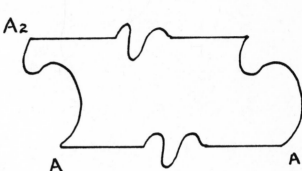

Any shape made in this way can be tessellated.

Activity 4 Tessellating any quadilateral

A more difficult investigation for children working singly or in pairs. Its purpose is to challenge the abilities of the brighter children.

Materials For each child:
- pencil and plain paper
- tracing paper
- ruler

What they do 1. Tell them that it is possible to tessellate a quadrilateral of any shape. (Note: we here mean quadrilaterals which are

convex   not concave   nor crossed.)

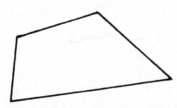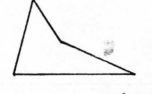

         Since the children have only encountered the first kind so far, we do not need to mention the other possibilities unless they do.)
2. They may like to try to find out how without help.
3. The method is to rotate the quadrilateral about the mid-point of each side in turn. By drawing a diagonal in a dotted line, and including this in the rotated versions, two sets of tessellating parallelograms result. For clarity this has been omitted from figure 29.

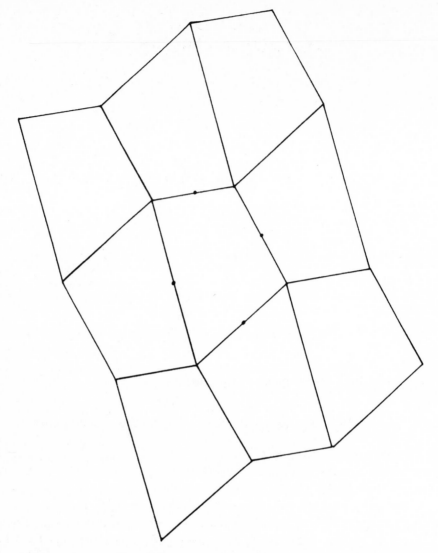

Figure 29 Tessellation of an irregular quadrilateral.

4. From this we see that the interior angles of any quadrilateral add up to 360 degrees.
5. Let the children draw their own tessellations of a quadrilateral of their own choice.

Discussion of activities	In a now-familiar sequence, we start with schema building by mode 1, physical experience, and progress to mode 3, creativity. Discussion plays an important part as always. This topic is open ended towards creativity of an artistic kind. If possible, do show the children some of the pictorial tessellations of the artist M. C. Esher. These are published both in book form, and as reproductions sold in art shops.

OBSERVE AND LISTEN   **REFLECT**   **DISCUSS**

THE NUMBER TRACK AND THE NUMBER LINE

Powerful support to our thinking about numbers

NuSp 1.7   UNIT INTERVALS: THE NUMBER LINE

Concepts   (i)   Unit intervals on a line.
(ii)   The number line.

Ability   To use the number line in the same ways as the number track, in preparation for other uses of the number line.

Discussion of concepts

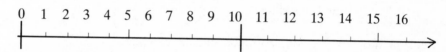

The difference between a number track and a number line are appreciable, and not immediately obvious.

The number track is physical, though we may represent it by a diagram. The number line is conceptual – it is a mental object, though we often use diagrams to help us think about it. The number track is finite, whereas the number line is infinite. However far we extend a physical track, it has to end somewhere. But in our thoughts, we can think of a number line as going on and on to infinity.

On the number line, numbers are represented by points, not spaces; and operations are represented by movements over intervals on the line, to the right for addition and to the left for subtraction. The concept of a unit interval thus replaces that of a unit object. Also, the number line starts at 0, not at 1. For the counting numbers, and all positive numbers, we use only the right-hand half of the number line, starting at zero and extending indefinitely to the right. For positive and negative numbers we still use 0 for the origin, but now the number line extends indefinitely to the right (positive numbers) and left (negative numbers).

Activity 1   Drawing the number line

This is a simple activity for introducing the concept.

Materials   • Pencil and paper for each child.

What they do
1. Ask the children to draw a line, as long as will conveniently go on the paper.
2. They mark off equal intervals.
3. They number these 0, 1, 2 . . . as in the diagram above.
4. At this stage, the two differences between the number track and the number line which need to be pointed out are: (i) With the number track, numbers are represented by spaces; with the number line, numbers are represented by points on the line. Though it is helpful to use different marks for tens, fives, and units, it is the points *on* the line which represent the numbers. (ii) The number track starts at 1, the number line starts at 0.

Activity 2   Sequences on the number line

NuSp 1.2/1, 'Sequences on the number track', may usefully be repeated here. Smaller markers will be needed. (See activity 3.)

Activity 3   Where must the frog land?

A game for two players. Its purpose is to introduce the use of the number line for adding.

Materials
- As long a number line as you like.
- A marker representing a frog for each player, occupying as small a base as possible.*
- 1 die 1-6, or 1-10 for athletic frogs.

* A short length (about 2 cm) of coloured milk straw, with a small blob of Blu-Tack on the end, makes a good marker for this and many other activities.

What they do
1. The frogs start at zero.
2. Player A throws the die and tells the frog what number it must hop to. This is done mentally, using aids such as finger counting if he likes. (To start with, children may use counting on along the number line, but should replace this by mentally adding as soon as they have learnt the game.)
3. Player B checks, and if he says 'Agree' the frog is allowed to hop.
4. If B does not agree, he says so, and they check.
5. If A has made a mistake, his frog may not hop.
6. Two frogs may be at the same number.
7. They then exchange roles for B's throw of the die.
8. The winner is the frog which first hops past the end of the line. (The exact number is not required).

Activity 4   Hopping backwards

The subtraction form of activity 3, starting at the largest number on the number line and hopping backwards past zero.

Activity 5 Taking

Another capture game for two, but quite different from NuSp 1.4/4 'Capture'. Its purpose is to give further practice in relating numbers to positions and movements on the number line.

Materials
- 1 number line 0-20.
- 3 markers for each player.
- 1 die 1-6.

What they do   *Form (a)*
1. The markers begin at zero.
2. The die is thrown alternately, and according to the number thrown a player may jump his marker forward that interval on the line.
3. A piece which is jumped *over* is taken, and removed from the board for the rest of the game.
4. An occupied point may not be jumped *onto*.
5. A player does not have to move at all if he doesn't want to. (We introduced this rule when we found that starting throws of low numbers were likely to result in the piece being taken next throw, with no room for manoeuvre.)
6. The winner is the player who gets the largest number of pieces past 20. (It is not necessary to throw the exact number.)

Form (b)
This may also be played as a subtraction game, backwards from 20.

Activity 6 A race through a maze

This is a board game for up to 3 players. Its purpose is to bring out the correspondence between the relationships smaller/larger number and left/right on the number line.

Materials
- Board (see figure 30).
- Number line 1-20
- Number cards 1-20
- For each player:
    1 coloured pointer for the number line.
    1 marker to take through the maze.

What they do
1. The pack of number cards is shuffled and put face down.
2. In turn, each player turns over the top card and puts it face up, starting a new pile. He may then use this number to position his pointer on the number line, or decide not to (since an extreme left or right position is not helpful). In that case he repeats this step at his next move.
3. When he does position his pointer, he also puts his marker at the start of the maze.
4. After taking steps 2 and 3, players at subsequent turns move forward through the maze if they can. The number they turn over determines whether they can or not.
    An example will make it clear.

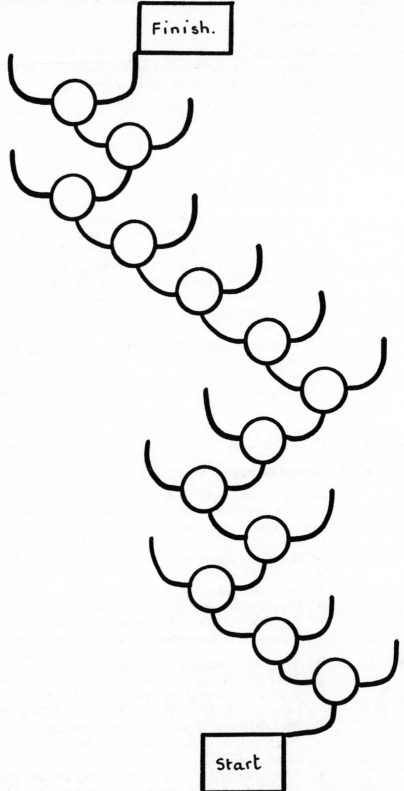

Figure 30 A race through a maze.

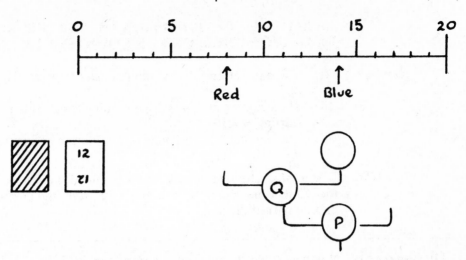

Since 12 is to the left of the blue pointer's position, player 'Blue' can move forward if he is at P on the maze, but not if he is at Q. However, the reverse is the case for player 'Red', since 12 is to the right of his pointer.

5. There is no limit to the number of players at a given position on the maze.

6. When all the cards are turned over the number pack is shuffled and used again.

7. The winner is the first player to reach the finish.

Note

If the children have difficulty in remembering their left and right, you could help with labelled arrows.

Discussion of activities

The first four activities are concerned first with introducing the number line, and then with linking it to concepts which are already familiar. Activity 5, 'Taking', is more difficult, since it involves mentally comparing a number of possible moves before deciding which one to make.

Activity 6 involves correspondence not between objects, but between two different relations. One is the relation of size, between two numbers, and the other is the relation of position, between two points on the number line. Here is another good example of the conceptual complexity of even elementary mathematics. Yet young children manage this without difficulty if we make it possible for them to use their intelligence to the full.

OBSERVE AND LISTEN   **REFLECT**   **DISCUSS**

NuSp 1.8   EXTRAPOLATION OF THE NUMBER LINE. EXTRAPOLATION OF THE COUNTING NUMBERS

Concepts   (i)   The number line as extending further than we could draw the whole of.

(ii)   The counting numbers as continuing further than we could count starting at zero.

(iii)   The number line as having other points and numbers as well as those marked.

Ability   Given satisfactory 'landmarks' on the number line, to construct that part of the number line mentally; and thereby to state the numbers of other points on that part of the line.

Discussion of concepts

When we have clearly seen a pattern, we are often able to extrapolate it, i.e. take the pattern further. Here we have two corresponding patterns: the spatial pattern of the number line, and the pattern of the counting numbers. Each of these has patterns within patterns: the 0-9 cycle is repeated anew for each decade, starting again at 10, 20, 30 . . . . The 10, 20, 30, . . . 90 cycle is repeated every hundred; and so on.

Since we can think of a line as continuing as far as we like, and as taking these patterns along with it, the number line is an excellent mental support for extending the more abstract concepts of the counting numbers.

Activity 1   What number is this? (Single starter)

An activity for children playing in pairs. Its purpose is to start them thinking in terms of a number line longer than one of which one could draw the whole.

Materials   For each pair:
* Two cards, each showing part of a number line.*
* Two pointers.**

* See illustration below. Card (a) is used for stage (a), card (b) for stage (b).

** E.g. cocktail sticks. We have found that a paper clip, with one end straightened out, also makes a good pointer.

Card (a)

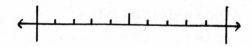

Card (b)

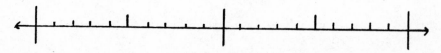

What they do   *Stage (a)*

1. Explain that the card shows part of a number line. The arrows at each end mean that the line continues back to zero on the left, and as far as we like on the right. The cross-lines mark tens, the smallest marks show units, and the fives are shown by slightly longer marks.

2. Child A begins by pointing to the left-hand mark, and says (e.g.)

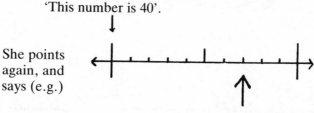

'This number is 40'.

She points again, and says (e.g.)

'What number is this?'

3. If child B says '47', child A would reply 'Agree' and they would change roles. If child B says something else, they would need to discuss.

4. Child A need not always name the left-hand point. E.g. she could begin by saying

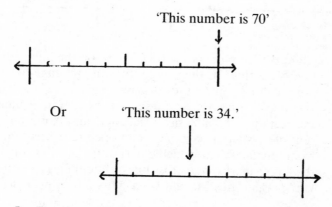

'This number is 70'

Or   'This number is 34.'

5. But A must keep to the tens, fives, units pattern of marking. E.g. she should not say

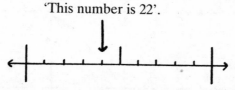

'This number is 22'.

If she did, B would say 'Disagree' and they would need to discuss.

Stage (b)

This uses card (b), which covers 2 decades. Otherwise it is played as in stage (a).

Activity 2   What number is this? (Double starter)

A continuation of activity 1, to be played in pairs. This is appreciably harder.

Materials The same as for activity 1.

What they do *Stage (a)* using card (a)

1. Child A now begins by placing *two* pointers and saying what number they represent. The smaller marks may now represent either unit intervals as before, or intervals of 2, 5, or 10. The larger marks and numbers lines must form part of a 'sensible' system. This is best shown by examples.

   Sensible.

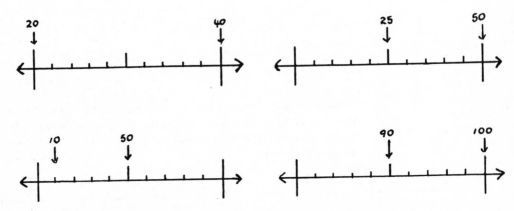

2. Child B then points to another mark on the line, and asks 'What number is this?' If they agree, they interchange roles and steps 1 and 2 are repeated. If not, they discuss.

3. If child B cannot think of a sensible system to explain where A has put the pointers, she may say 'Challenge' and A must explain. What is a sensible system is to some extent open to discussion. Such a discussion would in itself be a valuable part of the activity. My own view is that the larger marks, and cross lines, should represent more important landmarks. Thus I would not see the following as sensible.

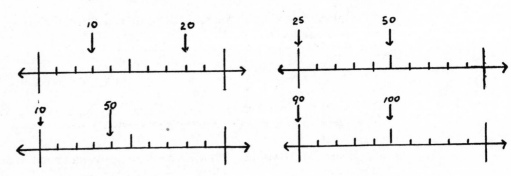

Stage (b)
This uses card (b); otherwise, as in stage (a).

Stage (c)
This uses card (b). The only difference between this and stage (a) is that the intervals used may be 1, 2, 5, 10, or multiples of these such as 20, 50, 100 etc.

Activity 3   Is there a limit?

A teacher-led discussion with a group of children. Underlying this is the difference between the finite nature of anything we can do physically, and the in-finite possibilities of thought.

Suggested sequence for discussion

1. Ask them how long a line they think they could draw. If they respond with answers like '100 miles', emphasise that you mean *actually draw*. Lead them in this way to realise the practical limitations of a line drawn physically.
2. Next, ask them how big a number do they think they could actually count – meaning, say the number words? Again let them come to realise the practical limitations.
3. Combine these in the number line. Show them a number line (say, 0-20) drawn on paper and ask them how far do they think this number line could be continued?
4. Now ask them: suppose we don't try to draw it, but just continue it in our imagination? What number would it take us to?
5. If they do not yet realise that there is no longer any limitation, then activity 4 will help to lead them towards this realization. If they do, this activity will consolidate it.

Activity 4   Can you think of . . . ?

A game for two teams. I think it needs to be teacher directed. It might be played with the rest of the class as spectators.

Materials   ● Blackboard?

What they do   *Stage (a)*
1. Team A writes a very large number, as big as they like.
2. Team B tries to think of a bigger one.
3. The task becomes easy as soon as they realise that all they need to do is to add 1.
4. When they do, they are ready to go on to stage b.

Stage (b)   Can you think of a further point?
1. Team B have now to think of a very long number line, and name (give the number of) its last point.
2. When they have done so, team A tries to name a point beyond this.
3. Again all they need is to name the point one further on.

There is no largest number!
There is no furthest point!

Discussion of activities   This topic is a good example of creative imagination. In activities 1 and 2, our thinking is supported by visual representations; but the meaning of these becomes increasingly a matter of choice. This choice is, however, neither random nor arbitrary. It has to 'make sense' in terms of what we already know about numbers and the number line.

In both of these activities we thus have mode 3 schema building, and schema testing by mode 3 (consistency with existing knowledge) and mode 2 (discussion). Activity 2 is suitable only for the more able children. It requires a well-developed feeling for number patterns. With very able children, I have used it without giving them any restriction on what the marks may mean, beyond saying that they must form part of a sensible system.

In activities 3 and 4, children are led to realize that the limitations of working with physical materials disappear when we move into the realm of thought. It then becomes all the more important to have an internally regulated orderliness, such as has been developed in activities 1 and 2.

OBSERVE AND LISTEN **REFLECT** **DISCUSS**

NuSp 1.9   INTERPOLATION BETWEEN POINTS. FRACTIONAL NUMBERS (DECIMAL)

Concepts (i)   Points marking tenth parts of a unit interval.
(ii)   New numbers, corresponding to these points, called decimal fractions.

Discussion of concepts

There are still a lot of 'unused' points on the number line, that is, points which do not yet have a number. And we do not need to go in the direction of infinity to find them – they are in between the points already in use, and correspond to fractional numbers. In this topic we shall be concerned mainly with decimal fractional numbers, usually and inaccurately called 'decimals'.

The relation between a fraction and a fractional number is discussed in Num 7. As long as we know this difference, there is no harm in following the custom of using the word 'fraction' for both. The currently established usage of 'decimal' is however less acceptable. 'Decimal' simply means 'related to ten' (Latin, *decem*). So 'decimal *notation*' means base 10 place-value notation as against, e.g., base 2, or binary, place-value notation. It is inaccurate to talk about decimal *numbers* and binary *numbers*, and very misleading. The *number* of objects in a set still remains the same if we *write* this number differently, just as it does if we use a French or German number-name.

'Decimal *fraction*' does, however describe a different kind of number from the counting numbers. It is a fractional number whose denominator is a power of 10: ten, a hundred, a thousand, etc. So

$$\frac{1}{10} \,, \quad \frac{7}{10} \,, \quad \frac{8}{100} \,, \quad \frac{47}{100} \,, \quad \frac{305}{1000}$$

are all decimal fractions, written in 'fraction bar' notation. Decimal fractions have the advantage that we can also write them in the place-value notation already in use. So

.1 .7 .08 .47 .305

are decimal fractions written in (decimal) place-value notation. A 'decimal' may or may not be a decimal fraction, and a decimal fraction may or may not be written in place-value notation.

We do not need to explain all this to the children, but we must try to avoid muddling them, which means we must try to clear up a long-standing muddle in our own minds. It is no accident that 'decimals' have long been the bane of generations of school children.

I suggest as a reasonable compromise that we accept 'fraction' with the dual meaning described above, but say and write 'decimal fraction' when we mean a fractional number of the kind described; and 'place-value notation' for, e.g., 17 , 0.17 , 1.7 . This, though not identical with general usage, is not in conflict with it, and therefore should not muddle anyone.

Activity 1   **What number is *this*? (Decimal fractions)**

This is introduced as a teacher-led discussion with a group of children after which it continues as in NuSp 1.8/1.

1. Draw, while you talk, an enlarged part of a number line, starting at zero, as shown below. Point half way between 0 and 1, and ask

What number is this?

'A half' is a good answer at this stage: we have not yet arrived at decimal fractions. Mark this point in pencil, and do similarly for the points which correspond to a quarter and three quarters.

2. We now have the unit interval 0-1 divided into four equal parts. Explain that these are useful divisions, but they don't fit in with the tens pattern of the rest of the number line.

3. So we rub these out (the half one can stay if you like) and mark the interval 0-1 in ten equal parts. We call these 'tenth parts'. ('Tenth' by itself has a different meaning, namely an ordinal number in the sequence first, second . . . ninth, tenth . . .) So the number for

this point

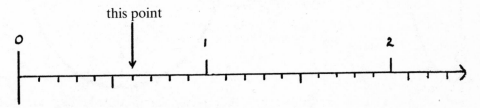

we will call for the present '6 tenth-parts'.

And the number for

this point

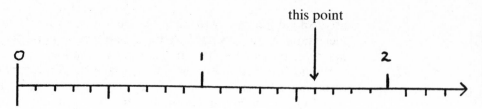

we will call '1 and 6 tenth-parts'.

Once they have grasped this, they are ready to repeat 'What number is *this*?' as in NuSp 1.8/1, using the same diagrams, but with the smaller divisions representing tenth-parts.

Activity 2   Snail race

A number line game for up to about four children. Its purpose is to provide a simple introduction to fractional points on the number line.

Materials
- Snail race board, see figure 31.
- Markers for each child to represent snails.*
- 1 die 1-6.

* These need to take up as little space as possible, as in NuSp 1.7/2 and 3.

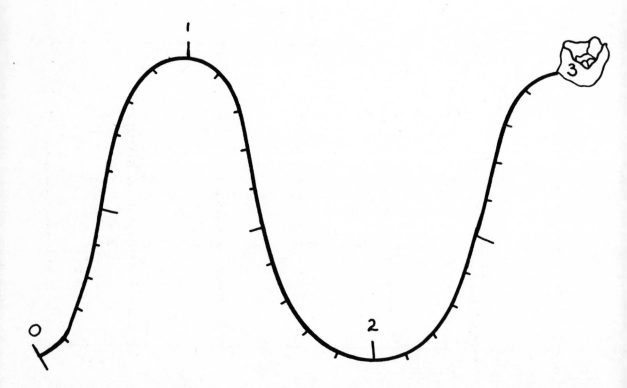

Figure 31   Snail race.

What they do 1. Players in turn throw the die, but move forward at a snail's pace! Each number thrown represents only that number of tenth-parts.
2. Overtaking is not allowed.
3. Two snails may not occupy the same point. Points are very small.

Activity 3 Snails and frogs

This game is played like the one before, with the following modifications. Its purpose is to make a contrast between whole and fractional numbers.

Materials • Snails and frogs board, see figure 32.
• 1 die marked 1, 2, 3 only.*
• Markers as before.
* This can be made from a base 10 single cube.

What they do 1. Normally a snail moves only that number of tenth-parts, as before.
2. However, if a move takes him exactly to a whole number, he is magically transformed into a frog for his next move, and hops the number of whole unit intervals shown by the die.
3. The spell is broken when he lands, however, and he must crawl snail-wise for his next moves.
4. To increase his chance of landing on a whole number, a player may decide not to use his throw. A snail may go into his shell and wait for a beneficial throw. Some children may even calculate the odds that this is a good tactic!

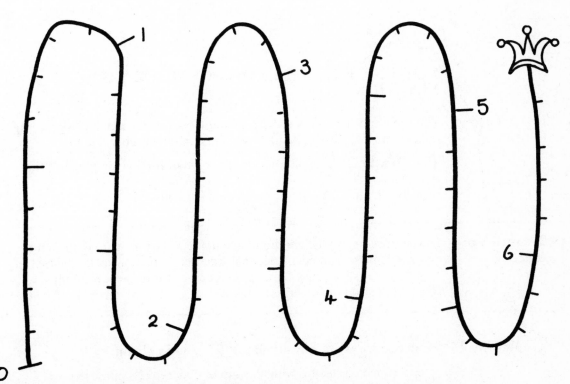

Figure 32 Snails and frogs.

5. Overtaking is allowed, but two snails may not occupy the same position unless this is a whole number.
6. Players should declare where they have landed e.g. '4 and 3 tenth parts'.
7. They must score the exact number to finish.

Discussion of activities	Here again we have a clear example of extrapolation – continuing a known pattern into a new situation. This is of a more difficult kind, since a new variety of number is being mentally constructed. In doing this, the visual support of the number line is a useful aid. Mixed numbers have been used from the beginning here because this gives continuity with the established decimal pattern. (This does not apply in Num 7, where fractions other than decimal are encountered.)
	I hope that you will share my belief in the importance of correct vocabulary when developing this new area of mathematics. I have tried to keep it simple as well as accurate. 'Tenth-part' may eventually be shortened to 'tenth' (etc.) when the meaning is clear from the context – but not until this meaning is well established.
	A muddled vocabulary is a hindrance to clear thinking. We correct bad English in our pupils, so we should not ourselves speak 'bad Maths'.

OBSERVE AND LISTEN   REFLECT   DISCUSS

NuSp 1.10   EXTRAPOLATION OF PLACE-VALUE NOTATION

Concept   The use of place-value notation, including the decimal point, for writing mixed numbers as represented by points on the number line.

Abilities   (i)   To write in decimal notation the number for a given point on the number line.
(ii)   To identify the point for a given mixed number.

Discussion of concept	In the preceding topic, children have made a start in forming the concept of a new kind of number, a decimal fraction, in the particular context of a number line. They also have spoken names for these new numbers. Now they learn how to write them.

Activity 1   'How can we write this number?' (Headed columns)

A teacher-led discussion with a group of children. Its purpose is to introduce the use of headed columns for writing fractional numbers.

Materials
- A number-line at least 30 cm long, using 1 decimetre (10 cm) as the unit interval. Centimetres will now represent tenth-parts, and millimetres hundredth-parts. (This may conveniently be made from graph paper). This is introduced in two stages.
- Pencil and paper for everyone.
- Pointers.

What they do

Stage (a)

1. Begin by saying, 'We've now learnt about new kinds of numbers, called decimal fractions, and we can say their number names. For example, the name of this number is . . . ?' (Here, use a few examples for revision, as in NuSp 1.9/1. At this stage use only the centimetre divisions, representing tenth-parts.)
2. 'Now we need a way of writing them'. Begin by drawing headed columns, like the ones already in use for units, tens, hundreds. Discuss the pattern: 10 times longer for each column to the left, 10 times smaller for each column to the right. This suggests a new column for tenth-parts, on the right of the units column. A double line separates whole numbers and fractions.
3. Draw this, and let the children draw their own.
4. What number is this?

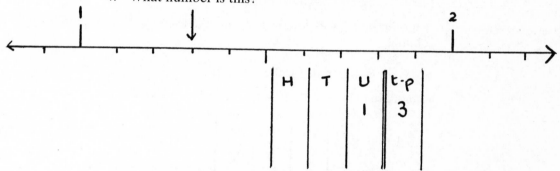

Ask how we should write the number shown by the pointer, spoken as 'one and three tenth-parts' and achieve agreement that we should write 1 in the units column, and 3 in the tenth-parts column. The children should say this aloud, and use the pointers to indicate what they mean.

5. The children may now take turns to point to positions on the line, keeping at this stage to the centimetre divisions. The others write the numbers for these points in their headed columns, and compare.
6. Repeat until they are confident.

Stage (b)

1. Point to one of the millimetre divisions and ask what they think these represent.
2. So now we need another column.

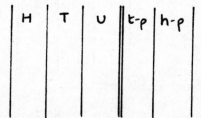

3. So what number is this?

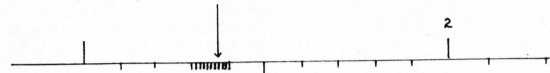

'One and three tenth parts, seven hundredth parts.' It is written

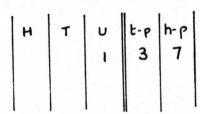

H	T	U	t-p	h-p
		1	3	7

4. The children then take turns to point while the others say and write the numbers in their headed columns.

Activity 2   Introducing the decimal point

A teacher-led discussion, introducing the use of a decimal point instead of columns.

Materials   ● Writing materials for the teacher.

What they do   Remind the children that for whole numbers like this one:

H	T	U
4	8	5

we can save having to write the columns every time, and write just:

$$4 \quad 8 \quad 5$$

as long as we remember that reading from right to left the digits mean units, tens, hundreds.

This only works if we have nothing smaller than units. As soon as we do, we can't simply leave out the columns, or these 2 numbers

H	T	U	t-p	h-p
		2	7	
			2	7

would both be written:

$$2 \quad 7$$

We need to know where whole numbers finish and fractional numbers begin. This is emphasised in headed column notation by the double line. So if we want to drop the columns and use place-value notation, all we need to do is show where the double line would be. A decimal point does this.

> We can now write the above
>
> 2.7   meaning 2 units, 7 tenth-parts, and
>
> .27   meaning 2 tenth-parts, 7 hundredth-parts.

These are read aloud as 'Two point seven' and 'Point two seven'. It is a good idea to write the second of these as 0.27 to emphasise that there are zero whole numbers. The second should *never* be read as 'Point twenty-seven'.

Activity 3   Pointing and writing

A game for a small group. Its purpose is to practise and test their use of place-value notation for decimal fractions, in conjunction with the number line.

Materials
- Number line marked in whole numbers, tenth-parts, and hundredth-parts.
- 2 packs of assorted number cards.*
- Pointer.
- Pencil and paper for each child.

* Mixed numbers in decimal notation. The pack for stage (a) uses whole numbers and tenth-parts. The pack for stage (b) uses whole numbers, tenth-parts and hundredth-parts.

What they do   Stage (a) and stage (b) are played in the same way, except that different packs of number cards are used (see above).
1. The cards are shuffled and put face down.
2. Player A takes the top card, looks at it, but does not let the others see it yet.
3. A now points to the appropriate point on the number line, and the others write the number in place-value notation.
4. Finally the number card used by A is compared with what the others have written.
5. If these agree, someone else acts as player A.
6. If not they discuss before continuing.

Activity 4   Shrinking and growing

A group game. This is an Alice-in-Wonderland kind of activity, which will stretch the imaginations of the more able children.

Materials
- Number-line 0-10.*
- Card with decimal point, see figure 33.
- Number cards 1-9.
- Paperclip for a pointer.

* This should be numbered at every whole number, with divisions marked at every tenth-part and every hundredth part. This may be made from graph paper with 10 mm and 1 mm squares. The unit interval will then be 1 decimetre, and the number line will be 1 metre long. A small part of this line is also illustrated here, in reduced size.

What they do

Stage (a)

1. The number cards are shuffled and put face down.
2. Player A turns over the top card (say 4) and puts it to the left of the decimal point. (I.e. on top of the zero, so that the zero is not showing but the decimal point is).
3. Player B points to the appropriate place on the number line and says 'Four units.'
4. The rest in turn say 'Agree' or 'Disagree'.
5. Player A moves the card to the right hand side of the decimal point. Player B should then say 'Zero units, four tenth parts' pointing as she speaks to the appropriate point on the number line. The others, as before, say 'Agree' or 'Disagree.'
6. Steps 2-5 are repeated using other number cards. Other players then take over the roles of players A and B, and the activity is repeated.

Stage (b)

1. The number cards are shuffled and put face down as before.
2. Player A now turns over the top two cards and puts one each side of the decimal point (e.g. 4.7).
3. Player B points to the appropriate place on the number line and says (in this case) 'Four units, seven tenth-parts.'
4. The rest in turn say 'Agree' or 'Disagree'.
5. Player A moves both cards to the right hand side of the decimal point, giving (in this case) 0.47. Player B should then say 'Zero units, four tenth-parts, seven hundredth-parts' pointing as he speaks to the appropriate point on the number line. The others, as before, say 'Agree' or 'Disagree.'
6. Steps 2-5 are repeated using other number cards. Other players then take over the roles of players A and B, and the activity is repeated.

Stage (c)

1. The number cards are shuffled and put face down as before.
2. Player A now turns over the top *three* cards and puts one to the left of the decimal point, the other two to the right (e.g. 4.72).
3. Player B points to the appropriate place on the number line and says (in this case) 'Four units, seven tenth-parts, two hundredth-parts.'
4. The rest in turn say 'Agree' or 'Disagree'.
5. Player A moves all three cards to the right hand side of the decimal point (giving in this case 0.472). Player B now has a more difficult task. A suitable response would be to say 'Zero units, four tenth-parts, seven hundredth-parts, two thousandth-parts' pointing as she speaks to the appropriate point on the number line, and continuing 'The thousandth-parts are too small to see.' When I was trying out this activity, Rosamund said '. . . and a very small move to the right.' The others, as before, say 'Agree' or 'Disagree.'
6. Steps 2-5 are repeated using other number cards. Other players then take over the roles of players A and B, and the activity is repeated.

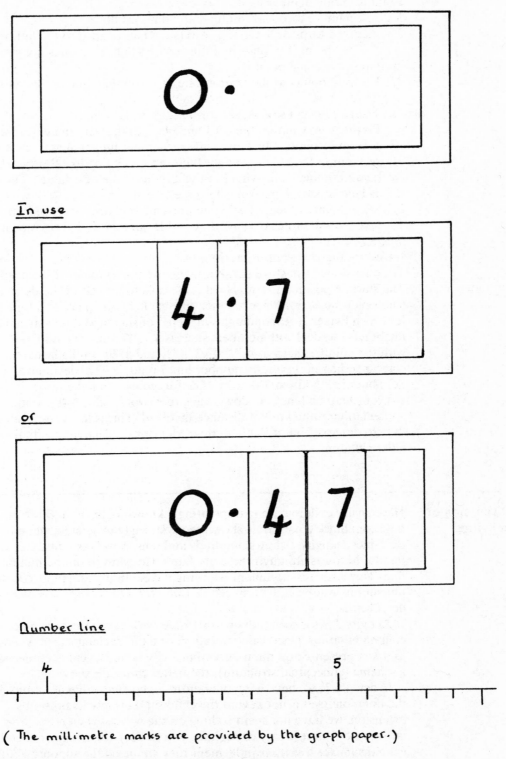

In use

or

Number line

(The millimetre marks are provided by the graph paper.)

Figure 33 Shrinking and growing.

Stage (d)

Activities 1, 2, 3 were about shrinking. Now we come to the growing. They begin with one number card, as in stage one.

1. The number cards are shuffled and put face down.
2. Player A turns over the top card (say 4) and puts it to the left of the decimal point (i.e. on top of the zero, so that the zero is not showing but the decimal point is).
3. Player B points to the appropriate place on the number line and says 'Four units.'
4. The rest in turn say 'Agree' or 'Disagree'.
5. Player A now moves the card one place to the left, giving (in the present example) 40. This is off the number line, 4 metres from the zero point. So player B might then say something like 'Forty. This will be off the line, somewhere in the middle of the next table.' The others, as before, say 'Agree' or 'Disagree.'
6. Steps 2-5 are repeated using other number cards. Other players then take over the roles of players A and B, and the activity is repeated.

Stages (e), (f)

Introduce these at your discretion.

They are done as in stage (d), but using two and three cards respectively. The starting position is always with one card to the left of the decimal point (on top of the zero). Player A then moves them one place at a time to the left, with Player B responding as in step 5 of stage (d). So in stage (e), he might have to deal with numbers such as 4.7, 47, and 470; and in stage (f), with the numbers such as 4.72, 47.2, 472, and 4720. In the last case, the corresponding point on the number line would be 4720 decimetres away, i.e. about half a kilometre away. The foregoing would be rather a good answer. 'Quite a long way down the street' would show sufficient appreciation of the kind of distance involved. This is less complicated to do than to describe, but it is still quite a sophisticated activity, suitable only for older children.

Discussion of activities	Here again, children are extrapolating a known pattern: in this case a notation. Since a pattern is shown more strongly by a larger number of examples, activity 1 shows hundreds and tens as well as units, and also hundredth-parts although these are harder to point to on the number line. This is also an argument for using mixed numbers. Hundreds, tens, units firmly establish the tens pattern which is now being extended downwards.
	Activity 2 is for consolidating the three-way relation between headed column notation, place-value notation, and the decimal fraction concept as it is represented on the number line. The more the connections within a schema (conceptual structure), the better the understanding.
	In activity 3, we have gone over entirely to place-value notation. Since the notation itself is not new to the children, but only its present extension, we have not spent so long on the way as when it was first introduced. But it is easy enough for you to keep them using headed columns longer if in your judgement they still need the support of this much more explicit notation.

Activity 4 is partly for consolidation, but especially for giving children a feeling of the great differences in the sizes represented in this very concise notation. Using a decimetre as unit interval, a digit in the hundreds column represents a length possibly too big to have in the classroom, while the same digit in the hundredth-part column represents a length too small even to draw. This activity also makes frequent demands for adaptability in children's thinking, so it is a good mental exercise for their intelligence.

Is all this talk about 'Four units, seven tenth-parts' etc., really necessary? In my belief, emphatically yes. This verbalisation is here being used, in conjunction with the number line, to help establish the concepts. The frequently-encountered problems with 'decimals' (decimal fractions in place value notation) are conceptual problems, problems of understanding. The importance of these early stages in establishing the right concepts can hardly be over-stated.

OBSERVE AND LISTEN   **REFLECT**   **DISCUSS**

GLOSSARY

These are words which may be unfamiliar, or which are used with specialised meanings. The definitions and short explanations given here are intended mainly as reminders for words already encountered in the text, where they are discussed more fully. This is not the best place to meet a word for the first time.

abstract	(verb) To perceive something in common among a diversity of experiences. (adj.) Resulting from this process, and thus more general, but also more remote from direct experience.
add	This can mean either a physical action, or a mathematical operation. Here we use it with only the second meaning, in order to keep these two ideas distinct.
addend	That which is to be added.
base	The number used for grouping objects, and then making groups of these groups, and so on. This is a way of organising large collections of objects to make them easier to count, and is also important for place-value notation.
binary	Describes an operation with two operands.
canonical form	When there are several ways of writing the same mathematical idea, one of these is often accepted as the one which is most generally useful. This is called the canonical form. A well known example is a fraction in its lowest terms.
characteristic property	Property which is the basis for classification, and for membership of a given set.
commutative	This describes a physical action or a mathematical operation for which the result is still the same if we do it the other way about. E.g. addition is commutative, since 7 + 3 gives the same result as 3 + 7; but subtraction is not.
concept	An idea which represents what a variety of different experiences have in common. It is the result of abstracting.
congruent	Two figures are congruent if one of them, put on top of the other, would coincide with it exactly. The term still applies if one figure would first have to be turned over.
contributor	One of the experiences from which a concept is abstracted.
counting numbers	The number of objects in a set. The cardinal numbers, 1, 2, 3 . . . (continuing indefinitely). Zero is usually included among these, but not negative or fractional numbers.
digit	A single figure. E.g. 0, 1, 2, 3 . . . 9.
equivalent	Of the same value.
extrapolate	To expand a schema by perceiving a pattern and extending it to new applications.
higher order concept	A concept which is itself abstracted from other concepts. E.g. the concept of an even number is abstracted from numbers like 2, 4, 6 . . . so *even number* is a higher order concept than 2, or 4, or 6 . . .

interiority	The detail within a concept.
interpolate	To increase what is within a schema by perceiving a pattern and extending it inwards.
low-noise example	An example of a concept which has a minimum of irrelevant qualities.
lower order concept	The opposite of *higher order concept*, q.v.
match	To be alike in some way.
mathematical operation	See *operation*.
mode 1	Schema building by physical experience, and testing by seeing whether predictions are confirmed.
mode 2	Schema building by receiving communication, and testing by discussion.
mode 3	Schema construction by mental creativity, and testing whether the new ideas thus obtained are consistent with what is already known.
model	A simplified representation of something. A model may be physical or mental, but here we are concerned mainly with mathematical models, which are an important kind of mental model.
natural numbers	The same as the counting numbers.
notation	A way of writing something.
numeral	A symbol for a number. Not to be confused with the number itself.
operand	Whatever is acted on, physically or mentally.
operation	Used here to mean a mental action, in contrast to a physical action.
pair	A set of two. Often used for a set made by taking one object from each of two existing sets: e.g. a knife and a fork.
place-value notation	A way of writing numbers in which the meaning of each digit depends both on the digit itself, and also on which place it is in, reading from right to left.
predict	To say what we think will happen, by inference from a suitable mental model. Not the same as guessing. Prediction is based on knowledge, guessing on ignorance.
schema	A conceptual structure. A connected group of ideas.
set	A collection of objects (these may be mental objects) which belong together in some way.
subitise	To perceive the number of objects in a set without counting.
sum	The result of an addition. Often used, incorrectly, to mean any kind of calculation.
symmetry	A relation of a figure with itself. If a line can be found which divides a figure into two congruent halves, the figure has symmetry about this line. This is the only kind of symmetry considered in this book. Rotational symmetry is another kind.
transitive	A property of a relationship. E.g. if Alan is taller than Brenda, and Brenda is taller than Charles, then we know also that Alan is taller than Charles. So the relationship 'is taller than' is transitive.
unary	Describes an operation with a single operand.

ALPHABETICAL LIST OF ACTIVITIES